# WHY UNIONS MATTER

# WHY UNIONS MATTER

## SECOND EDITION

Michael D. Yates

MONTHLY REVIEW PRESS
*New York*

Copyright © 2009 by Monthly Review Press

Library of Congress Cataloging-in-Publication Data

Yates, Michael, 1946-
Why unions matter / Michael D. Yates. -- New ed.
    p. cm.
Includes bibliographical references and index.
ISBN 978-1-58367-190-0 (pbk.) -- ISBN 978-1-58367-191-7 (cloth)
1. Labor unions--United States. I. Title.
HD6508.Y38 2009
331.880973--dc22
                            2008054520


Monthly Review Press
146 West 29th Street, Suite 6W
New York, NY 10001


5  4  3  2  1

*To my mother, Irene Yates,*
*for all her hard work, encouragement, and love.*

# CONTENTS

# ACKNOWLEDGMENTS

I first want to thank two former Monthly Review Press editors: Ethan Young for helping to get this book started and for his helpful comments and criticisms along the way, and Christopher Phelps for his editorial skills and attention to detail. Historian Paul LeBlanc read the entire manuscript of the first edition. He made many useful comments and corrected some glaring errors and omissions. Historian Priscilla Murolo graciously provided me with an annotated bibliography of books and articles concerning the labor history of women. Louis Proyect, a friend and longtime champion of the working class, made helpful comments and gave generous encouragement. My longtime friends and colleagues, the late Bruce Williams and Monica Frolander-Ulf, have helped me to think and write about, as well as try to organize, unions. Several members of the Progressive Economists Network (PEN-L) suggested useful resources: Doug Henwood, Bryan Thompson, Richard Robbins, Ellen Frank, Elaine Bernard, Ellen Dannin, and William Puette. Donald Spatz, Treasurer of Workers' Education Local 189 of the Communications Workers of America, kindly sent me a copy of the local's Directory of Labor Education, an indispensable guide to resources for workers. Labor educator and activist Fernando Gapasin provided much useful information on Central Labor Councils and on current labor insurgencies. Special thanks go to Howard Harris for first hiring me as a labor educator; it has been through teaching workers that I learned how to write a book like this.

I am indebted to the late Paul Sweezy and Harry Magdoff of *Monthly Review* for their friendly and consistent encouragement. Their lives and work are an inspiration to all of us. I am also grateful for the special kindness shown by the late Judy Ruben of Monthly Review Press. Her untimely death saddened us beyond words. I am pleased to acknowledge, too, the inspiration of the work of *Monthly Review's* cofounder, the late Leo Huberman. His 1946 pamphlet, *The Truth about Unions*, provided the model for this book, and his work as a labor educator, union activist, and popular writer gave me a model for my own working life.

This second edition owes much to Carol Lambiase of the United Electrical Workers (UE), who updated the materials in the book on her union, and to Ellen Dannin, who provided me with useful information on labor law and collective bargaining. I have drawn heavily from new works by Kim Moody and my friends Fernando Gapasin and Bill Fletcher, whose recent books are cited liberally in the updated parts of the text. I am grateful also to Seth Weiss for his fine copyediting and helpful comments and suggestions.

Finally, I want to thank my partner, Karen Korenoski. Not only has she been a keen critic, but she has also given me the kind of love that makes life worth living.

# PREFACE
# TO THE SECOND EDITION

The first edition of *Why Unions Matter* was published in 1998. In it I argued that unions mattered because they were the one institution that has dramatically improved the lives of the majority of the people and had the potential to radically transform both the economic and political landscape, making both more democratic. I showed with clear and decisive data that union members enjoyed significant advantages over nonunion workers: higher wages, more and better benefits, better access to many kinds of leaves of absence, a democratic voice in their workplaces, and a better understanding of their political and legal rights. What is more, unions benefited nonunion workers through their political agitations and through what is called the "spillover" effect; nonunion employers will treat their employees better if only to avoid unionization.

This assessment of the impact of unions has not changed in this second edition. What was said ten years ago is true today. I have updated the numbers, but they still show that *unions matter*. Maybe they matter even more today. Working men and women are more vulnerable to a host of problems than they were in 1998:

- Because of the electronic revolution, the radical reorganization of the labor process, and the political deregulation of impor-

tant product and financial markets, employers are more likely
to move operations to parts of the United States with lower
wages and to poorer countries. They are also more inclined to
threaten to do so. Try to buy U.S.-made shoes, toys, jewelry, and
a host of other consumer goods. If your automobile is made in
the United States, chances are good that it was manufactured in
the union-free southern states.

- Employers are more likely to contract out to lower-wage states
  and nations both labor-intensive operations such as call centers
  and higher-wage labor like computer programming and medical service work. When we make inquiries about our comput-
  ers, our credit card bills, or our health insurance, the person on
  the other side of the phone will very likely be in a foreign country.

- As local economies become more enmeshed in the global economy, aided and abetted by anti-labor trade agreements, peasants and working people in poor countries like Mexico are displaced from their land and livelihood. Large numbers have
  come to the United States, intensifying competition in some
  labor markets, allowing employers to divide and conquer their
  workforces, and giving an excuse for xenophobes like CNN's
  Lou Dobbs to foment anti-immigrant hysteria, which helps to
  keep domestic workers from seeing that it is their employers
  (and the employers' allies in government) that are their true
  enemies. As we shall see in Chapter Seven, the influx of immigrants offers the labor movement new and enthusiastic troops
  for rebirth and revitalization.

- Over the last ten years and especially during the administration
  of George W. Bush, our government has been increasingly
  under the thumb of corporate interests. The failure of organized labor to provide a counterweight to this (something we
  examine in detail in this book) has allowed a corporate-politi-
  cal alliance to sweep away most of the safety nets that protect us
  from the vagaries of the market and the inevitable occurrences

of failing health, old age, and workplace injuries. Our health insurance system is in tatters, with nearly fifty million people without insurance and tens of millions more with inadequate and expensive coverage. These numbers grow each year. Today, few workers have traditional defined benefit pension plans, which guarantee a predictable monthly income upon retirement. Instead, the declining fraction of workers who have pensions must accept defined contribution plans, in which they put up the money, sometimes with an employer match, and then must decide in what type of stock or bond fund to invest. How much money is available depends on how much money they were able to put into their funds, the size of the employer match, and the performance of the funds. The Social Security system, which is well-managed, financially sound, and capable of providing decent pensions for all, has been attacked by labor's enemies in a propaganda campaign aimed at privatization. Workplace safety has become a dead letter, as has the enforcement of our labor laws. Those programs aimed at the poor, including those who lose their jobs, have been shredded or have become less generous in terms of both coverage and benefits. Workers were encouraged to consider their homes as security blankets, assets they could sell or borrow against to deal with emergencies or just to supplement incomes. But now the notion that a house is an asset that always rises in value is another big joke, one made at the expense of the working class. All in all, we can say with certainty that workers have lost ground economically, while those who hire them and invest in their companies, those who loan them money or hold their mortgages, have taken what workers have lost and lined their own pockets. Inequalities of income and wealth have not been as great as they are now since the 1920s.

- While our government has eagerly helped employers beat down workers, it has just as fervently wasted hundreds of billions of dollars waging war. In fact, the two phenomena are connected. War spending starves social programs and socially useful public investments. The war in Iraq may cost more than a trillion dollars, money enough to implement a national healthcare system, expand Social Security, and begin to make the public investments needed to restore the health of our badly ravaged environment. Wars also are always harmful to the rights of workers. After the terrorist attacks of September 11, 2001, the federal government put in place measures to deny the right of many federal workers to unionize and threatened to invoke antiterrorism laws to stop strikes. A climate of war is a climate of fear and accusation. One right-wing pundit said on Fox Television that a national health care system would encourage terrorist physicians, willing to work for less, to come to the United States. Here, it is interesting to note that in Iraq, where the United States was supposedly engineering a democratic society from scratch, unions and strikes are for all practical purposes illegal.

- Compounding worker insecurity has been the collapse of two financial bubbles, first the stock market crash that began in 2000 and then the real estate debacle that commenced in 2007. The recovery from the first was one of the weakest on record, and working-class living standards never returned to where they were at the end of the last century. Some were able to maintain their incomes or make up for money shortfalls by borrowing, with credit cards and by taking out home equity loans. Both allowed consumer spending to grow faster than it would have otherwise. Now, however, the bursting of the housing bubble has left workers with a mountain of debt and no way out.[1]

It is difficult to imagine that this litany of working-class woes can be challenged and eradicated without strong unions and a vibrant labor movement. What has organized labor done to redress the many grievances of those who work for a living? One would think that the events of the past ten years have sown fertile grounds for the development of a powerful labor movement.

Perhaps no phrase better captures what has happened in the labor movement of the United States than the old saying that "the more things change, the more they stay the same." When the first edition was published, labor activists and scholars in the United States had high hopes for the "New Voice" movement, which in 1995 captured power in the AFL-CIO, the nation's largest labor federation (see Chapter Eight for details). Led by John Sweeney, Richard Trumka, and Linda Chavez-Thompson, New Voice promised a thoroughgoing transformation. Union membership would grow again; labor's political power would reassert itself; international solidarity would become the order of the day. There would, once again, be a labor movement.

Thirteen years after New Voice's inauguration, not much has changed. Workers are not joining unions. In 1995, union density (the share of all employed workers who could reasonably be union members who are union members) was nearly 15 percent. In 2007, it was around 12 percent. There are fewer union members today than there were in 1995. The private sector has so hemorrhaged union members that union density there is now about 7.5 percent, below what it was before the Great Depression. A few unions, most notably the Service Employees International Union (SEIU), have grown, but, in the case of SEIU, there is considerable controversy over the manner in which the union has gained new members, with critics arguing that its growth has not strengthened the labor movement.

Organized labor in the United States has never had the formidable political presence workers' organizations have in other parts of the world. However, there have been times when labor wielded some political clout. The record of New Voice here is not a good one. The AFL-CIO and its member unions have spent hundreds of millions of dollars trying to get sympathetic politicians elected to office, and with some success. Yet this has not translated into legislation that empowers working men and women. Except for a couple of badly needed increases in the minimum wage, quite the opposite has occurred. Whether the president has been Democrat or Republican, labor has gotten the short end of the stick: "free trade" agreements, an end to most federal aid to the poor, worsening health care, more working class people in prison, the refusal to enforce the nation's labor laws, and endless wars that have drained public coffers of funds that might have been used to enhance the lives of ordinary folks. And as critic of the labor movement Kim Moody points out, there is a direct correspondence between the increase in the amounts of money and effort labor has expended politically and the decline in organizing efforts.[2]

New Voice did change the international approach of the AFL-CIO. It got out of bed, at least partially, with the CIA and the U.S. State Department, eliminating the various labor "institutes" established during the Cold War to help suppress radical labor organizations around the world and assist those labor unions and political parties that allied themselves with the imperial interests of the United States. New Voice created the Center for International Labor Solidarity (CILS) and showed a new willingness to support labor efforts around the globe that it would have opposed in the past. But, Kim Moody tells us:

> There are still troubling signs. For example, the AFL-CIO's backing of the Venezuelan Confederation of Labor (CTV) whose strike appeared to lead off the coup against Hugo Chávez. Here, the CILS claimed they used money from the National Endowment for Democracy, the neo-conservative-run government agency that funded AFL-CIO Cold War foreign activities since the early 1980s, to support progressive forces within the CTV. The AFL-CIO still takes NED money, but claims there are no strings attached. They will not report on where or for what the money is spent. They don't reveal what they do in most of the forty countries where CILS is active.[3]

All things considered, it would be difficult to argue that New Voice has succeeded, even on its own terms. The new AFL-CIO was a breath of fresh air compared to the moribund and badly compromised administrations of Sweeney's predecessors Lane Kirkland and George Meany.

But the air has gotten pretty stale, so much so that new rumblings began inside the federation as early as 2000. Ironically, the sharpest criticisms came from Sweeney's old union, the SEIU, whose president, Andrew Stern, has become the most famous labor leader in the United States. Stern and his allies said that the AFL-CIO and most member unions were not serious about organizing. They suggested that they should pay lower per capita dues to the AFL-CIO, so that they would have more money for organizing. Gradually several unions formed a coalition called the New Unity Partnership (NUP) to press for changes in the AFL-CIO. Labor activists and scholars Fernando Gapasin and Bill Fletcher Jr. point to four key changes Stern and company wanted. First, the AFL-CIO had too many unions, causing many overlaps in jurisdiction. Some unions would have to merge with others to ensure greater efficiency of operations. Second, the AFL-CIO had to establish core jurisdictions (for example, health care) and a specific union had to be given the sole right to organize the workers in this area. Whatever union this might be would have the needed resources once the necessary mergers had created unions that could take advantage of economies of scale. Third, unions and the federation should practice more international solidarity, making direct contact with foreign unions, organizing with them, and even forming true international unions. Fourth, labor had to reevaluate its relationship with the Democratic Party. The party had to be held accountable for promises made to organized labor.[4]

The NUP consisted of the SEIU, the Laborers, HERE, UNITE (merged restaurant, hotel, garment, and textile workers), and the Carpenters (which had already left the AFL-CIO). To some this seemed an odd alliance. The Carpenters and Laborers had done good organizing work, but they had long histories of corruption and had never been in the forefront of labor's progressive forces. Perhaps there was more to the NUP than simply revitalizing a moribund labor movement. Maybe these unions wanted to keep more of their members' dues money. Perhaps there were personality and other conflicts between Stern and Sweeney. Maybe the NUP saw good opportunities for organizing in the service sector, which is not as threatened by off-shoring and outsourcing as is the goods-producing part of the economy, and did not want to support the unions in manufacturing. Certainly there were those in the rest of the AFL-CIO who agreed that more organizing was critical to labor's survival and that some reorganization of the AFL-CIO would be a good thing.

In any event, the NUP disappeared in late 2004, but a new organization appeared in June 2005—the Change to Win Coalition (CTW). This group included two more unions, the Teamsters and the United Food and Commercial Workers, which raised more suspicion, since these unions were also far removed from labor's progressive elements.

Change to Win proponents now argued that it would be necessary to greatly streamline the AFL-CIO—reducing the funds available to it from member unions that committed to organizing, while at the same time giving it power to merge unions, prevent mergers, and eliminate central labor councils—if union density was to increase. While it is difficult to say what the initial goal of the CTW was *vis-á-vis* the AFL-CIO, it soon became clear that unless the AFL-CIO agreed to CTW demands for dues rebates and restructuring, the CTW unions would secede. Curiously, CTW leaders never went out of their way to negotiate with the rest of the AFL-CIO and to try to work out compromises, much less call for a far-reaching debate on rebuilding the labor movement. The leading actor in all this was the SEIU, which usually put the issues at stake in terms of organizing. Stern and the SEIU said that unless every step possible was taken immediately to raise union density, the labor movement would die. Stern's allies began to make references to the formation of the CIO in the 1930s, implying that the growing split between CTW and the rest of the AFL-CIO could lead to a labor revolution.

CTW, now including the once iconic United Farm Workers union, did break with the AFL-CIO, and in September 2005 in St. Louis the breakaway unions formed the Change to Win Federation. Just as they did with New Voice, many labor activists and progressives jumped aboard this new agent of change. Three years later, it is fair to ask why. CTW has made little headway in building a new labor movement, no more so than has the AFL-CIO. Comparisons with the CIO rang hollow from the start, and now they seem preposterous. Some CTW unions have organized new members, but the manner in which the major organizing union, the SEIU, has done so has raised serious questions, as we shall see in this second edition. Some CTW unions have made good on their promise to consolidate their operations into fewer but larger locals, but this too has generated much controversy. CTW has done little to establish core jurisdictions assigned to specific unions, and it is doubtful that it will. As have their AFL-CIO counterparts, CTW and its affiliated unions have thrown gobs of money at the Democratic Party, especially in the 2008 presidential race. But to describe the Democratic Party nominee and president, Barack Obama, as a strong supporter of unions and the labor movement would be a stretch. When he was president-elect, he did not appoint a single labor person to his transition team. He has said that he supports the Employee Free Choice Act, which would make it easier for unions to organize workers (see Chapter Five for details). But we will see if words are followed by actions. Not much in the way of international solidarity has been achieved by CTW either, certainly nothing that would distinguish its unions from any number of AFL-CIO affiliates.

The devotion of CTW and its main affiliate, the SEIU, to the language of corporate management is also troubling. As Kim Moody explains, "the language of [CTW] leaders had the sound of corporate-speak." The new federation would "grow the labor movement" through increased "market share" and "value-added integration." SEIU hires business experts to train staff and lead seminars, and staff, in turn, comb the pages of journals like the *Harvard Business Review* for guidance.[5]

First New Voice, then Change to Win. The more things change, the more they stay the same. Unfortunately, these efforts to change the lives of workers have done little to affect what has really been changing, namely the conditions under which working people labor. As I shall argue in the book, neither New Voice nor Change to Win has done anything to change the ideological terrain. An important part of the employers' attack on labor has been an assault on the notion that collective organization and action are good things. Relentlessly, the bosses and their apologists tell us: Unions are outsiders interested only in dues money. The government is a denier of individual freedom and a thief that takes our hard-earned money. Its only legitimate function is to defend the country from the collective hordes bent on destroying our hallowed way of life. We are, each of us, on our own, and this is a good thing. When we act in groups, we inevitably act against our own interests and trample the liberty of others.

The labor movement has not challenged this worldview effectively. It has not come out foursquare for publicly funded universal health care. It has not rejected *in toto* the imperialism evident in every aspect of U.S. foreign policy, one that endangers workers everywhere in the world. It has not begun a national discussion on race, the main divider of workers. It has continued to embrace the reactionary idea of partnership with employers, which is a cornerstone of the program of Change to Win. Tellingly, it has, with a few exceptions, failed to edu-

cate its members in any but a superficial way, leaving them in the dark
on the issues that matter most. It has in the internal structure of its
unions replicated that of its class enemy. Some union leaders sneer at
the very thought of democracy.

We all need a compass to find our way. For workers, unions and a
labor movement must provide that compass. They have not. Until they
do, no amount of top-down reform, no new union federation, no
increase in union density will provide for workers the freer and richer
lives they deserve.

Amidst the many failings and shortcomings of unions and the
labor movement, there have been bright spots, too. Not long after the
first edition was published, many unions joined the fight for global
justice and against the uncontrolled globalization that had been driv-
ing wages and working conditions downward worldwide. The most
famous struggle occurred in Seattle in 1999. But just as this movement
was gaining traction, the events of September 11, 2001 created conditions in the United States that made it difficult for a labor movement
so tied historically to U.S. foreign policy to continue to participate. To
its credit, the AFL-CIO and many member unions did not give the
full-throated support for the "War on Terror" that its predecessors had
given to the war in Vietnam. And unionists opposed to it formed a
group that continues to exist—United States Labor Against the War
(USLAW). Fernando Gapasin and I described this group as follows:

> This organization, comprised of individuals, unions, and other pro-
> gressive organizations, is not only opposed to the U.S. war in Iraq but
> to U.S. foreign policy itself. Its statement of principles—a just foreign
> policy, an end to U.S. occupation of foreign countries, a redirecting of
> the nation's resources, bringing U.S. troops home now, protecting
> civil rights and the rights of workers and immigrants, and solidarity
> with workers and their organizations around the world—is remark-
> able in light of the sordid history of organized labor's support for U.S.
> imperialism.[6]

Just as remarkable is that the AFL-CIO has not only tolerated
USLAW but also given it tacit support by itself condemning the war in
Iraq.

Dan Clawson, in his book *The Next Upsurge: Labor and the New Social Movements*, describes and analyzes several important and successful organizing campaigns:

- Unionization by women that focused on nontraditional issues such as child care.

- Union alliances with community groups, most notably the famous Justice for Janitors campaigns of the SEIU, but also efforts by unions and community groups in Hartford, Connecticut, to win affordable housing for workers.

- Campaigns waged by Worker Centers, sometimes independently and sometimes in alliance with labor unions. Janice Fine defines such centers as "community-based and community-led organizations that engage in a combination of service, advocacy, and organizing to provide support to low-wage workers. The vast majority of them have grown up to serve predominantly or exclusively immigrant populations. However, there are a few centers that serve a primarily African American population or bring immigrants together with African Americans."[7] I will have more to say about Worker Centers in Chapter Seven. As Fine says, they are intimately connected to growing immigrant communities in the United States, and they will be a critical component of any future labor renewal.

- Living wage campaigns and anti-sweatshop organizing, which have been successful in forcing many cities to pay workers employed by firms with public contracts a wage that would yield an income at least equal to the federal poverty level of income and compelled universities to stop selling apparel produced under appalling conditions in low-wage countries. College students have expanded their anti-sweatshop actions to include the organizing of poorly paid employees on their campuses.[8]

Some of this organizing has borne fruit in terms of union membership. During the end of 2007 and the first half of 2008, this increased in

two important cities—Boston and Los Angeles. In Boston, cab drivers, security guards, truck drivers, communications technicians, and
home-care assistants, among others, added more than 6,000 workers
to union rosters.[9] Most of these employees were organized through
atypical means, that is, outside of the purview of the National Labor
Relations Board, something that will be discussed later in the book. In
Los Angeles, union density rose from 15.9 percent in 2007 to 17 percent by mid-2008, while in California it increased from 16.7 to 17 percent. Both increases reversed many years of declining density.
Remarkably, union density also went up half a percentage point in the
nation as a whole, from 12 to 12.6 percent. This is not enough time to
establish a trend, but it is heartening nonetheless.[10]

I am not as optimistic as Clawson that there will soon be a labor
upsurge. Still, his book shows that there are important and interesting
things happening in the world of organized labor. For the past twen-
ty-eight years I have been a labor educator, teaching union workers
and students in union halls, motel and hotel meeting rooms, in college
and university classrooms, and through the Internet. I know from this
experience that unions are as needed as ever, that there are thousands
of thoughtful union brothers and sisters out there, struggling to
rebuild their unions and give back to unions the local and national rel-
evance they once had. There are union officers around the nation trying to mobilize and educate their members, not just to empower them
in their own workplace, important as this is, but also to help them
grasp the economics and politics of the times in which we live. They
are trying to build the multiethnic, multiracial unions and labor
movement of men and women that will really mean it when saying,
"An injury to one is an injury to all."

# INTRODUCTION

Meadville, Pennsylvania, is a small town located ninety miles north of Pittsburgh. A few miles outside of town there is a factory that manufactures plate glass. It is owned by PPG industries, a large, profitable conglomerate, once one of the glass industry's leaders. When the plant was built, the company was known simply as Pittsburgh Plate Glass, but it took on the more impersonal initials as it diversified. In 1994, it employed 330 production workers in rotating shifts, making plate glass twenty-four hours a day, seven days a week. Most of them are white men, although a significant number of women work the lines as well.

In the fall of 1994, one of the workers telephoned and asked me to speak to his coworkers about their legal rights.[1] They were in the middle of a union organizing drive, and the management was turning up the heat. I said that I could not come unless the union trying to organize the plant approved. A few weeks later, he called to say that the union, the Aluminum, Brick, and Glass Workers (ABG, but now part of the United Steelworkers), had agreed that I should visit. In a fire hall close to the plant, I spoke twice to about sixty men and women. My talks were videotaped and later circulated around the plant. Six months after my visit, I returned at the request of the national union to speak again, the day before the election. I gave three speeches, one for each shift, to about a hundred workers. Unfortunately, our efforts were not sufficient to beat the corporation's anti-union campaign. The

next day the union was defeated by twenty votes. The union supporters were devastated, but they vowed to try again.

My experiences at the Meadville plant were instructive and emotionally intense. I went to high school with some of the union's
strongest supporters; they had moved to Meadville from our hometown, which once boasted the largest glass factory in the world. I had
not seen them in thirty years, and we had traveled different paths, but
we still had much in common. They remembered our town as a union
stronghold, a place where working people could make a decent living,
where they stuck together, where your identity depended on where
you stood, with the company or the union. Although, like me, they did
not know then what the union had meant to their hardworking parents, they knew now. Experience had taught them the hard lesson that
when you are unorganized, you are at the mercy of the company, and
that, as a rule, despite pronouncements to the contrary, the company
did not show much mercy.

The Meadville plant was one of many built by PPG to defeat the
union after the strike of 1958. The company began to locate glass
plants in isolated rural areas with few or no union traditions, especially in the South. New hires were carefully screened to avoid hiring
workers infected with the union virus. Not too many people from any
one town were hired, so that the company could be assured that their
workers would not socialize much. Hourly wage rates were close to
union rates, and workers could earn more through incentives and
bonuses. Sometimes all workers were paid a salary, just like the managers. New methods of personnel management were utilized, including the formation of teams.[2] Team leaders were selected by supervisors
for special training, often at hotels with all expenses paid.

Most workplaces are profoundly alienating, and unions can help
workers to overcome their isolation. Employers know this, and therefore try to devise company-dominated arrangements that they hope
will serve as substitutes for unions. The basic idea is to group the
workers into "quality circles," which then brainstorm more efficient
ways to work, or into "teams," which serve as problem-solvers for management. Each team member is trained to do every other member's
job. Management provides special training for circles and teams, often
outside the workplace and under the supervision of supposedly neu-

tral experts. This training deliberately imparts the impression that the employer is concerned with the workers as human beings with needs beyond the workplace. Employers may even provide special technical training and give workers access to company data so that the teams can solve problems and take on some of the work previously done by lower-level management.

Workers, desperate for any kind of attention, are often enthusiastic about teams. But, in time, most find that management uses them for one reason only—to increase productivity and profits. Since most jobs have been engineered to require as few skills as possible, the fact that team members know each other's jobs means that management will not have to hire replacements when a member is sick or injured. Workers may find it interesting to keep exact track of every move they make on a job, but employers have them do this to reduce the amount of labor used. When workers make suggestions for increasing productivity, they are giving to their employer knowledge that will eventually allow the employer to speed up their work or eliminate their jobs. When jobs are reevaluated with team assistance, workers may be helping the employer to discover which jobs can be profitably contracted out. When team members are called "associates" instead of workers, the employer is using manipulative psychology to give workers the trappings of power without relinquishing any real control.

The company's anti-union strategy was successful, leaving the union a shell of its former self. To survive, it had to become a catchall union, organizing anyone it could. It was also forced to merge with other unions; first it merged with a brick and aluminum workers' union, and then with the United Steelworkers of America. Yet, despite all that PPG has done to remain union-free, it has not been able to stamp out its employees' yearnings for something better. Nothing has erased the benefits of a union from the memories of my old classmates. At the Meadville plant, everyone was an employee "at will." This meant that a worker could be fired or otherwise discriminated against for any reason not protected by a written law. No employee could be discharged for union activity or because of race, sex, religion, ethnicity, national origin, age, or disability. But employees could be fired for any other reason: a disagreement with the foreman, an argument with a coworker, a political difference, a refusal to attend a company function, or a failure to perform work that they thought too dangerous. Every year, tens of thousands of people are discharged for these and many other reasons.

But if they had been in a union, they could not have been fired except for just cause. Every union contract includes a grievance procedure, giving each worker the right to file a complaint against the company for any discrimination. Nearly all contracts provide that a neutral "arbitrator," not employed by the company, will resolve the dispute if the parties themselves cannot do so. In other words, with a union the employer must have a good reason to fire someone.[3]

While the base wages at Meadville were comparable to those earned at union plants, the fringe benefits were not. At one of our meetings a pensioner spoke. His voice cracking, he told us that after thirty years of hard labor, he now received just $400 a month. If he died, his wife would get half as much. The company had already reduced his health benefits and was threatening to cut them off altogether. The pensioner implored those at the meeting to vote union. With a union, employer-provided benefits are the employer's contractual obligation. They cannot be changed without the consent of the union. (My father retired from a union PPG plant in 1984, and his pension was nearly twice that of the nonunion pensioner. My father had full health coverage as well, better than that received by the current workers at the nonunion facility.)

Our work lives are full of uncertainty and insecurity. At any time, we might find ourselves out in the street without work. In this era of corporate downsizing, plant closing, outsourcing, and offshoring, it is a rare worker who has not faced job loss. Workers are often fired or laid off without notice. At the time of the union election, the Meadville plant was about to close one of the tanks in which the glass is made for rebuilding, a project slated to take about a year and a half. The workers "enjoyed" (again at the will of the employer) recall rights—they would be automatically called back to work when there were job openings—-for thirteen months after a layoff; after that they would be considered new hires. Many feared that when the tank work was done, they would have no recall rights and would be hired back as temporary or part-time workers. In the union plants employees had unlimited recall rights. Of course, no union can guarantee employment, but if there is work, its members will get it. If a plant closes, the union members may be able to transfer to another plant with no loss of wages, benefits, or seniority.

During my visits, I heard again and again something else that a union would do. It would force the company, so long accustomed to seeing its employees as simply costs of production, to treat workers as human beings, with the respect that all people deserve. In the words of the old labor anthem "Solidarity Forever," the union would "make them strong," literally. I know that many of the people gathered in that fire hall would have voted for the union for this reason alone. In fact, the union organizing drive had already made them strong. To show their support, more than one hundred workers wore bright red union t-shirts to work. It took tremendous courage to take this symbolic action, which showed their supervisors that they were no longer just individuals who would meekly do what they were told. The bosses hated these shirts and tried to get the workers to stop wearing them, but this only reinforced the sense of power the shirts gave them. The shirts must have made them feel like the auto workers who pulled the stop switches on the assembly lines right before the great sit-down strikes of the 1930s. Observers said that you could feel the power the workers now knew they had. Of all the things a union brings, this understanding of workers' power is the most important.

Most people in the United States are workers, although this is difficult to discern from our media, scholarly journals, and popular culture. Somehow all we hear about are the rich, a very broad middle class, and the underclass of poor. Much attention is paid to the poor, who are presumed to be sociopathic and in need of special consideration. The middle class includes everyone not in the underclass and not filthy rich: the clerk at Sears is middle class, and so too the doctor and the lawyer. This is the "silent majority" of solid citizens extolled by our presidents and editorial writers. The rich avoid scrutiny altogether except when one of them does something outrageous or when, through pluck and courage, some former nobody fights his or her way into their ranks.

This threefold social division obscures what is most important to know, namely that we have a capitalist economic system that by its nature divides society into two classes: those who own the workplaces

and those who work for them. Ownership is highly unequal. A good
90 percent of the people own nothing, while a fraction of the rest own
almost everything.[4] This monopoly gives the owners a great advantage, namely, that everyone else depends on them to live. That is, we
have to sell to them our ability to work, or we will be in serious trouble. It takes no leap of the imagination to realize that, all other things
equal, we will not get the better of this transaction. We will be subject
to the threat of job loss anytime our employers can find cheaper labor
or get machines to do our work, or whenever the economy sinks into
recession.

The working class in the United States has suffered great hardships
for the past thirty-five years. The purchasing power of its wages is
barely higher now than in 1973, and workers have suffered dramatic
losses of benefits. Millions of workers have lost their health insurance
and an increasing proportion of new workers have none to begin with.
Those working must work longer hours to make ends meet, and more
and more families have to send at least two members into the workforce. More and more workers are "contingent," without full-time status or long-term security. At any given time, at least eight million persons are unemployed. It is no wonder that families are under siege and
that society confronts homelessness, violence, rampant drug abuse,
and mass imprisonment (especially of minorities), to name a few of
our social ills.[5]

Much has been written about the decline of the "middle class," in
actuality the decline of the working class. This decline is attributed to
a variety of sources: the increasing sophistication of technology and
the inability of most people to understand it (in turn, the fault of our
public schools); the loss of a work ethic due mainly to the generosity
of the welfare state; high taxes; overpopulation (especially if the focus
is international); foreign aid; and savage foreign competition.[6]

One issue is almost always missing from these analyses: class
power. The decline in working-class living standards corresponds
closely with the decimation of the primary defender of workers: the
labor union. In a society structured like ours, it is impossible for any
given individual to safeguard his or her economic position. Only by
acting together, in union, can most of us hope to face the owners of the
nation's vast wealth with anything approaching a level playing field.

Somehow this has become a great secret in this country, but it is easily proven that when workers are organized in unions they are demonstrably better off than when they are not.

This book will argue that no amount of education and training, no cut in taxes, and no rise in productivity can do for workers what their unionization and political organization can achieve. In this book, we will explore what unions are, how they work, what they do, and why they improve the lives of their members. We will learn the difference unions make, both in terms of overall statistics and individual case studies. We will become familiar with important aspects of trade union activity: picketing, strikes, and corporate campaigns, as well as shop stewards, grievances, arbitration, and collective bargaining.

This book's picture of unions is positive, but it does not obscure grave difficulties. A majority of the workers at the Meadville glass factory did, after all, vote against the union. Given the overwhelming benefits of unionization, why did they do this? If unions are so good, why do so few American workers belong to them? In examining the reasons for low and declining union density in the United States, this book will make a distinction between reasons external to the labor movement and those internal to it. With respect to external obstacles, we will look at the anti-labor bias of the laws, the exceptionally close alliance between business and the government, and the deep animosity of the media toward organized labor. With respect to the internal failings of trade unions, we will direct our attention to the failure to aggressively organize new members; racism, sexism, and corruption in the labor movement; the need for consistent union democracy; and the lack of an independent labor politics.

How can unions regain their former strength and increase it? The most important idea developed here is that unions can only grow when they are a part of a larger social and political movement. However, a working class social movement can best be built with unions as one of its primary components. Therefore, the growth of unions and the development of a wider movement for social change must occur together, and we will describe concrete steps that can be taken to make both events a reality.

What ultimately happened to the glass workers in Meadville? Employment has fallen since my visit fourteen years ago. As of

September 2007, there were 257 workers. PPG has decided to shed its glass division. In 2007, it made a deal with Platinum Equity, one of the private equity funds that have bought so many of our industrial facilities, to buy the entire glass division. Platinum claimed that PPG had been less than honest in valuing the glass division and sued to dissolve the agreement. In 2008, PPG agreed to sell 60 percent of its plate glass facilities to another equity firm, Kohlberg and Company. I don't know what will happen to the factory once this sale is completed. Usually a private equity buyout means significant employment cuts, as the new owners consolidate production to cut costs. To the best of my knowledge, no union drives were attempted after the ill-fated efforts of 1994.[7]

chapter one

# WHY UNIONS?

Let's be honest. Almost every person who works for a living works for someone else. We work in all sorts of jobs, in all types of industries, and under all kinds of conditions. But no matter what the circumstances, we do not work for ourselves or for each other, which means that the most fundamental aspects of our work are not controlled by us. Furthermore, our employers try to organize their workplaces so that we cannot exert much control by our own actions. For example, each of us needs to work; we do not labor for the fun of it, but to pay our bills and support our families. Yet none of us can guarantee that we will have work on any given day, let alone for an entire working life. If our employer decides to shut down the business, move it, or introduce labor-saving machinery, none of us, acting alone, can do anything about it.

I was a college teacher, and I worked for the same school for thirty-two years. By most accounts I was a good teacher; I once won an award for my teaching. Most people would say that my job required a lot of skill; I certainly had to be a student for a long time to qualify to do it. Suppose that I had believed that I was being paid too little for my work. I go to my supervisor, and I tell him this. He is sympathetic and says that he will see what he can do. Weeks go by and nothing happens, so I go back to his office. He tells me that he would like to give me more money, but the budget for the school is tight and there is nothing he can do now. If, at this point, I tell him that I cannot work for the money I am being paid and that I will have to seek other employment at the end of the school year, what do you suppose he will say? Will my threat to leave get me more money? I doubt it. He will know that if I do leave, the college will do one of two things. It may place advertisements for my replacement, and at least one hundred applicants will seek my job. They will all work for less than my salary, and the college will be under no obligation to grant them the type of job security that I now have. Or, the college will not replace me and simply eliminate my classes, assigning them to the remaining teachers or hiring part-timers to teach some of them. In other words, I am replaceable, and nothing I can do myself can change this. When push comes to shove, my employer holds all of the cards.

What was true for me is true for the overwhelming majority of workers. If you do not believe me, just ask yourself what your boss would say if you insisted on a significant raise and said that you would not work without one. Naturally you do not have to confine yourself to a pay hike. Try insisting that your hours be cut with no loss of wages, or that your employer finance a pension for you, or that your employer purchase expensive safety equipment so you can do your job without risking your health, or that your buddy who was fired be reinstated. You can ask for these things, but you cannot force the employer to give them to you.

If we are honest, we must admit that our employers have power over us. Some of them may be nice and some of them may be nasty, but none of them will spend money just because it would be good for us. They know that as individuals we are less powerful than they. We have only our ability to work to sell, but they have the jobs. In our economic system, these jobs belong to them and not to us, and they can do with them whatever they want. It is a simple but powerful truth that working people and their employers do not face each other as equals. Their employers have the jobs they need, and workers are replaceable.[1]

### STRENGTH IN NUMBERS

While most working people know that they cannot do much on their own, some choose to ignore this fact. Perhaps they are afraid, or maybe they believe that they will become supervisors some day, or maybe they think that they deserve to be controlled by someone else. Sooner or later, however, most workers will draw the obvious conclusion: if they stick together with their fellow workers, they can change things. Usually something will happen at work that sparks general anger and resentment. My wife and my daughter once worked at a daycare center run by a large national corporation. Despite the pitifully low pay, most of the women there enjoyed working with young children, and most of them showed little day-to-day animosity toward their employer. Yet they were unhappy about nearly every aspect of their work. Once a month, the supervisor had an after-work staff meeting to inform the workers of changes in policies and to give them the impression that management was concerned about employee welfare. Ordinarily, none of them had the nerve to openly challenge the office manager at these meetings, despite the fact that most of them couldn't stand her personally and had the deepest dislike for the company. Right before one meeting, the company issued a directive that each worker had to wear a uniform and a nametag. This led to much grumbling and discussion. A few people said that they would not comply with this policy, and if they were forced to, they would quit. At the meeting, my wife brought the issue out in the open, along with other complaints, including direct criticisms of the manager. Her courage stiffened the backbones of others, and before long a barrage of angry comments filled the air. Faced with such a revolt the supervisor was forced to retreat and make promises that she would investigate some of the complaints. And no one wore a uniform!

Direct actions such as this occur every day in thousands of workplaces around the world. Through them workers learn the power of solidarity and begin to understand the great gap between what is and what could be. At the daycare center "what is" is the minimum wage, few benefits, onerous working conditions, favoritism, and no respect.[2] In 2006, median annual salary for daycare employees was $17,630. But this is certainly not "what could be." Surely, those who care for our children deserve better, but the corporation's greed and the inability of the workers to exert their collective power prevents "what could be" from becoming reality.

After the meeting, a few of the women began to discuss their work situation more seriously. Out of these discussions, they came up with a plan of action based upon their knowledge that the center's contract to provide daycare was about to expire. The daycare provider is under contract with a large university hospital, and many of the children's parents work for the hospital. A contingent of daycare workers went to see the hospital administrator who deals regularly with the provider, and workers also began to speak with sympathetic parents. Their message was that unless the hospital chose a new provider, they would quit the center. This was especially upsetting to the parents, whose children were attached to the workers, and who frequently had to hire sitters to care for their children at home in evenings and on weekends. The hospital also did not want a mass exodus of skilled and caring workers. Ultimately, the company's contract was not renewed, and a new provider was chosen, paying higher wages and offering better benefits. On the other hand, not all of the workers were hired by the new center.

While the spontaneous organizing just described occurs all of the time and often results in gains for the workers, it is not enough to insure permanent results. First, workers quit, retire, and move, so the workers who win a particular struggle may not be there for the next fight. Second, workers may not always have the energy for direct actions, especially in situations that they may not perceive as important. For example, suppose a worker is fired unfairly, but he has a spotty work record and is not universally loved by his coworkers. It is unlikely that they will threaten to quit unless he is reinstated. Third, long-term improvement in the conditions of employment may require money and constant attention. Thus, it is not surprising that working people have come to the realization that more formal organizing is necessary. In all capitalist societies those who toil for others have formed labor unions to defend themselves and advance their interests in the face of powerful employers.[3]

In many ways a labor union is like any other voluntary organization. Say some residents in a community are unhappy with the condition of their streets, schools, and playgrounds. Some activists call a meeting at a local church and a large number of people show up. After they voice their concerns, someone proposes that they form a neighborhood association to pressure the town's leaders to do something about their problems. Some temporary officers are elected and regular meetings are established. Plans of action are formulated and tactics for achieving the groups' goals are worked out. A committee is formed to devise a set of bylaws for the organization; these include provisions for the selection of officers, outlining the purpose of the organization, conditions of membership, and so forth. As the group grows and achieves some successes, its members decide to assess dues on members, rent office space, obtain some used office equipment, and hire an office manager. The more or less spontaneous actions that led to the original formation have generated a more formal, structured, and hopefully permanent institution.[4]

What distinguishes labor unions from other voluntary organizations is that they are formed in response to the daily grind of working for others. The understanding that workers, as individuals, are powerless leads to a recognition that they share this powerlessness with others. They begin to identify with their workmates and this identification, based upon shared work experience, is the root cause of the formation of a labor union. When this sense of identity as working people combines with enough frustration at work, actions follow: spontaneous walkouts or slowdowns, forced meetings with the bosses, the stopping of the work process. Sooner or later, the need for a permanent defender, an independent organization standing ready to take on the employer, is felt—and the labor union is born.

## THE FIRST U.S. UNIONS[5]

In 1776 there were not many wage laborers in the United States. Most workers in the South were, of course, slaves. In the North, most people were farmers. What little manufacturing existed was carried on in small shops organized on a guild model, with young apprentices learning a trade taught them by skilled journeymen and master craftsmen. The masters owned the shops but they worked alongside their men, most of whom aspired to become masters themselves. With the onset of the nineteenth century, however, things began to change dramatically. The possibility of making large sums of money grew with the development of mass markets for items like shoes and clothing. Masters began to see that if they organized their shops in a more hierarchical way they could increase their profits. They began to take on more apprentices, but they confined them to doing unskilled work. And they began to resist any demands by their journeymen (skilled manufacturing workers) for higher "prices" for their work—that is, more pay. At the same time, the invention of labor-saving and skill-reducing machines such as power looms led to the construction of factories in which large quantities of goods could be produced. These factories, especially the textile mills of New England, began to hire young farm girls to do the work. In these factories, there was a clear separation between the workers and the owners from the beginning, whereas in the small craft shops it took the journeymen some time to see that their interests were separate from those of the masters.

As the differences between workers and owners sharpened and became clearer, the journeymen did what workers always do. They began to organize to protect themselves. In Philadelphia in 1806, shoemakers (or cordwainers as they were then called) presented the city's shoe masters with a "price list" for the various types of work they did. When the masters refused to honor their list, the cordwainers said that they would not work for any master who would not pay them their prices. And they would not work alongside any cordwainer who would work for less than the proposed rates. What they were trying to do was to create a "closed shop," that is, an arrangement in which the masters could not hire anyone who was not a member of the journeymen's union. Likewise, the young women in the textile factories struck to protest wage cuts. A strike in Lowell, Massachusetts, in 1834 encompassed one-sixth of the city's workforce.[6]

These early attempts at unionization met with a host of obstacles. The economy was subject to sudden depressions and the resulting unemployment quickly destroyed the unions. The employers aggressively resisted the efforts of their upstart workers and the press and many politicians condemned the unions as threats to liberty. The Philadelphia cordwainers were taken to court by the masters and the judge ruled that their union was a "criminal conspiracy," worthy of fines and jail time for the members. The law was uniformly hostile to any attempts by workers to organize.[7] Women workers faced special difficulties in organizing.

Not only did they have to contend with the normal greed of their employers, but they also had to confront the hostility of men, including most male workers, toward any acts of female independence. As one woman put it, "It needs no small share of courage for us, who have been used to impositions and oppression from our youth up to the present day, to come before the public in defense of our own rights."[8]

Yet workers persevered, moving forward in good times and backward in bad, but always creating the memory for their heirs that only collective actions could improve their lot in life. By the middle of the 1880s, skilled workers, at least, had finally managed to achieve a permanent organization, the American Federation of Labor or AFL.[9]

## DO UNIONS WORK?

We are regularly told by employers and by the media that unions are neither necessary nor beneficial for workers. When employers get wind of an attempt by their employees to unionize, they usually begin a disinformation campaign. They say that workers are no better off with a union than without one, and most likely worse off. Unions, they charge, are undemocratic outsiders whose leaders are interested only in their own power and in filling the union's treasury. They ask workers a simple question: why should they vote in a union when the only "benefit" they will get will be the privilege of paying dues? By their argument, a union will inevitably lead them out on strike, forcing them to lose their paychecks, with no guarantee of any gains; these strikes tend to be violent, and their only result will be the breakdown of workplace harmony. Here is part of an actual letter sent by management to some restaurant workers trying to form a union:

Dear Fellow Employees:

As you know, there will be a Union election on July 9. At that election each of you will have the opportunity to vote to determine whether or not you want to be represented by the restaurant workers' union.

You are much luckier than the employees at Fiorello's, our restaurant on the west side. Some time ago those employees voted to be represented by the restaurant workers' union. They were led down the primrose path by Union promises of increased wage benefits. In fact, after the Union negotiated a contract with the restaurant management which, in my opinion, gave the employees at Fiorello's no more than they would have gotten had there been no union—and probably gave them less [sic]. In addition, I believe that many of these employees will be hurt by the inflexibility of the Union contract. . . .

On the other hand, you know from the experience of Fiorello's employees exactly the kind of contract the Union would negotiate if it became your collective bargaining representative. A contract which produces nothing more than you would expect to receive were there no union in the picture. For that, you are afforded the privilege of paying Union dues. . . .

The restaurant does not want a Union at Fiorello's! Our experience on the west side has shown that we can negotiate an agreement with the Union which does not cost us any more in wages and benefits than without the Union and may even cost less. But our experience on the west side has also shown us that the presence of the Union results in a tense working relationship with extreme disharmony among the employees.

This is a real cost to everyone. It can result in a loss of customers and a loss of income to our employees who serve those customers, as well as the restaurant itself. The Union benefits no one but itself.[10]

The media seldom present unions in a favorable light, ignoring their positive features and highlighting and exaggerating the negative ones. Strike violence[11] always makes the front page, although it is seldom mentioned that employers nearly always instigate such violence. If employers hire scabs to replace the strikers, the media will not question whether the companies should have the right to do so. Instead, they will highlight the confrontations between the strikers and the police brought in to insure that the scabs can get through the picket lines. The daily work of unions in securing higher wages and benefits, safer workplaces, and the right to a fair hearing for complaints against the employer is ignored completely. In the more artistic media, such as films, the collective struggles of working people rarely take center stage, and when they do, they tend to be tainted with violence and corruption. Try to remember a popular movie showing unions in a favorable light. The only one that comes immediately to mind is *Norma Rae,* the exception that proves the rule.[12]

I mention the negative, and, as I shall show, false, popular image of unions for two reasons. First, workers need to be aware of the lies employers will tell them when they attempt to act in their own interests. Second, we must understand that the very nature of our society is disguised and hidden by elaborate propaganda repeated so often that most of us have come to think that it is true.[13] It is only a slight exaggeration to state that whatever is good for working people will be presented to us as bad—in newspapers, on radio and television, in the movies, and on the talk shows. Nowhere is this more the case than with unions, and the reason is not hard to discover. The corporate pursuit of profits is the underpinning of our social order, from the daily newspapers to the halls of Congress. Maximum profits require the maximum corporate control of our workplaces, which, in turn, means that our employers must be free to control us. Anything that interferes with this control will be portrayed as evil, not just to the employers but also to the social order itself. Since a union tries to win some control for us over our lives at work, it provides a direct threat to management. Therefore, unions will be portrayed as evil incarnate, as viruses that must be stamped out for the good of society. The fact that unions are *good* for workers makes the attack upon them all the more important.

One way to show the union advantage is simply to compare the wages and benefits of union members with those who are not in unions. Table 1 gives us the basic data. In addition to wages, the table also compares differences in two important benefits—insurance (including health insurance) and pensions. Given the insecurities of working life, these are probably the most important benefits, since they protect workers against the ravages of sickness and old age.

Two things should be noted about this data. First, the benefits are given in terms of their wage per hour equivalent; the overall union advantage for pensions, for example, is equal to an additional one dollar and sixty-seven cents per hour. Second, the compensation advan-

TABLE 1[14]

Union Wage and Benefit Advantage, 2005

|                | Wages | Insurance | Pension | Compensation |
|----------------|-------|-----------|---------|--------------|
| ALL WORKERS    |       |           |         |              |
| Union          | $24.10 | $3.63    | $2.39   | 33.17        |
| Nonunion       | 18.81  | 1.54     | 0.72    | 23.09        |
|                |       |           |         |              |
| UNION ADVANTAGE |      |           |         |              |
| Dollars        | $5.29  | $2.09    | $1.67   | 10.08        |
| By percent     | 28.1   | 135.7    | 231.9   | 43.7         |

tage, which includes the benefits, is greater than the wage advantage. This is because union members enjoy both more and better fringe benefits than do nonunion workers. For example, in the early 2000s, 71.9 percent of union workers had pensions, while only 43.8 percent of those without a union had them.[15] Data also show that the union advantage is greater for blue-collar workers and those with less formal education than it is for all workers, reflecting the fact that unions are of most benefit to workers of lower social status.[16]

Table I shows what we might call the "gross" union advantage. We cannot know from these data alone whether the differences between the wages and benefits of union and nonunion workers are due exclusively, or even primarily, to the fact that one group of workers belongs to unions. There may be other characteristics of the workers that would cause their wages to be unequal. For example, workers with more education and greater experience ordinarily earn more money, so some of the difference might be due to the fact that union workers have more education and experience. To take this possibility into account, we have to hold all of the other wage-determining factors (that is, all of them except the workers' union status) constant. In this way, we would be comparing two groups of workers that are alike in all respects except union status. Fortunately, economists use a technique that allows them to do this, and, while it will not prove without any doubt that union wages and benefits are higher, it will go a long way toward making the case.

In Table 2 (see page 43), the union wage advantage (excluding the benefit advantage) is presented for a variety of employee groups. The following variables that might influence wages besides union status are held constant: experience, education, region of the country, industry, occupation, and marital status.

While the effect of unionization (with all other variables held constant) varies from group to group, it is always significantly positive. For example, Hispanic men in unions earn wages 21.9 percent higher than do nonunion Hispanic men, even after we have accounted for all of the other factors that might make the union wages higher. These data also show that, contrary to the view of many conservative economists, unions reduce the wage gap between whites and blacks and between whites and Hispanics. This can be seen in the table, where the union impact on black and Hispanic wages is greater than the union effect on white wages. As we shall see, where there is a union, the principle of "equal pay for equal work" is guaranteed by the collective bargaining agreement. A black worker doing a certain job will get the same pay as a white worker. And a senior Hispanic worker will normally have a better chance in bidding for a higher paying job than a less senior white. Over the past three decades, wage inequality has risen. One reason for this has been the steady decline in union density (the share of those employed who are in a union), something we will discuss later in this book.

It is interesting to note that nonunion workers also gain when other workers are in unions. Unionization gives rise to what is called a "spillover effect." Where unions are strong, nonunion employers will pay higher wages and benefits to discourage their employees from organizing unions. So if a high proportion of high school graduates are unionized, the wages of nonunion high school graduates will be higher than they would otherwise be. As with the inequality-reducing impact of unions, the "spillover effect" has weakened as union density has fallen.[17]

## UNIONS AND DIGNITY

That unions improve the wages and benefits of workers is something all workers should know, since it directly contradicts the anti-union propaganda with which we are more familiar. It also shows that there is nothing sacred about the almighty market. Workers make low wages not because the market dictates that this is so but because they are not powerful enough to make their employers pay them more. Companies often pay low wages to their U.S. workers but pay similar workers much higher wages in their European operations. They are compelled to do this because the European workers are either organized or subject to generous minimum wage laws secured by the labor movement.[18]

In a society in which access to money is a life-or-death matter, the fact that unions bring workers more of it is important. However, unions do much more. One of the peculiar features of our economic system is that most of us must sell our ability to work in order to live. When our employers buy this ability, they think of it as their private property, and as with the rest of their property, they think that they have the right to do with it as they see fit. In other words, to them we are just "costs of production" to be minimized, and our ability to work will be treated no better than the tools and machines—and, to the extent that we are easy to replace, probably worse. The nature of our society allows our employers to objectify us, to treat us as mere means to the end of making money. Yet we do not think of ourselves in this way. Our ability to work cannot be separated from us; we are human beings, with a multitude of memories, hopes, and aspirations. Our awareness of ourselves as living beings inevitably comes into conflict with our employers' view of us as objects. We want to be treated with dignity and respect, but whether we are or not is a matter of chance, depending upon whether or not our particular employer is a decent person. And even if bosses are decent, they will not and cannot hesitate to sacrifice us for the good of the company.

A fundamental goal of a union is to change the relationship between labor and management. Again and again, when workers are asked why they support the union or what the union has meant to them, they say that their fight for a union was a fight for dignity and respect. Automobile workers in the 1930s said that the supervisors would call them by their badge numbers, not their names.[19] A worker in a company that manufactures chain links says that the boss would just whistle for them.[20] Legally, without a union, workers are "at-will";

TABLE 2[21]

Union Wage Advantage for Different Demographic Groups, 2007

| Group | Union advantage (dollars) | Union advantage (percent) |
| --- | --- | --- |
| All workers | $1.50 | 14.1% |
| Men | 2.22 | 17.1 |
| Women | 1.06 | 10.7 |
| | | |
| Whites | $1.19 | 12.4% |
| Men | 1.86 | 15.0 |
| Women | 0.81 | 9.1 |
| | | |
| Blacks | $2.44 | 18.3% |
| Men | 3.29 | 22.7 |
| Women | 1.82 | 14.5 |
| | | |
| Hispanics | $3.07 | 21.9% |
| Men | 3.53 | 23.4 |
| Women | 2.38 | 18.7 |
| | | |
| Asians | $2.51 | 17.4% |
| Men | 3.75 | 23.2 |
| Women | 1.69 | 12.6 |
| | | |
| New Immigrants (<10 yrs.) | | |
| Men | $2.05 | 16.5% |
| Women | 2.29 | 16.2 |
| | | |
| Other Immigrants (>10 yrs.) | | |
| Men | $2.10 | 16.4% |
| Women | 0.98 | 10.3 |

they can be discharged, demoted, or transferred for any reason other than those privileged by laws, such as race, sex, disability, and union activity. Our employers are free to treat us as they please, even to cut our wages and eliminate our benefits. A union can, and usually does, change all of this. Union members can take action against their employer whenever the boss shows disrespect for them. They can do this through the grievance procedure of the collective bargaining agreement, and, in addition, the union may stand ready to take direct action on behalf of any of its members.

In scholarly language, what a union does is give workers a "voice" in their workplaces, a way to put themselves on a more equal footing with their employers.[22] Here are two examples. I once worked for two summers in a glass factory. My "office" was in the plant's fire hall. During the first shift the firemen were on call, so they spent most of the day waiting for trouble, drinking coffee and shooting the breeze. Every morning the local union's officers would stop by for a coffee and trade stories about work and the union with the firemen, who might then relay them throughout the plant when they made their safety inspection rounds. The union president was a feisty old-timer with one arm. He had gotten his arm caught in a grinding machine, and legend had it that he had the arm amputated on the spot. He would daily regale us with stories of confrontations with the company and how he had stood up to the plant manager. Even if his tales were exaggerated, what if there had been no union when he had lost his arm? He would have been thrown onto the industrial scrap heap to fend for himself as best he could. But the union contract allowed him to take a job as a gate guard, a job without great physical demands. He used this job as the base from which he built support for himself as a union leader; everyone who passed through the gate knew him, and he had a lot of time to think and to plan. He had dignity despite his lack of an arm, and he owed this to the union. So too did all of the men and women who had their breath stolen from them by emphysema, one of the consequences of working in a glass factory. Some jobs involved lighter duties, and these were allocated by seniority and not by company decree.

The fate of another worker again shows the union advantage in terms beyond dollars and cents. I was the arbitrator in a case in which a man had been unemployed for two years before finally getting a job with the local water company. The employer had a policy that required the workers to wear shoes with steel toes. It also had agreed to reimburse the employees for shoe purchases up to an amount of $50.00. The man was too poor to buy the shoes, so his grandmother bought them for him. He took the receipt to the company, expecting to get the $50.00, since the shoes had cost more than this. Without warning, his supervisor called him in to his office and accused him of doctoring the receipt, saying that the company knew that the shoes were priced at only $37.95. In other words, he was accused of stealing $12.05 from the company. At the meeting, the worker, flustered because he did not want the employer to know that his grandmother had purchased the shoes, lied and said that he had himself purchased them for the amount shown on the receipt. At this point the worker was fired for theft.

Without a union, the matter would have ended there, because the company could have discharged him for no reason at all. But as a union member, he had rights which the employer had to respect. The collective bargaining agreement stated that no one in the bargaining unit could be discharged except for "just cause." He filed a grievance against the company, demanding his reinstatement with full back pay. The grievance procedure contained a series of steps by which the union and the company could try to resolve the dispute. The employer was out to make an example of this worker because, as it turned out, he had become a solid union member and recently had been elected the shop steward, the first-level union representative inside the plant. He had been aggressively pursuing grievances, trying to make the union stronger by showing the members that it would stand up for them. This is the type of person a company hates, so it decided to fire him, expecting that his short tenure and his lie at the meeting would be enough to convict him.

But the employer was wrong. When the two sides failed to settle his grievance, the union invoked the arbitration clause of the agreement, which forced the employer to place the case before a neutral outsider called an arbitrator. At the arbitration hearing, the company's attorney tried to bully the union's witnesses and the arbitrator as well. But he could not prove that the employee had altered the receipt. So I, as the

arbitrator, ordered the worker back to work with no loss of pay, benefits, or seniority. The employer then took a sentence from my award
and used it as the basis for firing the worker a second time. But it fared
no better before a second arbitrator or before the state court to which
it appealed both awards. After collecting the large back pay due him,
the worker resumed his duties as shop steward, a position he still holds
today.

A worker standing alone is a worker in trouble. For every LeBron
James, whose amazing talent gives him tremendous bargaining power,
there are millions of the rest of us, eminently replaceable. Our only
hope is to stand together, and, as we have seen, when we do, we can
greatly improve our lot in life. There is no doubt that unions force
employers to pay their workers higher wages and to provide them with
more and better fringe benefits. And furthermore, unions compel
employers to listen to their employees and to respect them as human
beings. Employers know these things, and this is why they fight our
collective efforts so viciously and spread lies about them. In their disinformation campaigns they have allies in the highest places: in
Congress, in the White House, in the corporate-owned media, and in
the universities. As we examine labor unions further in the following
chapters, it is important that we always remember this: if unions are
just in it for themselves, how do we explain their known benefits and
why is it that most employers are in an all-out war against them?

# chapter two

# HOW UNIONS FORM

Up until the end of the 1930s, the formation of a union was mainly a contest of power. Employers were intent on keeping their workplaces union-free, and they took whatever steps were necessary, no matter how ruthless. Acts of anti-union violence were common and, though illegal, were seldom punished. In fact, public authorities were often complicit in corporate violence against working people. In the coal towns of Pennsylvania, for example, the notorious coal and iron police hired by the companies to intimidate the miners and their families were actually sanctioned by the state legislature. Union supporters could be fired and blacklisted legally. Employers were free to coerce their workers into signing "yellow dog" contracts in which they promised not to join a union. These were legally enforceable, and union organizers risked fine and imprisonment if they tried to get workers to break these agreements by joining a union. The courts took a dim view of labor organizations and readily issued court orders called injunctions forbidding workers to strike, picket, or boycott. More than a thousand of these injunctions were issued in the 1920s alone.[1]

Yet, despite the combined force of the corporations and the government, workers did manage to organize to protect their interests and improve their circumstances. The living conditions of unskilled workers, including most African Americans, were too harsh to allow for much success in forming unions, but skilled workers were sometimes able to overcome the employers' antagonism. They did this through what came to be called direct actions. For example, iron molders might force their employer to give in to their collective demands by striking and enforcing their strike with pickets. The molders would typically be white men of the same nationality and with strong community ties. No one would cross their picket lines, and occasionally the local police would not do the employers' bidding. A strike by one group of workers might spread to other groups, who would strike in sympathy. Workers came to understand that the more they stuck together, the better were their chances.[2] A powerful tool of the skilled workers was the boycott, asking consumers not to buy products from particular companies charged with unfairness to labor.[3] During the 1880s, thousands of boycotts were called and honored, helping workers to bring recalcitrant employers into line under threat of losing their customers. Once organized, workers could maintain union wage scales and conditions only so long as they were prepared to use direct action against their employers any time the employers refused to honor their agreements with the union.

Skilled workers extended their organizations in several ways. First, as their employers began to expand from local to national markets, local unions in different cities and towns banded together to form national unions. One of these that has stood the test of time is the United Mine Workers of America, founded in 1890. Not only was it one of the first successful unions of unskilled and skilled workers, but it was also one of the few unions that actively organized African Americans.[4]

Second, all of the unions in a city began to form central labor bodies or councils. Through these local umbrella organizations, unions could coordinate their boycotts and sympathy strikes, as well as labor political activities.

Third, the various unions of skilled workers attempted to build a federation of all national unions. Such a federation could publish a national labor newspaper, act as an arbiter in disputes between national unions, lobby for political reforms, develop a staff of experts on labor affairs, and directly organize new workers into unions, making labor a force to be reckoned with on the national scene. After several attempts, the national unions succeeded in creating the American

Federation of Labor (AFL) in 1886, and this federation of many national unions has survived to the present day.

Fourth, unions at all levels saw clearly the need for a political response to the alliance between government and business. It might prove impossible to expand organization if the police, the courts, and the legislatures stood ready to stifle labor at every turn. Workers groped for the most appropriate political response, but there was much disagreement. Some argued for the formation of a labor party: a party of, for, and by workers, on the model of the labor parties in Europe. Others argued that the situation in the United States made such a party doomed to failure because the two major parties were too powerful to be challenged. The best political response for labor, they said, was to fight for labor-oriented candidates and policies within the major parties. As the first president of the AFL, the English-born cigar maker Samuel Gompers, put it, labor should "reward its friends and punish its enemies" regardless of their political affiliations. As it turned out, this second argument won the day. It is still the position of organized labor, although the party with which labor is most closely allied is the Democratic Party. But the discussion about labor and politics, and how the alliance of labor and the Democratic Party has failed to promote the interests of workers, is far from finished.[5]

## A LITTLE HISTORY

In the decades after the Civil War, which ended in 1865, our economy took on its modern form, one dominated by large corporations. As the opportunities diminished for people to own land for farming or to gain economic independence through owning small businesses, most people were forced to become wage workers. This made them vulnerable to the vagaries of the business cycle—the periodic ups and downs in economic activity characteristic of economies like ours. Over and over, vicious competition among the corporations led them to expand their production too much; they produced more than they could sell. This led to price wars and falling profits, which, in turn, led to massive layoffs and unemployment. The resulting depressions sometimes lasted for many years. During such periods it was difficult for workers to build their unions because the competition among workers for jobs was so severe. People desperate for work would take the jobs of others if they had to. However, as hard times continued, workers at times became so angry at their circumstances that they revolted.

The first worker revolt occurred in 1877, the year of "'The Great Uprising."[6] The railroad companies were the nation's largest employers and among the most ruthless. The economy had been in depression since 1873, and the railroad companies had responded to the crisis by repeatedly cutting the wages of their hard-pressed workers. When the B&O Railroad cut wages by 10 percent in July 1877, workers at its yards in Martinsburg, West Virginia, walked off their jobs in a spontaneous strike. President Rutherford B. Hayes sent in federal troops to stop the strike, but this so angered workers that the strike spread north and west, soon becoming a national insurrection. Pittsburgh railroad workers struck the Pennsylvania Railroad on July 19, 1877, and when local militia could not stop the strike, the state government ordered the Philadelphia militia into the city. Hostile crowds met the soldiers. When rocks were thrown, the militiamen opened fire and killed twenty people, including one woman and three children. In response, the workers revolted and destroyed the railroad's property. The workers themselves restored order, although they were defeated later by federal troops. Similar events took place throughout the country, from Chicago to St. Louis to San Francisco. When the strikes were finally crushed, the nation's newspapers condemned the strikers as thugs, tramps, and communists. Citizens were urged to buy guns to protect themselves from the working-class rabble.

Other rebellions arose after this first uprising, most notably in 1886, 1892, 1894, 1919, and during the Great Depression of the 1930s. In 1886, workers throughout the country struck, boycotted, picketed, and marched to win the eight-hour day. During a rally in Haymarket Square in Chicago, a bomb was thrown, perhaps by a police agent, which killed eight policemen.[7] The Chicago police reacted violently, killing a number of workers and wounding scores more. Eight radical labor leaders were arrested soon afterward and charged with murder. Without evidence that they had committed any crime, they were quickly tried and sentenced to death. Four of the eight were hanged, and one committed suicide in jail. Governor John Altgeld, whose political career was ruined by this act of mercy, later pardoned the others. 1894 was the year of the great Homestead steel strike.[8] War broke out in Homestead, Pennsylvania, when steel magnate Andrew Carnegie and his lieutenant, Henry Clay Frick, shut down the Carnegie Steel Works and then tried to reopen it with nonunion labor. Workers actually took over the government of the town, fighting a pitched battle against a private army of Pinkerton detectives and forcing them to surrender. The strike was defeated only when government troops were brought in. Two years later the Pullman strike erupted. This strike, led by working-class hero Eugene V. Debs, began when the workers in the company town of Pullman, Illinois, home of the factory that made the Pullman railroad cars, struck over repeated wage cuts. This monumental battle between employers and workers was again broken by federal troops and court injunctions. Debs was actually sent to prison after the strike for not obeying the injunctions.[9] After the First World War, a massive strike wave, notably in steel, shook the American economy. Historian Philip S. Foner called the 1919 wave "an unprecedented series of uprisings which, if only temporarily, vigorously challenged employers' control of the work force."[10]

There were so many rebellions during the 1930s that it is not possible to examine them all here.[11] In the famous sit-down strikes to organize the unskilled workers in our mass production industries, workers would literally sit down in industrial workplaces, refusing to work or leave. The unemployed took to the streets as well. A strike on the San Francisco docks spread to all workplaces in the city in a general strike in 1934. In Minneapolis, truck drivers led a similar strike, complete with roving bands of picketers and sophisticated logistics.[12] More than one hundred thousand people demonstrated in Chicago in 1932 to protest the murder of several people by police, who were trying to enforce an eviction of a family from their home. While police and troops again intervened on the side of the employers, the rebellions of the

1930s could not be defeated. Workers consolidated their unions and were able to win significant political victories.

Apart from a short-lived postwar upheaval in 1945 to 1946, there have been no great labor upheavals since the 1930s. There are two major reasons for this. First, workers have not been able to overcome racial and sexual divisions. With some notable exceptions, the labor movement has been dominated by white men, who have often acted in racist and sexist ways, even during the labor rebellions. During the 1930s genuine gains were made in and through many unions against racism and sexism, but after the Second World War organized labor failed to live up to a cherished principle in earlier times: "an injury to one is an injury to all." This meant that the great revolts against racism and sexism of the postwar period, the civil rights movement and the women's movement, were not intimately connected with the labor movement, despite the fact that women and people of color were becoming increasingly important in the workforce.[13] Second, all of the labor rebellions were motivated by a search for alternatives to the wage labor system itself, which many workers could see was the source of their bondage to employers. The challenge to wage labor was part of the politics of the labor movement and the basis for the formation of labor political parties. In the 1930s conditions were right for forming a labor party and renewing labor's historic antagonism to the system of wage labor. Unfortunately, labor's leaders instead accepted the class structure of American society, allied with the Democratic Party, and eventually purged the left-wing unionists from the labor movement. The result was a more conservative trade unionism, which saw itself more as partner than opponent of employers. So, while there have been many strikes and other militant labor actions since the Great Depression, there has not been a widespread labor rebellion.

## HOW UNIONS FORM

During the Great Depression of the 1930s, unskilled workers also relied on the direct-action tactics used by skilled workers in the nineteenth century. However, the depth of the economic crisis combined with the breadth of the labor movement helped to secure for working people significant political concessions. Renewed militancy led to the formation of a new national federation of unions, the Congress of Industrial Organizations (CIO). Feeling the pressure from below, the federal government under Franklin D. Roosevelt passed laws, which, for the first time, gave workers certain fundamental rights.[14] The Norris-LaGuardia Act of 1932 strictly limited the ability of employers to obtain injunctions in labor disputes. The Fair Labor Standards Act of 1937 provided for the payment of a minimum wage and overtime pay for hours in excess of forty per week. These laws represented major victories for workers, but the most important law enacted during the Great Depression was the National Labor Relations Act (NLRA). Section 7 of the NLRA gives workers the right to form labor unions without employer interference and compels employers to bargain collectively with unions chosen by the employees. A federal agency, the National Labor Relations Board (NLRB), was established by the NLRA to investigate employer violations of the act and to conduct elections in which workers can freely choose whether or not they want to be represented by a union.

Since the passage of the NLRA, the vast majority of unions have been formed through NLRB-conducted representation elections. This is not to say that a union cannot be formed through direct actions. But the law itself places serious roadblocks in the path of direct actions. So if you are ever part of a unionization effort, you will most likely use the NLRB or some similar agency.[15] Over the past few years, especially during the administration of George W. Bush, when the NLRB was dominated by members extremely hostile to organized labor, many unions have tried to find ways to secure employer recognition without going through normal NLRB procedures. One tactic has been to use economic, political, and community pressure to force the employer to recognize the union on the basis of some showing of majority support, either through a majority of the members of a proposed bargaining unit signing authorization cards or through holding an election under the auspices of an entity other than the NLRB, such as a religious or community organization. Another has been for a strong union, such as SEIU, to use its bargaining power in one area to get an employer it has organized in that area to agree to remain neutral in a union organizing campaign at a facility of this company in another area. Such a neutrality agreement precludes an employer from using the tactics normally used in an anti-union campaign.

The NLRA does not cover all employees. Farm workers, domestic workers, railroad and airline workers, and public employees are the most important groups not covered. However, Congress and many state legislatures have passed laws similar to the NLRA that protect these workers. For example, railroad and airline workers can use the Railway Labor Act to get a union, and state and local government workers in most states can use state public employee laws. Therefore, the procedure described below for those covered by the NLRA will also be useful for most of the uncovered workers.

The principles underlying the NLRA are that, first, if a majority of workers in a workplace want a union, they should have a way to get one without having to engage in direct actions, and, second, only one union should represent any particular group of workers. Further, the workers who decide to form a union must have common interests by, for example, doing the same type of work. These workers form the bargaining unit.

Once the workers have carved out a bargaining unit, they must convince the NLRB that there is a sufficient interest in unionization to warrant an NLRB election. The board uses the yardstick that 30 percent of the members of the shop must express an interest in being represented by a particular union. This means that the workers must affiliate themselves with a union. They could constitute themselves as an independent union; glass factory workers could form the "Meadville Glassworkers Union," or some similar organization. However, it will probably be wiser for employees to contact an already existing union to help them organize. This is because winning an election or forcing the employer to recognize the union without an election is a time-consuming, expensive undertaking. Unions have organizers, legal staffs, and money, all of which may be essential for victory.

Great care must be taken in choosing a union. Although many unions today know that they must organize new members or die, it is still the case that too many unions devote too little effort to organizing. So when workers make contact with a union, they should ask questions and get assurances that the union will do right by them. For example, suppose that a group of nurses want to unionize. There are several unions with nurse members; the two most important are the SEIU and the CNA. The former organizes many kinds of workers, including nonprofessional hospital employees, such as those who clean rooms and serve food in the cafeterias. The latter, on the other hand, is a craft union and only organizes nurses. There are advantages in affiliating with either union. SEIU might be able to organize almost all of a hospital's workers, and this would give it ways to put more pressure on the employer than would a union that organized only nurses. But the CNA might argue that it knows more about the specific problems faced by nurses, since nurses make up its membership as well as the core of its staff. It would be appropriate for our nurses to contact both unions and ask questions: are you interested in helping us unionize? What resources are you prepared to provide us? What do your collective bargaining contracts win for nurses? Will our demands be neglected because you have more members who are not nurses? Will you be able to make cooperative agreements with other groups of workers given that you only have nurse members? How independent are locals in you union? Who will actually do the bargaining, professional staff or the nurses themselves? It might be that either union will do a good job. As Mike Parker notes:

> Both the craft [CNA] and industrial [SEIU] models address important parts of our work experience. Any union movement that wants to win power for workers needs to address both.
>
> In principle, it shouldn't be so difficult to pay attention to both kinds of issues. An industrial union can have subdivisions that address the specific needs of its craft sectors. Within the UAW, for example, skilled workers have their own stewards and elect their own representatives to the executive board. People with technical jobs such as engineers have their own locals. In the West Coast longshore, dockworkers, clerks, and warehouse workers have their own locals.
>
> Likewise, craft unions can form councils to deal with a common employer. A bargaining council at a university, for example, could bring together separate unions for professors, teaching assistants, lab techs, clerical workers, and maintenance.[16]

The glass workers in Meadville chose the Aluminum, Brick, and Glass Workers (ABG), which has won contracts from major glass manufacturers. The ABG has since merged with the United Steelworkers of America (USWA), a very large union that has committed itself to organizing and has a large and sophisticated staff. But while size and staff are important, experience in the industry is critical as well. The United Auto Workers (UAW) failed to organize the glass workers at the sister plant in Carlisle, Pennsylvania, despite the fact that it had the early support of 80 percent of the bargaining unit.

The typical way in which workers show interest in unionization is by signing union authorization cards; these state that each worker authorizes the union to represent them for the purpose of collective bargaining. The union can petition the NLRB for an election once 30 percent of the members of the bargaining unit have signed the cards, although no union should ever go into an election without at least 50 percent of the cards signed—and probably a lot more. Not everyone who signs a card will wind up voting for the union. Another way to show the necessary support for the union is for the workers to sign a petition, which can also be presented to the NLRB instead of, or along with, authorization cards. As a tactic, this is actually better than signing cards, because each person signing a petition will see the other names on it, whereas card signing is a private matter. To win an election, workers have to publicly commit themselves to the union, and a petition forces them to do this.

Once the requisite number of cards has been signed, the union petitions the NLRB for an election. The board notifies the employer. At this point, the employer is free to recognize the union or consent to an election. Most employers will do neither of these things. Instead they will ask the board to conduct a hearing, at which the union must show that it has enough support for an election and an appropriate basis for the bargaining unit. Employers often use these hearings just to delay the union drive and give them more time to develop their anti-union efforts. In addition, the employer may be able to convince the board that the bargaining unit is not appropriate. It may have jobs in it that are beyond its proper scope, or it may not include enough workers. The university at which I worked once held up union elections for more than two years by continually challenging the bargaining unit. The NLRB has recently made it easier for employers to challenge bargaining units on the grounds that some of the workers in it are supervisors and therefore not legitimate unit members.[17]

If the union successfully makes its case, the board will set a date (or dates) for the election. The employer is then free to try vigorously to get the workers to vote against the union. Amendments to the original NLRA, as well as NLRB and court decisions, have greatly expanded the range of anti-union activities that an employer can use. Often employers hire consultants to run their anti-union campaigns, and many of these are notorious for their semi-legal and illegal tactics.[18] But even the legal tactics are appalling. Under current law it is legal for an employer to:

- Barrage the workers with anti-union propaganda, including sending letters (even videos) to the employees and their families at their homes. This propaganda does not have to be true, and as long as it is not directly threatening, it can suggest that certain bad things will happen if the workers vote in the union.

- Assign supervisors to engage in daily face-to-face "discussions" with union supporters. Prohibit union organizers who are not employees from being anywhere on company property.

- Hold captive audience meetings at the workplace. At these mandatory meetings, supervisors will pull out all the stops to convince the workers that disaster awaits them if they vote for a union. They will tell the workers to give them another chance and things will get better. An organizer told me that one boss actually pulled out a handkerchief with an onion hidden in it, so that he could look like he was crying during one of these spiels.

Most employers will go further and commit illegal acts during the union campaign; they will transfer workers who support the union, threaten them, offer them bribes, or fire them in order to defeat the union. One researcher found that since the passage of the North American Free Trade Agreement (NAFTA) employers have more frequently threatened to move their plants to Mexico or close them if a union won an election.[19] Under current law, the penalties for such dirty tricks usually come too late and hurt the employer too little to make a difference.

On the election date, the workers vote by secret ballot. The union must win 50 percent plus one of the votes cast to be certified by the NLRB as the sole bargaining agent for the workers. If the union loses, it can challenge the results if the employer has violated the law by committing unfair labor practices. The board will hold a hearing and has the power to overturn the election results. If it does, it may simply order another election. It can also overturn the election and order the employer to recognize the union despite the lost election, but that does not happen very often—only when the employer has so egregiously violated the law that the board feels that a fair election can no longer be held. Once the union has been certified as the bargaining agent, it has the duty to notify the employer that it wants to negotiate a contract with the employer.

## SUCCESSFUL UNION ORGANIZING

It is difficult to force an employer to recognize a union, despite the protections provided by the labor laws. Over the past forty years, unfair labor practices by employers have mushroomed, and union victory rates in elections have declined. For example, the unfair labor practices most germane to union election campaigns rose fourfold between the early 1950s and 1990, while refusals to bargain increased eightfold during the same period. In the 1950–1954 period, unions won 72.1 percent of NLRB elections, but by 1990 this ratio had fallen to 49.5 percent. Today it is a bit higher, but the number of elections held has fallen, as has the number of workers who are ultimately covered by collective bargaining agreements. The data available now must be viewed carefully because more unions have been refusing to use the NLRB at all. But while we don't have accurate figures on elections, workers covered by agreements, and unfair labor practices, there is no reason to believe that unions are surging or employers have become more law-abiding. And empirical studies still indicate that employers' tactics, including the illegal ones, have a negative impact on union success rates.[20]

Yet it is not impossible for unions to win recognition from employers. Some unions have decided to organize unions outside of the National Labor Relations Act. They do this in a variety of ways, usually involving direct actions. The United Food and Commercial Workers tries to organize boycotts against stubborn employers, telling them, in effect, that the boycotts will be ended when the employer recognizes the union. Others focus attention upon an entire community, trying to raise citizen awareness of the rights of workers and participating actively in community life. Then, when particular employers are targeted for organization, the union has already built a favorable climate which the employer will have difficulty combating. A union might then hold an *ad hoc* representation election under the supervision of a community organization, and if the workers vote for the union, community pressures can be brought to bear upon the employer to recognize it. Recently, unions have used their power in one place to compel employers to sign "neutrality agreements" for workers the union is trying to organize in another region.[21] Labor law scholar Ellen Dannin, while not opposed to such organizing strategies, cautions that unions should not abandon the NLRB and the NLRA. Both still have much potential to protect workers. She argues that union attorneys need to learn to educate judges, who have been trained in a legal tradition innately hostile to the interests of employees. Most judges do not know that the NLRA makes it the duty of the federal government to encourage the settlement of industrial disputes by collective bargaining.[22]

## WITH THE CALIFORNIA NURSES' ASSOCIATION IN TEXAS[23]

In the summer of 2007, I went with my wife Karen on a four-month nationwide book tour. For one week in mid-July we made our way across Texas promoting my latest book (*Cheap Motels and a Hot Plate: An Economist's Travelogue*) and talking union with members of the California Nurses Association (CNA). We made stops in San Antonio, Austin, Houston, and Dallas, meeting in two restaurants, a union hall, and a nurse's home. Along with the new book, I sold dozens of copies of the first edition of this book, discovering once again that workers, no matter the kind of work they do, have grievances against their employers that cannot be remedied unless employees organize.

The CNA was founded in 1903 as a professional association for nurses. As the social and legal climates changed, nurses, like public school teachers, converted their organization into a labor union and began to agitate for recognition from their employers and collective bargaining. CNA has enjoyed great success unionizing nurses in California, winning collective bargaining agreements that establish considerably better pay, benefits, working conditions, and voice than those enjoyed by their nonunion counterparts. (Labor scholar Gordon Lafer notes that where nurses are unionized, patients are safer.)  The union has also been a strong advocate for the general public, sponsoring legislation in California that mandates the nation's first minimum registered nurse-to-patient ratio.  When governor Arnold Schwarzenegger suspended this law in 2004, the union aggressively picketed his appearances around the state and galvanized other unions and the public to protest. Then, as Mark Brenner of *Labor Notes* tells us:

> But rather than retreat, the governor upped the ante, calling for a special election in November and personally working to put four propositions on the ballot, including two that were explicitly anti-union.
>
> .The first measure extended the probationary period for teachers from two years to five, which would make it easier to fire teachers for any reason (or no reason at all). The second required public employee unions to get annual written permission before using any member's dues for political purposes.
>
> California's unions responded by pooling an unprecedented amount of money, spending over $100 million to defeat the four propositions. The California Teachers Association provided the lion's share, more than $53 million, while SEIU put in more than $20 million between its umbrella California State Council of Service Employees and the large state workers Local 1000.

Working through the Alliance, labor also blanketed the airwaves, sponsoring 24 separate television commercials and countless radio ads.

As the election approached, the Alliance worked with local labor councils and the state fed to coordinate precinct walking and phone banking, with more than 10,000 people working on voter turnout statewide.

But it was the nurses' performance that really stole the show. Wherever Arnold went, from Washington to Wall Street, the nurses weren't far behind. The CNA even followed Schwarzenegger to a $100,000-per-ticket fundraiser at the Rolling Stones concert in Boston's Fenway Park.

"People recognized us right away, and they even know about the ratio issue," said Nguyen, who followed Arnold to Boston to protest outside of the concert. "They knew exactly why we were shadowing our governor."

The nurses never let up, staging more than 100 protests in 12 months. These efforts struck a chord both with union members and with the public. At the November 8 election, all four of Schwarzenegger's propositions were defeated.[24]

The CNA has been a steadfast champion of single-payer national health care. The union's concern for patients and the public has given it a high and positive profile in California. To expand its base, in 2004 CNA formed the National Nurses Organizing Committee (NNOC) and began to organize nationally.

One place where CNA is concentrating its efforts is Texas, where many nurses work in public hospitals. Texas does not have a collective bargaining law for public employees, which means that while workers in state and local government have a constitutional right to join a union, they cannot compel their employers to bargain with them. An employer can voluntarily recognize a union, but this rarely happens. For nurses at private hospitals, workers can use the National Labor Relations Board or try for voluntary recognition. However, Texas is a right-to-work state, so even if a union secures representation rights, it cannot negotiate a union security agreement with an employer.

CNA, like some other unions (including SEIU, with which CNA has had an often rancorous and competitive relationship), has employed innovative tactics to compensate for these difficulties. For example, it used corporate campaigns and aggressive organizing in California to get Tenet Healthcare, one of the industry's largest corporations, to sign a "neutrality agreement," in which the company agreed not to interfere in certain organizing efforts in Texas. Since employer interference in organizing efforts, often illegal but seldom punished effectively, is a major reason for low union success rates, such agreements can give the union a considerable advantage. There has been much debate about neutrality agreements, with some critics arguing that unions have made unreasonably restrictive concessions to employers to win them. However, if a union uses its power in one place to get an employer to maintain neutrality in another location, it can organize workers in might not have been able to in ordinary circumstances. On March 28, 2008, CNA's neutrality agreement with Tenet bore fruit with a victory at Houston's Cypress Fairbanks Hospital, the first hospital to be unionized in Texas.[25]

CNA has also lobbied the Texas legislature to secure staffing ratios such as it won in California and freedom for nurses to act as patient advocates. It has held demonstrations in the state capital, Austin, and other cities across the state, as well as informational pickets to inform the public about the working conditions of nurses and the need for healthcare reform.

Our first visit was in San Antonio. I spoke to a spirited group of about forty nurses, spouses, and staff persons. They asked pointed questions, showing a good grasp of workplace problems and what needed to be done about them, as well as a knowledge of unions and the labor movement. CNA has made a point of developing rank-and-file leaders and using female and minority staff. Most nurses are women, and in San Antonio many are Latina. It has also understood that a union must educate its members not just about the nuts and bolts of unions and collective bargaining but also about the larger society and political economy. Workers need a political compass and an ideological code or creed that fits their needs and galvanizes them into action. To do so they must learn much more than what they see on television or what all too many unions teach them.

The meetings in Austin, Houston, and Dallas were less satisfying, but the fact that working nurses came to hear me at all was gratifying. And I learned once again why unions matter. Nurse after nurse told horror stories about their work—unconscionable patient loads and twelve-hour shifts, which, even if done in a shorter workweek, leave nurses exhausted and patients at risk. One nurse told us of working such shifts for two weeks straight before getting a break. Another worked sixteen-hour shifts! All the nurses spoke of constant harassment from supervisors and some doctors. Hospital treatment of patients was described as profit-driven and often unsafe. One nurse described a hospital evacuation in which seriously ill and injured patients were forced to leave their rooms without adequate support, and without the nurse's intervention patients might have died. Nurses are time-studied and subjected to lean production tactics made common by the automobile companies. Poorly trained and less skilled workers allow hospitals to economize on the use of regular nurses. Patient loads are incrementally increased and necessary supplies are curtailed. Nurses must "do more with less," in an occupation where both mean worse care for the sick. Not one nurse to whom I spoke said that she would encourage her daughter or son to become a nurse. As they shared their stories, encouraged by the union staff persons, I could see the seeds of the solidarity necessary for successful union-building sprouting. From small meetings to talking at work to reading and reflecting to wearing union insignia at work to confronting a supervisor about patient loads to a public protest to the signing of a petition. Gradually, day-by-day, you come to understand that your life circumstances can only improve if those of your coworkers do as well. If the time is right, if the union is right, you come to realize that you are a part of something larger than yourself—the struggle of an entire class, the working class, for liberation.

No matter whether unions organize under the NLRA or not, we have a good deal of evidence about what it takes for a union to succeed. To overcome the obstacles employers and the law put in the path of union organizing, union tactics matter. In fact, researchers Kate Bronfenbrenner and Tom Juravich say that "union tactics as a group played a greater role in explaining election outcome than any other group of variables, including employer characteristics and tactics, bargaining unit demographics, organizer background, or election environment."[26]

A successful union often takes time to build. Those workers who strongly support the union must, with the help of the union's organizers, build a rank-and-file organization inside the workplace right from the beginning. This means meeting and talking with coworkers to build understanding and support long before asking them to sign petitions or authorization cards.

We often think of unions as organizations whose only purpose is to get their members more money. Yet Bronfenbrenner and Juravich found that "unions which focus on issues such as dignity, justice, discrimination, fairness, or service quality were associated with higher win rates than those which focused on more traditional bread and butter issues, such as wages, benefits, and job security."[27] The sanitation workers on strike in Memphis, Tennessee, whom Martin Luther King Jr. was supporting at the time of his assassination in 1968, wore signs that read "I Am a Man." The women clerical workers who organized at Yale University in the 1970s wanted respect and dignity, plus an end to racial and sexual discrimination, and not merely more pay.[28]

To achieve these goals, a "culture of solidarity" must permeate every aspect of the union drive. In general terms, the employer must come to be understood as the *class enemy* of the workers, one that can be defeated only if the workers stick together, acting as if "an injury to one is an injury to all." The union should encourage a gradual escalation of solidarity actions, allowing workers to discover through action that unity is both possible and beneficial. For example, once an internal organizing committee is formed, its members can begin to have informal meetings with other workers outside the plant or arrange to visit workers at their homes. Then, a petition of union support might be circulated. Signing a petition might be the first step in getting a person's commitment; once it is obtained, the worker's further commitment should be invited and secured. Once sufficient numbers have signed a petition, a rally of signers might be organized. An open rally means people stand up for what they have done and makes further actions easier. Regular events, from meetings with speakers to social events, can further solidify the workers. People must be made aware at these events of what the employer is doing or will be doing to undermine the union effort. It is relatively easy for the union to predict the employer's tactics, since they all use basically the same ones. In addition, the workers' families and the larger working community must be brought into the campaign from the beginning. Workers from other union bargaining units can be excellent organizers, since they speak from direct experience. As soon as possible, workers should begin to formulate the demands that they will bring to the bargaining table when their union drive succeeds. Perhaps demands can be presented to the employer before the election.

In their research, Bronfenbrenner and Juravich found specific tactics that were especially helpful in winning elections:

- **Forming an organizing committee.** This workplace committee should include as high a percentage of workers as possible. It should be representative of the composition of the workforce in as many ways as possible. Each department of the workplace should be represented, and the sexual and racial composition of the committee should reflect those of the workplace as a whole. Optimally, the union staff people will also reflect these compositions. For example, in plants with mostly Asian women workers, the organizers should be Asian women, or at least women familiar with their circumstances. Similarly, organizing in the South requires unions to use African American organizers, since it is still the case that most African American workers labor in the South. Those who originally form the organizing committee should make a diagram of the workplace to aid in the organizing.

- **House calling.** Successful unionization demands face-to-face contacts. For example, I participated in four failed attempts to unionize college teachers. One of the reasons why these efforts failed is because the teachers would not speak directly to their coworkers even at work. College teachers are too caught up in the middle-class view that it is not polite to infringe upon another person's privacy. It was unthinkable for many union supporters to buttonhole their colleagues in the hallways, much less in their homes. Therefore the union relied too heavily upon mass mailings and letters to newspapers. We had missed the point that the formation of a union is an emotional as well as an intellectual experience. Getting people to take actions that they have been taught all their lives are not appropriate requires that they be moved, that they get angry, that they come to see that there are principles at stake. Only through personal contact is there any hope of winning the emotional commitment without which a union cannot succeed. Both union-supporting workers and organizers should make house calls, for the obvious reason that potential recruits are bound to be more receptive to people whom they recognize.

- **Holding mass and small group meetings.** Unions are collective organizations and, as such, require regular meetings to work effectively and democratically. At meetings, not only can workers hear what the union is all about, they can also learn the fundamentals of democratic organization and begin to gain the confidence that will help them confront their employers. Meetings can also be social events, places at which workers can solidify friendships and make new ones. At larger meetings, people from other workplaces can inform the workers of how unions have benefited them and can help the new union develop its strategies.

- **Using solidarity days,** on which union supporters do something to show their solidarity. At the Meadville glass factory, the workers showed their unity, pride, and dignity by wearing red union t-shirts. Depending on circumstances, a solidarity day can also be an occasion to challenge managerial authority in a more direct way, such as a group of union supporters formally grieving some particularly outrageous management action.

- **Forming a bargaining committee** before the election. People begin to see that something may become a possibility as they actually begin to do it. As workers develop concrete contract proposals, their ingenuity is tapped and they become impatient that their proposals are not already the law of the shop. The idea is to make unionization a more or less self-fulfilling prophecy.

Not only do such tactics make it possible to win unionization even when the employer vigorously resists the workers' efforts, but they are also crucial to the union winning a first contract. Management does not stop fighting the union once it wins the election. It will try to prevent the union from getting the critical first collective bargaining agreement, and it will succeed about a third of the time. It will do so by using legal and illegal tricks to delay the bargaining. In order to detect and to prevent this, the union must continue to build the rank-and-file movement after the election. Finally, to be effective, a union must convince most or all of the members of the bargaining unit to actually become members of the union. Under current labor laws, it is not possible to negotiate a contract provision that forces workers to become union members.[29] However, the tactics that work in organizing and in bargaining also work in building union membership.

chapter three

# UNION STRUCTURES AND DEMOCRACY

In the 1996 presidential election, Republican candidate Bob Dole, no friend of working people, repeatedly disparaged the union "bosses" who were supporting President Clinton. In 2008, John McCain did the same thing (although Barack Obama downplayed his strong union support so much that McCain's anti-unionism did not resonate much with the electorate). What made this remarkable is that Dole and McCain, like Clinton and Obama, got gobs of money from corporate officials—who really are bosses! Yet, although Obama and McCain railed against the fat cats on Wall Street when the financial system melted down, they would never have thought to call them "bosses." Unions are routinely accused of being undemocratic bureaucracies, more interested in enriching their leaders than in serving their members. Even those who are generally sympathetic to unions refer to union leaders as "bosses." Working people often tell pollsters that they believe that union leaders are not trustworthy, although the public's overall view of unions is generally positive and large numbers tell pollsters that they would join a union if given the opportunity.[1]

Is it true that unions are top-down organizations with bosses, just like the corporations that they claim to be fighting? While many unions are not as democratic as they should be, there is no doubt that unions, especially at the local level, are among the most democratic institutions in the country. And even the most top-down union has a potential for democracy that every business lacks. General Motors is organized as a hierarchy with orders emanating from the top and carried out below, and this is true of most employers, both private and public. If the board of directors of GM decides that the corporation is going to do a certain thing, there is no way that the employees can bring about a change in the corporation's hierarchy to reverse course. The workers do not elect the board members, nor do they have the power to force a change so that they could elect them. In other words, most employers do not have democratic organizations, and they cannot be made to have them. The power is at the top, supported by the property rights of the owners and the government that stands ready to enforce them.

In a union, the situation is much different. Unions are organizations that workers have formed voluntarily and in such a way that they, the members, have or can exert real power. All unions have constitutions or bylaws that provide for democratic structures, and important federal laws promote union democracy. This is not to say that all unions act democratically, but they all have a democratic potential absent in employers. History gives us all too many examples of undemocratic, even corrupt, unions, although it also gives us plenty of examples of union democracy. However, there are no unions in which democracy is completely absent. Consider the International Brotherhood of Teamsters, the union that comes to everyone's mind when the words "corrupt union" are spoken. For at least fifty years, this union was mired in corruption, controlled by organized criminals who used its pension funds as banks for their casinos in Las Vegas. Yet the national Teamsters union was comprised of hundreds of local unions that were not corrupt and that carried out the wishes of their members. In Minneapolis in the late 1930s, the Teamsters led one of the labor rebellions of the Great Depression, establishing a model of democratic and progressive unionism in the process. And in the early 1980s and 1990s, courageous reformers built a rank-and-file movement called Teamsters for a Democratic Union (TDU), whose aim was to win back control of the union for the members. They stood up to the gangsters and their union stooges and eventually succeeded in getting the federal government to press racketeering charges against them. The government also agreed to oversee open and fair elections. As a result, reformer Ron Carey and his allies in the TDU won control of the union and began to implement an ambitious program of democratic reforms.

Of course, there are many problems yet to be solved. Carey won reelection in 1998 against the son of the legendary and corrupt Jimmy Hoffa by a slim margin. Then, in a tragic turn of events, Carey himself was accused of using union funds to aid his election by means of a scheme that funneled money from the union to certain liberal organizations, which then gave the money to Carey's campaign. Democratic Party and AFL-CIO officials were also involved. Carey was forced by the government overseer to step down as president and was disqualified from running again. Given that chicanery is commonplace in political campaign financing, the penalty against Carey was excessive, and he was later exonerated of any personal corruption.[2] But a union must be controlled by its rank-and file and not by its bureaucrats, who should serve the members not dictate to them. And a labor movement must be politically independent and not in league with its class enemies in any political party.

Yet, despite this terrible turn of events, the Teamsters union has been radically changed by the efforts of the TDU in a way that would be utterly impossible in a privately owned business or government agency.[3] You can bet that the UPS strike, carried out under Carey's leadership in 1997, would never have occurred under the Teamsters' old guard, which probably would have signed a sellout contract with the company. It will be up to the TDU and its rank-and-file allies to continue to fight for democracy in the union, irrespective of who the officers happen to be.

## LOCALS AND INTERNATIONALS

When workers form a union they usually form a *local* of a larger *national* or *international*. (Some U.S. unions are called *internationals* because they have members and locals in Canada.) The union will have a constitution to which the local must subscribe, but the local will also have its own bylaws, binding for all local members. The bylaws will establish which officers the union will have and how they are to be selected, and the local's rules of operations: who is eligible to run for office, whether or not the officers will be paid, the duties of the officers, the lengths of the terms of the officers, the frequency and times of the union's meetings, the behavior expected of union members, the dues of the local (these may be specified in part by the national or international union), etc. In the United States, there are thousands of local unions (though the number is declining as national unions force local mergers, presumably to gain economies of scale). Almost all of these local unions are members of national or international unions.[4] There are a few independent locals unattached to a national or international. In some cases, these independents are closely allied with the employer and may be *company unions*; they do not independently pursue the interests of the workers.

While there is diversity in union structures, in most cases the local union has autonomy but is still bound by the rules and policies of the national or international union of which it is a member. A union may also contain intermediate bodies between the levels of the local and the national. For example, the American Federation of Teachers (AFT), of which I was a member for many years, is a national union of school teachers and related workers. My local was called the United Faculty (most locals are simply designated by their numbers, as in Local 3 of the International Brotherhood of Electrical Workers). We had our own constitution and bylaws and, in general, set our own policies. We had not yet won bargaining rights, but if we had, we would have established our own bargaining agenda. As part of the AFT, we were required to pay a part of our dues (called the per capita) to an intermediate group, the Pennsylvania Federation of Teachers, and to the national union. The role of the state federation is to service the locals, publish a newspaper, form alliances with other unions in the state, and act as a lobbying group with the state legislature. This last role is of great importance for teachers, most of whom are public employees and whose employers are, therefore, dependent upon the state for funding. The national union sets the overall program of the union. It hires a staff of researchers, organizers, lawyers, lobbyists, and the like, who service the locals, help the union to secure new members, lobby various political bodies, and promote public support for teachers and education.

The most common schema, therefore, is: local—intermediate body—national. However, even within this structure there is variability. First, local union autonomy differs from union to union. Some locals might be able to call strikes irrespective of the wishes of the national officers, while others might have to first secure the approval of the national union. Some unions have large strike funds, but before a local's members can gain access to it they must get permission to strike from the national. Second, locals vary in size and in the complexity of their tasks. A local union of electrical workers may represent all of the electrical workers in a large city and negotiate with an association of construction contractors. These contractors may contribute money into a pension fund—so many cents for each hour a union electrician is employed by one of them—and the local union may help to manage a fund. By contrast, a local union of GM automobile workers would not be involved in pension fund management; the national would attend to that.

Third, unions differ in how they select their officers. Local officers are normally selected by secret ballot by the members. The officers, then, may have the power to appoint staff. In a factory setting, the first-level union official, the one in most direct contact with the members at the workplace, is called the shop steward. In some unions, stewards are elected, while in others they are appointed by the officers. The same thing might be true of the local's bargaining committee.

Intermediate body and national officers are usually chosen in one of two ways. They are either elected by the direct vote of the membership or they are elected by delegates to the national union's periodic conventions. The delegates are local union officers, appointed staff persons, or some combination of the two. Both systems can be democratic, although the direct election method is the most democratic and therefore the most desirable. Before the reform of the Teamsters union, for example, delegates to the national convention elected national officers, but most of the delegates were appointed staff persons. Such a situation, in which it is nearly impossible to unseat an incumbent union officer, is tailor-made for corruption.

Nearly all of the national and international unions in the United States are, in turn, a part of one of two federations of unions, the American Federation of Labor and Congress of Industrial

Organizations (AFL-CIO) and the Change to Win Federation (CTW). As we saw in the Preface to this edition, there are seven national/international unions in the CTW. According to the AFL-CIO's website, there are sixty-two such unions in the AFL-CIO. This represents a nearly 40 percent decline in the past ten years, the consequence of numerous union mergers.[5]

In some ways the relationship between the AFL-CIO and CTW and their member unions is similar to the relationship between a national union and its locals. The AFL-CIO publishes a newspaper; it has a large staff of researchers; it hires organizers and sponsors an "Organizing Institute"; it has a contingent of lobbyists in Washington, D.C.; and in general it acts as the spokesperson for working people. However, the AFL-CIO has limited powers over the affiliated national unions; these maintain their autonomy. The AFL-CIO can try to work out disagreements among the member unions, getting them to agree not to raid each other's members, for example. But it cannot dictate policies to them. If a national union wants to end a strike, the AFL-CIO cannot prevent it from doing so, even if its officers believe that the union is making a bad mistake. The AFL-CIO can, of course, expel unions from membership, and it has done this a few times, most notably when it expelled the Teamsters for corruption, a decision since rescinded.  Not all national unions are members of the federation. The nation's largest teachers' union, the National Education Association, is not a member although there are places in the country where NEA affiliates are merged with AFT (an AFL-CIO union) locals. Nor is the smaller United Electrical, Radio, and Machine Workers of America (UE). All in all, the AFL-CIO and CTW can best be described as weak federations. This is good in terms of member union independence, but bad for forging united worker actions. They are of considerable importance, though, and we will have more to say about them later in the book.

Within certain geographical areas, such as cities, the AFL-CIO affiliated unions form another kind of organization: central labor councils. These councils serve a variety of functions. Historically they have served as coordinators of local union organizing. Suppose that the United Steel Workers union is trying to organize a steel fabricating company in Pittsburgh, Pennsylvania. The unions in Pittsburgh's

Central Labor Council could agree to support the organizing effort with money and organizers from the member unions. The council could support a boycott of the target company's products. In a strike, council unions could help with the picketing. Members of the unions could refuse to cross the picket lines to make deliveries or to do construction work on the struck premises. Central labor councils can sponsor labor education classes for union members or, indeed, for any workers in the area. In these ways, central labor councils can help to build strong local labor movements. Unfortunately, while a few central labor councils still do these things, many of them are inactive and devote most of their energies to helping local charities such as the United Way, and to getting out the vote for labor-friendly candidates. Recently, there has been considerable literature on the need for a renewal of the original organizing and solidarity-building activities of central labor councils.[6]

## UNION STRUCTURE AND THE LAW

While union structures exhibit much diversity, they all must conform to an important federal labor law, the Labor Management Reporting and Disclosure Act, more commonly known as the Landrum-Griffin Act.[7] Congress enacted this statute in 1959, in the wake of several congressional investigations into union corruption. Since employers do not typically mind dealing with corrupt unions (which, incidentally, often make large contributions to the campaigns of conservative politicians), it follows that "corruption in unions" was a smokescreen for the real purpose of the hearings—to give labor a black eye. Employers and their governmental allies wanted to create the impression that unions were in fundamental conflict with their members, who needed protection from corrupt and autocratic union leaders. Yet, as is sometimes the case, the anti-union intentions of the Congressional investigators produced legislation of potentially great importance to union members.

The act is divided into a number of parts or "titles." The most important provisions of which are the following:

Title I: The union member's "bill of rights." It guarantees that a union cannot deny the rights provided by its constitution and bylaws to any member. No member can be denied the right to speak out at union meetings, to run for union office, or to have access to the union's newspaper. A union's president cannot arbitrarily replace a staff person who has been elected by the membership. A union cannot deny a member running for union office the right to place advertisements in the union paper if the incumbent has such a right. A member whose rights have been violated can sue the union in state court. Of great importance: "No member of any labor organization may be fined, suspended, expelled, or otherwise disciplined except for nonpayment of dues by such organization or by any officer thereof unless such member has been (a) served with written charges; (b) given a reasonable time to prepare his defense; (c) afforded a full and fair hearing."

Title II: Unions must file various membership and financial reports with the Department of Labor, and all of this information must be made available to the members upon request.

Title III: Strict limits are placed on the right of the national union to implement trusteeships. The constitutions of most national unions give them the power to temporarily take over the affairs of their locals or intermediate bodies. This is called putting the local in trusteeship. It is not a bad thing, if the local has fallen prey to gangsters or if local officers have stolen funds. However, in some unions, trusteeships were forced upon locals in order to consolidate the power of the national union's officers and to deny the democratic functioning of the locals. Title III stipulates against such abuses of power, although critics say that this title is inadequately enforced and easily subverted by unions intent on imposing trusteeships.[8]

**Title IV: Unions must have regular elections of officers. Local unions must have such elections at least once every three years and national unions once every five years. All elections must conform to minimal democratic standards; for example, they must be by secret ballot. A union cannot establish discriminatory eligibility rules such that, for example, a member had to be present at 90 percent of the union's meetings in the past year to be eligible for office. The Department of Labor, which administers most of the act, has the power to overturn a union election and to oversee a new one. This is what happened in the United Mine Workers in 1972. Incumbent Tony Boyle had won reelection in a tainted election in 1969. In fact, he had his main rival, Joseph "Jock" Yablonski, murdered right after that election. The Department of Labor, upon petition from Boyle's challengers, overturned the election. This paved the way for the election of Arnold Miller, the candidate of the miners' reform group, Miners for Democracy, and for the revival of democracy in that great union.[9]**

## AN EXAMPLE OF UNION DEMOCRACY

The United Electrical, Radio, and Machine Workers of America, better known as the UE, was one of the unions in the forefront of the movement for industrial unionism during the labor wars of the Great Depression.[10] A charter member of the pre-merger CIO, the UE had, by the end of the Second World War, organized most of the large firms that produced both industrial and consumer electronic goods, most notably General Electric and Westinghouse. The UE established an admirable record of both rank-and-file democracy and progressive politics and, in the process, won significant gains in wages, hours, and working conditions for hundreds of thousands of electrical, machine, and radio workers. Unfortunately, the union fell victim to the anti-communist frenzy of the Cold War. The UE was ultimately expelled from the CIO because its officers would not sign the non-communist oaths required by the Taft-Hartley laws. Taft-Hartley, passed in 1947, amended the National Labor Relations Act, adding many anti-labor provisions to it. Taft-Hartley required that all union officers sign oaths stating that they were not members of the U.S. Communist Party, at the time a legal political party. Not only was this a violation of civil liberties, but it also served to drive the left out of the unions. Communist Party members and supporters had done yeoman work in establishing the CIO, often taking the greatest risks and doing the most difficult organizing, and had gained considerable influence in some of the CIO unions, including the UE.[11] Especially noteworthy was the Communist position on the rights of African American workers; radicals in the unions led the way in organizing black workers, most of whom worked in the South.[12] The left-led unions struggled and won collective bargaining agreements second to none in the industrial unions.

After the UE was purged from the CIO, other unions raided its members, a practice made easier by the denial to the UE of the protections of the NLRA and the NLRB and by the constant harassment of the employers and the Red hunters in Congress. Yet somehow the union survived, and, after losing most of its members in the 1950s, began a comeback in the next three decades. Today, the union has about thirty-five thousand members and is headquartered in Pittsburgh, a city that has seen some of the greatest UE victories and defeats. It no longer organizes only within the industries indicated in its name, but, like most unions today, will organize any workers who agree with its principles. Recently it has been working to organize public sector workers in southern states—North Carolina, Virginia, and West Virginia—that do not have laws giving such employees the right to collective bargaining. It has worked cooperatively with the Black Workers for Justice (a worker center), forming Local 150—the North Carolina Public Service Workers Union—to organize janitors and similar workers at all of the public colleges and universities in the state. In doing this work, it has formed the International Workers Justice Campaign, which has successfully petitioned the International Labor Organization (ILO) to censure North Carolina for denying public employees from exercising their internationally recognized human right to unionize and bargain collectively.[13]

The vitality of the union is partly explained by its vibrant internal democracy. The UE has a tripartite organizational structure.[14] At the top there is the national union. The constitution of the national union states that the object of the union is "to protect, maintain, and advance the interests of working people, to organize local unions at places of employment, and to promote the advancement of such bodies." The union seeks to organize any private and public sector workers "who desire organization on the basis of rank-and-file control in order to pursue a policy of aggressive struggle to improve their conditions." The union promises to accept members irrespective of their "skill, age, sex, nationality, color, race, religious or political belief or affiliation, sexual orientation, or immigration status." The constitution provides for the election of a general president, general secretary-treasurer, director of organization, and a general vice-president for each of the union's geographical districts. These officers comprise the union's general executive board, which is responsible for the running of the national union. In addition, there are three trustees and two alternates who audit the union's books, take a yearly inventory, and generally safeguard all of the union's properties.

The national officers of the UE serve only two-year terms and must stand for election at the biennial conventions of the union. The locals of the union select the delegates to the convention by secret ballot of members in good standing. The delegates have voting power in proportion to the membership of their locals, but no local can have more than fifteen delegates, irrespective of its number of members. Thus, this union guarantees that the officers will be elected democratically, and it also protects the voice of smaller locals. This is in contrast to many other unions, which, although they operate in a reasonably democratic manner, allow convention delegates to be appointed by national officers, thereby making it difficult for alternative points of view to be heard. Even when anticommunist dissidents, often sponsored by outside groups, were ripping the UE apart, it maintained its standard of spirited and democratic debate. Perhaps most remarkably, its constitution places strict limits on the salaries of the officers: "Where not defined in the Constitution, the General Executive Board may fix the compensation to be paid to any officer, member, or other person employed by the National Union provided that such compensation shall not exceed the maximum weekly wage paid in the industry. . . ." In 2009, the president of the union could be paid no more than

$56,805.12. In this way, the union makes sure that the officers stay close to the members and identify with them, as opposed to the employers with whom they negotiate. The constitution also provides another check on the officers. Any of them can be recalled through a petition procedure initiated by the locals.

Beneath the national union (organizationally, that is, not in terms of power) are three regions: the Eastern, Northeast, and Western. In each there is a regional council. The goal of each council is to "secure mutual protection, harmonious action, and close cooperation among all locals within a given region, in all matters relating to the United Electrical, Radio, and Machine Workers of America (UE)." The local unions elect the officers of the councils. Each council must have its own constitution. Recently, the General Executive Board was expanded to provide additional rank-and-file positions based on the number of dues-paying members in each region.  Carol Lambiase, a longtime union staff person, says that "the goal was to provide for greater leadership development at the national level."

The base of the union consists of the local unions in each district. Each local must have a constitution, which spells out the number of officers, the duties of the officers, the times of the local's meetings, the local's standing committees, the procedures for calling strikes, and the rights of a member brought up on charges by another member for violating the union's rules and regulations. Each of the constitutions (national, regional, and local) includes procedures to guarantee basic due process rights to any accused member. The national constitution provides for the chartering of new locals, and the basic dues structure is established by the national convention. Sister Lambiase told me that "dues are now set on a sliding scale, given the wide divergence in wages throughout the union. They are now based on the average wage of the shop [workplace]. Currently [mid-2008] the minimum dues range from $4.38 per week to $6.92 per week, but locals can vote to set their dues higher. Similarly, per capita is set on a sliding scale based on the average wage of the shop as well."[15]

In the UE, strikes are called by the locals. Still, any strike must be in conformity with the union's constitution. Specifically, "any strike related to the negotiation of a new collective bargaining contract or the renewal of an existing collective bargaining contract and all contract settlements must be approved by vote of the membership of the local or locals involved. . . ." Each local must establish a strike defense fund to support members when they are on strike. In collective bargaining, "no representative of the United Electrical, Radio, and Machine Workers of America (UE) shall negotiate alone with the employer."

The UE goes to great lengths to insure that the members actually control the union, from the national convention to the daily operations of every level of the union. Article 25 of the national constitution is titled "UE Rank-and-File Principles," which includes the following statement: "The UE staff is employed by the membership through the national officers and general executive board and implements the leadership's decisions to build the union membership, to assist the locals and districts in solving their problems, and to effectuate UE programs and policies. Staff members have no right to interfere with UE rank-and-file control, including election processes, at any level of the union. To deviate from this policy would lead to a staff controlled union."

Naturally, a union may not act as democratically as its constitution might suggest, but the UE has, in fact, operated throughout its history in accord with its principles. Therefore, it can serve as a measuring rod for the evaluation of other unions. A few unions do provide for greater due process for union members charged with a violation of union rules. The United Auto Workers (UAW) has an independent review board to which a member can appeal an adverse ruling. But the UAW is much more dominated by its staff than is the UE. In many unions today, there are rank-and-file movements that are insisting on greater union democracy. The labor movement will succeed in rebuilding itself only to the extent that these movements achieve success.

## A LOCAL UNION MEETING

**For many years, I was a member of the American Federation of Teachers (AFT). My local was named the United Faculty, and our goal was to organize the teachers at the University of Pittsburgh, which is where I worked. Every aspect of our union was democratic. We wrote our own constitution and bylaws, and we made our own decisions with respect to strategies and policies. The AFT has**

state federations and a national office, and we were affiliated with both the Pennsylvania Federation of Teachers and the AFI. We set our own dues, but we had to pay a per capita amount of money to both the state and national federations as well as to the AFL-CIO, with which the AFT was affiliated. The AFT provided us with funds for our organizing drives as well as with organizers and staff. Of course, we were bound by the AFT's constitution and the AFT could decide not to back our efforts, but all in all, the local ran with a remarkable amount of autonomy. Eventually, the AFT agreed to a merger of our AFT local with that of another union, the American Association of University Professors (AAUP), and so we then had a joint union.

We held our meetings in a building owned by a Protestant church, which was used for a variety of purposes. We conducted them according to a standard form, with any member present free to speak his or her mind about any issue brought forward. We made our decisions by vote of our executive board or by a mail ballot of the entire membership, depending on the issue and the rules in our constitution. There were times when the meetings were routine, and there were times when the meetings got heated. We had many disagreements with the AFT staff and sometimes with our attorneys. We did not always like the positions taken by the national AFT. But our union was always an exercise in democracy, and much the same can be said of the operations of the vast majority of local unions.

If we look at the history of the labor movement, we discover that its periods of growth were in times when the movement came to symbolize a path to a better life for all working people. Researchers are now also finding that the more democratic the union movement, and the more militant and class-conscious its leaders, the better off the workers end up being.[16]

chapter four

# COLLECTIVE BARGAINING

Once a union has been formed, it seeks to establish the terms under which its members will work. Once, unions simply set these conditions, and workers refused to labor unless the employer agreed to them. Today, however, wages, hours, and the terms and conditions of employment are normally worked out through a process known as collective bargaining. A union formally recognized by the employer, either because of an election or voluntarily by the employer, has the right to negotiate with the employer, and the employer has an obligation to do so. The National Labor Relations Act requires the employer to bargain in "good faith."[1] This does not mean that the employer must come to an agreement with the union, only that the employer has "intent" to reach agreement. The union is the sole bargaining agent for all of the people in the bargaining unit (whether they are members of the union or not); this means that the employer must bargain with this union, with no other, and not with individual workers.[2]

Reaching agreement with an employer—arriving at a written collective bargaining agreement or contract—is difficult. Employers often engage in a variety of stalling tactics known as *surface bargaining*, that is, going through the motions of negotiating without having an intent to reach agreement. They may cancel or delay meetings; they may agree to minor and costless union proposals but refuse to consider important ones; they may refuse to offer counterproposals to the union's demands; they may add new proposals just when it appears that agreement is close; and they may take back agreement on bargaining items already concluded. These tactics are illegal (in bad faith), but the labor laws do not have enough teeth to deter employers from using them. If the union files an unfair labor practice grievance, it may be many months before the NLRB or a related agency makes a ruling. In the meantime, the workers may become demoralized at the failure of the union to get a contract, and the employer will take advantage of this by blaming the delay on the unreasonableness of the union. In addition, there is turnover in any workplace, so some union supporters may quit, retire, get injured, or die. All of which may sap the union's strength. Worst of all, if the board does rule against the employer, the typical penalty is simply to order the employer back to the bargaining table. There is no monetary penalty for an employer's refusal to bargain in good faith.

The weakness of the law has led to a sharp rise in refusals to bargain and other unfair labor practices. Between the early 1950s and the beginning of the 1990s, these increased by nearly eight times, which is all the more discouraging since union membership was declining throughout most of this period.[3] The most important consequence of employer lawlessness is that it has become much more difficult for a new union to win its first collective bargaining agreement. In fact, a large number of all first negotiations end without the union achieving an agreement with the employer. In other words, although the union wins recognition, it is ultimately defeated.[4] The situation is not so bad for established unions, although even here a refusal to bargain can have serious consequences, especially if the union is not prepared or able to force the employer back to the bargaining table.

This means that if a union is to win a good agreement, it must approach bargaining in the same way it approached the initial organizing. The tactics that researchers have found essential to successful organizing are also necessary for collective bargaining: one-on-one meetings, solidarity days, house-calling, rank-and-file-mobilization, community support, and, above all, skillful preparations.

## THE IWW'S CASE
## AGAINST COLLECTIVE BARGAINING

The American Federation of Labor, the trade union association created in the late nineteenth century, was mostly made up of unions of skilled or craft workers. These workers, overwhelmingly male and concentrated in particular ethnic groups (German, Irish, Jewish, etc.), often had disdain for unskilled workers, who were much more ethnically and racially diverse and contained a higher proportion of women. The AFL made little effort to organize the unskilled. In addition, while skilled workers were willing to utilize militant actions such as strikes and boycotts to force employers to deal with them, once they achieved a stable union they placed most of their efforts on negotiating contracts. The AFL's conservative approach to unionism, which included an acceptance of the wage system and a willingness to work within the two-party political framework, won it the enmity of more radical elements within the labor movement. Such radicals, led by men like Eugene Debs and "Big" Bill Haywood and women like Elizabeth Gurley Flynn, formed other kinds of unions. The most famous of these was the Industrial Workers of the World, better known as the IWW or the Wobblies. Founded in 1905, the IWW had a base among hard rock miners in the West and agricultural, lumber, garment, and other highly exploited workers around the country.[5]

The IWW did not believe in craft unions or collective bargaining. Instead, it favored "one big union" for all workers regardless of skill or any other factor, including race and sex. And it championed direct actions, such as strikes, mass demonstrations, sit-ins, and sabotage of the employer's property. Bargaining and contracts could, in the Wobbly view, only serve to create a union bureaucracy whose job it would be to enforce the contract and prevent the members from using direct actions to protest the employer's actions. Instead, it would be better if the workers enforced their will upon the employer by always standing ready to act together to force the employer into submission.

The IWW did organize some of the nation's most downtrodden workers, and it won some spectacular strikes. Wobbly agitators helped to make free speech a reality for working people by "soapboxing." That is, giving unannounced public speeches in parks and on street corners in towns across the nation. Usually, these would be broken up when the police made mass arrests.

Ultimately, the IWW was defeated by a combination of employer and government violence, AFL antagonism, and its own internal weaknesses. A small remnant still exists today, and Wobblies continue to play an important role in a variety of worker campaigns, including living wage struggles in places like Duluth, Minnesota, and organizing campaigns among Starbucks employees in some of our major cities.[6]

Some unionists continue to believe that collective bargaining is a conservative strategy likely to discourage worker solidarity. A cogent argument has been made, for example, that the NLRA, with its strong discouragement of militant collective actions, such as strikes, and its encouragement of collective bargaining helped to set the stage for the gradual takeover of the mass workers' movement of the early 1930s by labor bureaucrats. That is, the government agreed that workers could form unions, but, in return, it and the employers expected union leaders to police their members so as to ensure that workers would obey their contracts and file grievances, instead of taking direct actions to settle disputes.[7]

On the other hand, the IWW's contempt for collective bargaining made it more vulnerable to employer and government attacks by making every victory wholly dependent on its own members' reserves. Every disagreement with employers or with government, no matter how small, had the potential to become an all-out battle, risking destruction when a more prudent strategy might have embraced the necessity of short-term compromise in a long-term war.

## STRATEGIES OF THE CONTRACT CAMPAIGN

When unions were more powerful in the United States, collective bargaining was sometimes an elaborate ritual. In the 1950s, for example, the United Steelworkers of America (USWA) represented most of the workers who labored in the nation's steel mills. The union had won contracts from each of the large steel corporations, using the agreement settled with the largest producer, U.S. Steel, as the pattern contract for all of the other companies. These contracts were negotiated by a small group of national union officers and staff, without much input from the rank and file, who often did not know what was negotiated until they read the final agreement. The contracts were, in effect, imposed upon the members without a ratification vote.[8] If the bargaining broke down, or reached what the labor law calls an impasse, the union would more than likely call a strike, and the workers would stay out until the company or the union conceded and an agreement was reached. The employers had little ability to hire replacement workers to break the strike, and sometimes only token picket lines were needed to enforce the strike.

Today the situation is different. Decades of union decline, along with slack labor markets and a hostile legal environment, have given employers the advantage.[9] Today's companies are more resistant to union demands and often come to the bargaining table with long lists of give-backs that they want from the workers. They do not necessarily mind strikes, seeing in them opportunities to hire replacement workers, draw down inventories, implement labor-saving technologies, and perhaps defeat the union once and for all. The United Auto Workers and other unions have been defeated by corporations, like International Harvester, which just two decades before would never have dared to challenge unions so strongly.[10] Even the Canadian Auto Workers (CAW)—which broke from the UAW in the 1980s because Canadian unionists saw the U.S. union as too willing to capitulate to management and which for twenty years was a model of uncompromising and successful bargaining—has not been immune to employer attack and defeat.[11] The old bargaining ritual is no longer viable, and unions have had to rethink how they go about bargaining. The best unions have come to see that negotiations must be approached as *campaigns*, with many battles and a wide array of tactics, all built upon the dedicated involvement of the members.

Suppose a union has been recognized by an employer and it wants to negotiate a contract. What happens next? First, the union must notify the employer of its desire to bargain; the employer is legally bound to do so. Then, the union must commence its campaign. What follows is an outline of a strategy developed by the Service Employees International Union (SEIU) in its Contract Campaign Manual.[12]

Most people probably think of collective bargaining in terms of what happens at the bargaining table. The most skilled negotiators win because, like good car salespersons, they know the tricks of the trade. But what really matters is power. While what goes on at the table is important and workers can learn to be good bargainers, what happens outside the bargaining room is far more important. The union must use the power it has effectively and develop more potency by building a strong bargaining campaign. The strength of a union derives from the fact that its members perform work without which the employer cannot function. As SEIU puts it, "the most important source of power we have as a union is the unity and organization of our members." Note the words "unity" and "organization." These things can never be taken for granted. In the normal course of events, workers may be divided in many ways: age, skill, sex, race, and experience. And workers may be in a union, but this does not mean that they will function as an organization. Unity and organization have to be built, carefully and constantly.

In a contract campaign, the leaders of the union, in close collaboration with the members, can begin to establish unity and organization by preparing a planning document that lays out what the union proposes to do, how it plans to do it, and a timetable for the plan's elements. The best time to begin is right after an old agreement has been signed (in the case of a contract renewal) or when the organizing of the union begins (in the case of a first contract). A contract campaign cannot get up to speed in a few days; time is required to put everything in place. Goals have to be established, both for the immediate bargaining and the long term. To set goals, the union must engage in various types of research. Questions such as the following must be answered: Who are the members of the union? How do they differ in terms of age, seniority, race, sex, marital status, job titles, and pay levels? What problems do the members face at work? How has the last contract worked? What parts of it have led to grievances or informal complaints? What changes in the workplace do the members want? What is the financial status of the employer? What types of relationships with suppliers, customers, banks, public officials, media, and so forth, are important to the employer? What does the union know about the managers of the plant and the company's negotiators?

Information can be gathered in several ways. The union can poll its members and conduct surveys, supported by one-on-one contacts, small group meetings, and union meetings. Most unions have research departments, and these can be used to get information, especially about the economic condition of the employer. The union will have a record of all grievances and arbitrations filed under the current agreement. Employers have to file a variety of reports, and these are often matters of public record; most of the records of public employers are also obtainable from the appropriate public agency. Reports may be available at the local courthouse (of lawsuits filed against the company or property transactions), the Internal Revenue Service (tax returns), or the Securities and Exchange Commission (various statements for stockholders). Government agencies such as the Bureau of Labor Statistics publish a wide range of reports on the overall economy and on specific industries, as well as wage and benefit trends. Private organizations such as the Bureau of National Affairs do similar research; the BNA publishes an annual *Source Book on Collective Bargaining* that contains much valuable information, including employer bargaining goals for the year and an update of legal changes. BNA also publishes many other valuable reference works for negotiators.[13] Other unions, especially ones that have dealt with this employer, can supply information. They can also provide collective bargaining agreements for comparison. Newspapers, trade journals, magazines, and research papers should also be sought.

Employers themselves are an invaluable source of information. Some information can be gathered informally from friendly (often disgruntled) people inside management. Data can also be gathered from the company's annual report, which a union might get from a private company by purchasing a share of stock. However, the union has the legal right to obtain from the employer, simply by asking, any information that the union can reasonably claim is necessary for the union to fulfill its bargaining duties.[14] A union might make all sorts of demands at the bargaining table, from obvious ones like hourly wage rates, overtime, pensions, and vacations, to others like moving expenses, sexual harassment, successorship (language in the agreement that commits a new owner to honor it), and video display terminal policies. Upon request, the employer must provide the union with the data it has concerning these matters, and it is an unfair labor practice for the employer to refuse or fail to do so.

There are some exceptions. The labor law makes a distinction between mandatory and permissive bargaining subjects. Mandatory subjects are those about which the parties must negotiate; these include the ones just mentioned, as well as hundreds of others dealing with what the NLRB categorizes as "wages, hours, and terms and conditions of employment." Permissive bargaining subjects are those that the parties are not legally obliged to bargain, although they can if they so desire. A union does not have the right to request information concerning permissive subjects, nor can it try to force the employer to negotiate them by using pressure tactics such as strikes and boycotts. Generally speaking, a permissive subject is one which, as the courts have put it, goes to the heart of the managerial function. That is, the courts have ruled that management has certain inherent rights simply because it represents those who own the property in the case of a private employer, or just because it is the management in the case of a public employer. Thus, a union cannot legally compel the employer to bargain about price of product, the selection of supervisors, the location of plants, the nature and types of product, a decision to close a plant, kinds of equipment used, the choice of health insurance carrier (as opposed to the level of health benefits), benefits for those already retired, and so forth.

Let us look at a couple of examples of when a union may want to request information. Suppose, as is often the case today, that the union suspects that the employer is going to seek to cut health insurance costs. The union can request at least the following: a copy of all health plans now in effect, employer and worker premium payments, administrative expenses, yearly cost to the employer per worker in total dollars and cents per hour, number of claims total and per employee, amounts of all claims, a distribution of the types of claims filed, complaints from employees about health insurance, any reports made by the employer or contracted by the employer concerning health care and costs, all utilization statistics, and complete patient data for each claim. Or suppose that the union wants to improve the employment circumstances of its female and minority members. It can request a list of all job classifications broken down by race and sex; any employer affirmative action plans, documents, and studies; reports filed to the Equal Employment Opportunity Commission (EEOC) or similar state agency; and copies of all materials relating to any discrimination lawsuits filed by employees. With so much information potentially available, it pays to do a little research on this aspect of the labor law.

Once the union has set its goals and fixed a timetable for achieving them, it must create an organizational structure that will be responsible for turning goals into reality. Committees must be formed, including a negotiating committee and a contract campaign committee and various specialized committees as well, such as a media committee, a civil rights committee, and a childcare committee.

The negotiating committee will actually sit down and bargain with the employer. Legally, a union can have whomever it wants on this committee; the NLRA specifies "representatives of their [the workers'] own choosing." The union should make sure that this committee, like all others, is broadly representative of the bargaining unit, in terms of departments, age, sex, race, and any other categories that are important for this group of workers. If a workplace contains more than one union, it is often a good idea to have someone from one union be on the negotiating team of another. This can insure, among other things, that the employer does not try to play one group of workers off against another by spreading rumors about what is going on at the table. The members of this committee should be trained carefully; the use of role-playing is an especially useful technique for training negotiators.[15]

The job of the contract campaign committee is to mobilize the membership in a series of actions aimed at convincing the employer that the costs of not bargaining in good faith and ultimately reaching agreement are greater than doing the opposite. The committee is responsible for everything from organizing a phone tree for rapid communications to logistics for all campaign events. The key is to build up solidarity by beginning with relatively simple and easy actions and then moving to more aggressive and riskier tactics, all timed to maximize the value of each action. Again, the participation of the rank and file usually means the difference between success and failure. Examples of pressure tactics inside the workplace include wearing special union insignia; circulating petitions condemning some particularly urgent abuse; conducting "work-to-rule" slowdowns in which workers obey just the letter of their work rules and no more (bus drivers, for example, obeying all safety precautions exactly, thereby continuously running behind schedule); one-minute work stoppages; "rolling strikes" in which workers strike for a brief period, return to work, and strike again, or similar actions in which different departments strike at different times; and demonstrations in management offices.

Outside the workplace, the workers can begin a corporate campaign, in which they identify through their research the pressure points at which their employer is most vulnerable.[16] Perhaps the employers' customers can be reached through a consumer boycott. Perhaps the banks and insurance companies that provide financing to the employer can be pressured through techniques such as withdrawal of union funds and boycotts. In the case of a public employer, perhaps the politicians who make key decisions affecting the employer can be convinced to encourage the employer to settle. Nearly every employer is subject to a variety of regulations and laws, and not many of them can withstand close scrutiny of their compliance with these. Research might uncover, for example, that the employer is ignoring important safety and health regulations. These can be reported to the appropriate agency or court, as well as to the media; the bad publicity received by the employer may pressure it to come to terms with the union. Most of these tactics can also be used in conjunction with other labor and community groups. Unions should maintain strong and reciprocal ties with all groups that might support them in their struggles with employers. Other unions might have relations with a certain employer; and their experience can be invaluable for a union dealing with that employer for the first time. Similarly, a union will want the support of other unionized workers in cases of strikes so that they do not cross picket lines. Community organizations, from churches to civil rights groups to environmental groups, can be convinced to make common cause with a union. Workers in a factory that is polluting a poor neighborhood are the natural allies of the local inhabitants whose health is being damaged.

Tactics must be coordinated in such a way that the employer experiences them as more and more threatening; the pressure must escalate. Suppose that this is a first agreement and that the employer argued throughout the campaign that the union was unlikely to win an agreement that improved the circumstances of the workers. As soon as—or even before—the election is won, or the employer otherwise recognizes the union, the union should initiate actions that demonstrate to the employer the seriousness of the workers. Workers could all wear special insignia to work, all of the time or on certain days; they could begin to present demands in small or large groups to supervisors; they could escalate to short work stoppages; they could build toward demonstrations timed to employer statements, or actions hostile to the bargaining; they could charge the employer with violations of laws and regulations, and distribute the facts to the media; they could hold a strike vote when the employer stalls in negotiations; they could picket on a regular basis during bargaining to alert the public to the situation.

One final point must be made about contract campaigns. The way in which these can be implemented, and whether implementation is easy or tough, will depend upon the *bargaining structure*.[17] When a single union local faces a one-plant employer, the structure is decentralized. If the workers in the bargaining unit all do the same type of work (for example, teachers), the structure is narrow, as opposed to a broad structure in which the unit consists of many different types of jobs (janitors, assembly line workers, packers). In a highly centralized structure, the actual negotiators may be far removed from the workers. For example, when the Canadian Auto Workers union (CAW) negotiates with General Motors, it bargains on behalf of the workers at all of GM's plants in Canada. The union leader and a small inner circle of advisors do the bargaining with a top official of GM. In fact, these two officials might conduct most of the negotiations one-on-one. However, the inner circle must report back to a much larger group consisting of the presidents of all of the locals. Then, the workers themselves must ratify the contract. The CAW is committed to securing good agreements for the members and the overall structure of the union is democratic. In addition, the CAW strongly supports a progressive and independent labor politics.[18] So, while the rank and file do not actually participate in the bargaining, they maintain reasonably strong control over their union, and will remove from office any leaders not attuned to their needs. Unfortunately, not all centralized bargaining is done along the lines of the CAW, and history offers us numerous examples of union elites negotiating with their corporate counterparts in complete isolation from the members of the bargaining unit, often in situations in which the workers do not even have the right to ratify the final agreement.

## BARGAINING IN WARTIME

The entry of the United States into the First World War in 1917 was not popular at first, and with good reason. The war was the consequence of intense international economic and political rivalry for overseas markets and colonies. There was no good reason why workers should have supported it and excellent reasons why they should not have. But, as usually happens in time of war, the government made it extremely dangerous for workers to oppose it, making it clear that opposition would be regarded as treasonous and actively prosecuting opponents under newly enacted wartime legislation. The AFL had earlier in its history espoused pacifism, but the federal government exerted strong pressure on it to support the war.[19] Eventually, it supported the war and its unions agreed not to strike, and in return the government encouraged employers to bargain collectively with AFL unions. As a consequence of this arrangement, union membership grew considerably and unions won collective bargaining agreements.

There were those in the labor movement, notably the IWW and many socialists, who actively fought against the war. These people and organizations were persecuted and prosecuted by the government, which also turned a blind eye to the many private vigilante actions against war opponents mounted by groups such as the American Legion. Sadly, the AFL cooperated with the authorities in these anti-radical attacks, which devastated the left wing of the labor movement. Socialist leader Eugene V. Debs was sent to prison for ten years for making an anti-war speech in Ohio. IWW leader "Big" Bill Haywood was hounded out of the country and forced to seek refuge in the Soviet Union. So, while the unions gained members and contracts during the war, the labor movement was dealt a serious blow, as those who took the most progressive stands on a wide range of social issues were expelled from the movement.[20]

Much the same thing happened during the Second World War. This war was much more popular than the First World War, and the purge of the radicals mostly took place after it. The AFL and the CIO strongly supported the war, and their member unions pledged not to strike. Once again, the government placed strong pressure upon employers to recognize unions in their plants and to bargain collectively with them. It sponsored arbitration to settle contract disputes, as a substitute for strikes. This system of labor-management cooperation was put into place by top national union leaders, along with corporate and government bigwigs, with little rank-and-file input. Union leaders got into the habit of sitting down with their corporate counterparts and working out settlements to their disputes without having to activate their members. Because of their allegiance to the Soviet Union, Communists in labor for the most part went along with this conservative arrangement. Radical politics and rank-and-file agitation were put on hold during the war, although workers did often strike in defiance of the no-strike pledge: the United Mine Workers, which did not concur with the pledge, actually conducted several nationwide work stoppages in 1943.[21]

After the war, the government and business went all out to crush the left wing of the labor movement.[22] This time the CIO unions did what the AFL had done during World War I and expelled the most radical and rank-and-file oriented unions, including the United Electrical Workers. This action marked the end of the mass movement of workers begun during the Great Depression. Bureaucratic, staff-dominated collective bargaining was extended after the war. A staff-controlled grievance procedure with arbitration as the final step used to resolve disputes became all but universal, and almost all collective bargaining agreements came to contain "no strike" agreements in which workers gave up the right to strike to settle workplace disagreements.

Some scholars have argued, as the IWW did, that modern collective bargaining is inherently bureaucratic and hostile to the interests of workers.[23] I take issue with this view. Both collective bargaining and grievance procedures can be of great advantage to workers. An effective collective bargaining campaign can permit unions time to regroup for battles to come. And a grievance procedure can be seen as just one more weapon to use in the ongoing war between employers and workers. Take the worker reinstated after being accused of falsifying a shoe reimbursement form. Ask him if he thinks that arbitration is inherently a bad thing for workers. Of course, arbitration today would be swifter and work more to the advantage of workers if labor had initially been bolder in its reactions to the great wars, but that should not discredit collective bargaining across-the-board.

## AT THE TABLE

Hundreds of books have been written about the art and science of negotiations.[24] A reader of many of these tomes might be led to believe that anyone can negotiate anything, if only one learns the right "table skills." While it is important to do the right things at the bargaining table, collective bargaining occurs within a social context. A union that has prepared its membership to view the bargaining as part of an ongoing struggle will do better than one that fails to involve the members. With this in mind, there are some useful things for the negotiators to remember when they sit down to bargain.

The items that the union hopes to get into the final collective bargaining agreement are called substantive issues. Before negotiating these, the union must bargain procedural subjects. These spell out the procedures the two parties are going to use to reach agreement. They include such things as the dates, places, and times of the meetings, whether the meetings will be tape-recorded, whether the negotiators agree not to take calls or leave the meeting room during the bargaining (except for caucuses), what relationships the bargainers will have with the media, whether or not attorneys will be present, how the parties will exchange information, how both sides will "agree that they have agreed," whether the meetings will take place during normal working hours, and, if so, whether the workers on the committee will be paid their regular wages. These are often crucially important points, and the union should give them the same care and preparation as the substantive issues. For example, the union should not agree to limit the people it can bring to the table, nor should it promise not to talk to the media. Most unions prefer to negotiate at a neutral site and not at the workplace, often a symbol of management's authority. The union should not agree to allow the employer to take care of the final preparation of the contract for printing, and it should be sure that it has good note-takers at each meeting.

At the table, the bargainers should maintain a tight discipline. It is not necessary that one person do all of the talking; it might be desirable to rotate the spokesperson each session to give as many people as possible this valuable experience. It is necessary, though, to anticipate and plan what will be said. The employer will be looking for signs of disagreement among the union's bargainers, so they should never show any such signs. Whenever there is disagreement or confusion among the union's negotiators, someone should call a caucus; that is, the union should say to the management that it wants to meet alone outside the negotiating room. A good rule of bargaining is to always have a ready excuse to halt the bargaining. Away from the table, the team can get a clearer picture of what is transpiring and not get caught up in a rush to reach agreement. Similar delaying tactics can be used at the table: you can ask the employer to repeat its proposal or say something like, "Let me see if I understand what you are saying." Sometimes silence is a good way to get the other side to repeat itself and give you time to think. Most people do not like silences and will say something to break the quiet. One negotiating expert calls these delays "going to the balcony." That is, pretending that you are on a balcony watching the bargaining below.[25] The distance gives you better perspective.

Union negotiators should always be well prepared for each session, using role-playing beforehand if necessary. On the first day of bargaining, for instance, the union spokesperson could just hand the union's proposed agreement to the employer. But it would be better to hold on to it and make a detailed presentation of what the union wants, complete with supporting documentation. Not only will the employer be forced to sit and listen, but its representatives will also see that the union has done its homework. This sends a message to the employer that the union is serious and has probably prepared a sophisticated campaign to secure an agreement. It is not that the union's presentation aims to convince the employer by the force of its logic. The two sides operate on entirely different premises; one side's logic is the other side's illogic. Instead, the union negotiators' skills at the table tell the employer that it can expect a hard struggle from the workers.

A critical element in the bargaining is for the union to know well what is called its "best alternative to a negotiated agreement."[26] The union must know its "resistance point," the point beyond which it would rather not reach agreement, and it must then know what it will do if this point is reached. In negotiations with GM, when the CAW was still part of the United Auto Workers, the Canadian union stuck firmly to its position that the workers deserved the annual percentage wage increase that the UAW had first won in the late 1940s. GM insisted on lump-sum wage increases; the workers would get a sum of money each year but their base wage rates would not change. Additional pressure was placed upon the CAW and its chief negotiator, Robert White, by the fact that the U.S. sector of the union had already agreed to lump-sum raises and the UAW leadership badly wanted White to go along. In the face of this, White and his staff refused to cave in. Their best alternative to a negotiated agreement was a strike, and they had prepared the membership for it. With its Canadian facilities shut down and its U.S. operations' profits threatened, GM relented. The Canadian workers kept their annual percentage wage increases.[27]

The CAW-GM negotiations are an example of *principled* bargaining.[28] The union based its position on a strong union principle, steady increases in real wage rates, and refused to compromise on the principle (though it was willing to make concessions on the amount of the increase). Bargaining based upon principle is difficult to counter, especially if the principle can be framed in terms of fundamental fairness, but that is true only if the principle has strong member support. Some years ago, the union of professional football players in the United States went on strike over the principle of free agency, the right of a player to sell his services to the highest bidder without his current team receiving any compensation from the new team. The union was convinced that this was an issue over which the membership would strike; it based this belief on a poll it had taken prior to the bargaining. The belief turned out to be erroneous, and not long into the strike the players began to cross their own picket lines and return to work, fearful that they would be permanently replaced. The error of the union was not that the principle was a bad one, but that it had not prepared its campaign properly. A poll is no substitute for a comprehensive bargaining strategy campaign.

Imaginative bargainers figure out ways to tie issues together so that both sides can win something. (In this regard, it is important to "cost out" all proposals and counter-proposals. Today there are computer programs that greatly simplify this. BNA has a book on this, too.) Here is an example. An organizer was negotiating an agreement with a commercial bank after the union had won a rare victory among bank employees. The union had prevailed in the representation election by a small margin, and the bank's chief negotiator was using the weakness of support for the union as a weapon to deny the union's demands. The union wanted to secure a *union shop*, an agreement whereby everyone in the bargaining unit had to join the union within a specified number of days. The employer eventually conceded to this demand, after the national union promised to deposit a large sum of union money in the bank! In this same negotiation, much of the actual bargaining was done away from the table by the chief negotiators. This is a dangerous tactic because it is done behind the backs of the members. A successful union is one that keeps its members informed of what is going on, so that when the negotiators come back to the members and urge ratification of the contract, the members feel that they were an integral part of the bargaining.

What if, despite a well-planned contract campaign and good negotiating strategies, the union fails to convince the employer to come to terms? This question needs to be answered in both legal and strategic terms. Under our labor laws, a bargaining stalemate is called an *impasse*. An impasse exists when the NLRB determines that further bargaining is not likely to lead to an agreement. If an impasse does exist, the employer is free to unilaterally impose its last contract offer upon the workers. What usually happens is that the employer declares that the bargaining is at an impasse and imposes its last offer. The union must then file unfair labor practice charges against the employer, accusing it of a violation of Section 8(a)(5) for bargaining in bad faith. It is then up to the NLRB to decide whether or not there is an impasse.[29] This gives the employer an incentive to come to the table with a proposal and refuse to offer any significant modifications. Then, when the union digs in and in turn refuses to make concessions, the employer states that the parties are at an impasse, hoping that a compliant board will agree. Labor law scholar Ellen Dannin has argued, most impressively with bargaining simulations, that the greater ease of employers getting an impasse ruling has led unions to make concessions simply to prevent this from happening. She has also shown that the ease with which employers can now declare impasse (and the power of employers to hire permanent replacements for strikers), knowing that the Board will support them, has subverted the purported purpose of the NLRA to encourage collective bargaining.[30] In the past, union negotiators had to avoid language at the table or in the media suggesting that an impasse might exist (such as saying "there is no way we will ever accept" a particular company proposal), but now this may not be enough.

Strategically, the possibility of an impasse should be considered as part of the overall contract campaign and dealt with accordingly. A strike may prove necessary. Employers are more willing to take strikes today than they were when unions had more power. They can and do hire permanent replacements for strikers, and the union-busting consultants know all of the devious tricks to defeat a strike, including using armed thugs. Yet strikes should not be rejected out of hand. The United Mine Workers would never have brought the Pittston Coal Company to heel without a strike, including the illegal occupation of one of the struck mines. The same was true in the UPS strike and several others.[31]

A strike is only one way to deal with an impasse. Some impasses can be resolved through the techniques of mediation and arbitration. In the private sector of the economy, these devices are voluntary that is, the parties have to agree to their use. But in the public sector, the law often mandates one or the other. In mediation, a mediator is brought in to try to get the parties to agree. The mediator will usually meet with each side independently and try to figure out if an agreement is possible. Then the mediator will begin to float proposals to see how the two sides react; these proposals may become the basis for a settlement. A union should be cautious about being completely honest with a mediator; there is no guarantee that the mediator will honor the union's assumption that what it tells the mediator will not be immediately disclosed to the management. A mediator can only recommend contract terms, not impose them. On the other hand, in arbitration, which is called *interest arbitration*, the arbitrator has the power to impose a settlement on the union and the employer. This procedure is rare in the private sector, but it is sometimes legally required for public employees, especially those who are denied the right to strike. If, for example, the police in a Pennsylvania city cannot reach a settlement with the city's managers, the law requires that a tripartite panel of arbitrators decide what the terms of the contract will be. In a few states, a special kind of interest arbitration, *"final offer" arbitration*, is in force. Once a dispute reaches an impasse, the arbitrator imposes either the union's or the employer's last offer but cannot dictate any sort of compromise solution. It is argued that this will force the parties to negotiate in good faith rather than just go through the motions until arbitration.[32]

## THE AGREEMENT

If the union's contract campaign has been successful, the workers and the employer will sign a collective bargaining agreement that will serve as the law of the workplace for its duration. A union should view the contract as a temporary truce in a never-ending class war.

The contract can be conveniently divided into four parts: union security and management rights, the wage and effort bargain, individual security, and contract administration.[33] A union will try to win in the contract provisions that secure the existence, continuity, and funding of the union; the parts of the agreement that do this are called *union security clauses*. One such clause is a *union shop* agreement, which dictates that every member of the bargaining unit must join the union within a specified number of days after being hired (such as the one negotiated with the bank mentioned above). An *agency shop* does not require membership, but it does demand that every unit member pay a dues equivalent to the union.[34] Another is a dues check-off provision, in which the employer agrees to deduct union dues from the members' paychecks and remit the money to the union. Such a provision is convenient for the union, but it denies the members a chance to directly confront the union with complaints when it comes around to collect the dues.[35]

Two important and controversial parts of most agreements today are management rights and no-strike clauses. Nearly all contracts have some sort of management rights clause, guaranteeing to the employer certain unilateral rights. The essence of management is control. A good collective bargaining agreement limits this control in significant ways, while a bad one allows the management to retain much of what it already had. Therefore, each part of the agreement should be scrutinized with an eye toward its effect upon managerial control. Some management rights clauses simply state that all matters not specifically dealt with in the agreement become the right of the management. Others spell out in great detail all of the things that the management reserves the right to decide unilaterally. Unions should try to keep management rights as narrowly defined as possible because the employer will refer to these rights in every dispute with the union over the meaning of the contract. However, even absent a management rights clause, both the NLRB and arbitrators often just assume that certain powers belong to the employer. As corporations continue to downsize, move, and adopt new technology, it will be important for unions to end their long-standing accommodation to the notion that the employer has a right to make all of the fundamental business decisions, while the union limits itself to bargaining over the share of the pie the workers will get. The 2008 financial crisis and the massive government bailout should set the stage for labor movements around the world to demand greater worker say in what employers can do with their capital.[36]

It is a rare contract that does not have a no-strike agreement in it.[37] In such a clause the union agrees not to strike during the duration of the contract; if the union does strike, it opens itself up to a suit under the NLRA and the payment of damages to the employer. The workers who strike in defiance of a no-strike agreement subject themselves to discharge. It has been argued that the no-strike clause is the *quid pro quo* for the employer's acceptance of arbitration to settle contract disputes. Unfortunately, in many unions arbitration is a long, drawn-out affair over which the aggrieved worker has little control. The NLRB and arbitrators take the view that a worker should almost always obey a manager's order and then file a grievance if she believes that the order violates the contract. This means that the worker might have a long time to wait before justice is done. With a no-strike clause in effect, direct action by the workers to resolve the dispute is legally prohibited.

Some unions have managed to exempt certain issues from the no-strike agreement. For example, in the automobile industry, the UAW has kept the right to strike over production standards, that is, the amount of work required of any particular job. Similarly, a union might insist on the right to strike over safety issues. In any event, the wording of no-strike clauses is critical. A general no-strike agreement, without any special wording, might be interpreted by the NLRB or the courts to mean that workers cannot refuse to cross another union's picket line.

The wage and effort bargain could contain literally hundreds of clauses, covering everything from basic wages and benefits to how the workers will be paid (hourly, by the piece, or some combination) to the myriad ways in which the employer seeks to guarantee that the workers will labor with at least some minimal level of intensity. Once the U.S. economy began to slow down and stagnate in the early 1970s, employers became obsessed with raising productivity. One of the outcomes of this was the movement toward various types of labor-management cooperation schemes, in which, in return for granting to the employer greater flexibility in organizing work, the workers were promised greater say in decision making.[38] Thus, many collective bargaining agreements embraced the "team concept." At GM's famous Saturn plant in Tennessee, traditional collective bargaining disappeared altogether, replaced with a system of joint decision making on a wide variety of issues. The dangers of the team concept are well documented. They usually weaken the grievance procedure and eliminate hard-won work rules yet never give the union real input into the most critical management decisions.

Still, the productivity bargaining of the last thirty years does illustrate the great flexibility of collective bargaining. Once the workers have formed a union, the management has to take the workers into account no matter what it does. The nation's shipping companies have been able to introduce labor-saving containerization technology to unload ships, but the unions have forced them to pay a high price for the right to do so.[39] In a nonunion workplace, only the employees bear the cost.

Individual security provisions include the grievance procedure and seniority rules. Through the grievance procedure, workers gain fundamental due process, similar to that to which citizens have a right when they come into conflict with the government. The grievance mechanism insures that the members of the bargaining unit are no longer employees "at will." If workers are disciplined "without just cause," they can file grievances. If workers are forced to do work outside of their job classifications, they can file grievances. If the contract has a broad "no discrimination" clause, workers discriminated against by the employer because of some personal characteristic such as race, gender, sexual preference, or political views can file grievances. Most contracts specify that a grievance is a claim by a member of the bargaining unit that the employer has violated the contract. The worker must file the grievance, usually through the first-level union authority (shop steward), within the time limit spelled out in the agreement. Then, the grievance goes through a series of steps in which successively higher levels of union and management authority try to settle it. If it cannot be settled, the union can insist that a third party, an arbitrator, be brought in to dictate the settlement.

The importance of the grievance procedure cannot be exaggerated. It is what separates organized workers from unorganized workers. Its significance can be measured by how rare such a system is in a nonunion company.[40] However, a grievance system is not a substitute for a militant and vigilant rank-and-file controlled union. The union should consider grievances as part of the overall struggle with employers. They should be handled with a bargaining campaign strategy, using education, publicity, solidarity actions, and whatever other tactics best insure victory in grievance resolution. Suppose that a worker is unjustly fired. The union could simply encourage that worker to file a grievance and then process it through the steps, ultimately letting the arbitrator decide whether or not the worker gets reinstated. Or the union could mobilize the membership to act immediately, with information pickets, work-to-rule, in-plant solidarity actions, short stoppages, and the like, as well as filing a formal grievance. The fired worker could become directly involved in the whole process and not just a passive observer hoping for the right outcome.

Collective bargaining cannot eliminate the uncertainty inherent in our economic system. It cannot prevent plants from closing, and it cannot stop a downturn in the business cycle. However, it can offer workers some job protection through the rule of seniority. Seniority is a powerful union weapon and should be guarded zealously. When my father could no longer breathe well enough to do hard physical labor, his long seniority gave him the right to bid on an easier job. In a nonunion shop, he would simply have been let go. In a layoff, seniority denies the company the power to choose who will go and who will stay. Of course, seniority gives older workers preference over younger ones, but no one stays young forever, and the abuses likely to occur when the employer makes layoff, recall, transfer, and promotion decisions unilaterally far outweigh any discrimination against the young. The fact is that the older we get, the more vulnerable we are; seniority protects us against this vulnerability. Care must be taken to make the seniority provisions of the agreement as strong as possible. For example, employers will insist on getting language that gives them the right to use ability along with seniority in making choices concerning promotions and perhaps layoffs and recalls as well, so the union must make sure that seniority is always the dominant criterion.

One problem with seniority is that it sometimes perpetuates various forms of discrimination. A plant may be divided into departments and the contract may grant departmental seniority. A force reduction in one department might result in the layoff of a person who has worked in the plant for more years than any other worker in a different department in which there is no reduction. Or a person with years of seniority in the plant might transfer into a more desirable department, but this means that his seniority in the new department is zero. A layoff in this new department will result in unemployment for him, while people with less plant seniority but more departmental seniority will remain at work. If the less desirable departments are dominated by racial minorities or women, such a system gives them little incentive to transfer. This perpetuates the past discrimination that placed them in the inferior departments to begin with. One way to deal with this inequity is to force decisions to be based upon the broadest seniority unit possible, in this case plant seniority. Or layoffs could be allocated in some fixed proportion by race (the least senior white worker is laid off, then the least senior minority worker, and so forth) until such time as such a system is no longer needed to avoid perpetuating discrimination.[41]

Once a contract is signed, it must be enforced. Again, enforcement should be seen as part of the ongoing campaign to increase the workers' power and should involve all of the members. A union should have democratically elected shop stewards to handle grievances and educate the members, and their powers should be spelled out in the contract. They must be given the contractual right to investigate complaints in the workplace on company time, to have space at work to do this job, to accompany workers to any meetings with supervisors, to meet upon request with managers, to post notices on union bulletin boards in the workplace, and to request and obtain all information needed to accomplish their tasks in an efficient and timely manner. The labor laws guarantee some of these rights, but they will be that much stronger if protected by the contract as well.[42]

Arbitration of contract disputes is such an important part of collective bargaining that it deserves some specific commentary.[43] As opposed to interest arbitration, *grievance arbitration* calls for the arbitrator to decide whether or not the employer has violated an already existing agreement. Once the last internal step of the grievance procedure has failed to generate a settlement of the grievance, the union has so many days, spelled out in the contract, to invoke arbitration. This done, the contract will specify how the arbitrator is to be selected. A few contracts provide for permanent arbitrators who preside over all arbitrations, but most contracts make each arbitration *ad hoc*. Anyone can be selected as an arbitrator; there are no specific qualifications that a person must have to be one. Naturally the parties will be wise to choose someone well versed in collective bargaining agreements. There are national associations of arbitrators, the best known of which is the American Arbitration Association. Some states maintain panels of arbitrators as well. Any of these organizations will send a list of arbitrators to the parties upon request, and this is something that may be included in the contract. Among public employees and employers in Pennsylvania, a common procedure is to request a list of arbitrators from a state panel maintained by the Bureau of Mediation in Harrisburg, the state capital. Upon receipt of the arbitrator list, the union and the employer will successively eliminate arbitrators until one is left. This person will be notified that the parties have selected him or her. The chosen arbitrator will then work out a date for the hearing agreeable to both sides. Unions should keep track of arbitration decisions, some of which are published and most of which are sent to the appropriate association or bureau. These rulings can give the union some idea of how it might fare with a particular arbitrator.

An arbitration hearing is a quasi-legal proceeding. Both the union and the employer will make opening statements, often through an attorney (union staff can learn to do this, though often lawyers are best suited for it). Both sides will present their cases through witnesses, who will be examined and cross-examined. Both sides will introduce documents as evidence (such as the collective bargaining agreement, negotiation notes, management memoranda, etc.). The parties may be requested by the arbitrator to write closing briefs, in which they are free to cite prior arbitration decisions for the use of the arbitrator. Formal rules of law, such as a prohibition of hearsay evidence, usually apply, although somewhat more loosely than in a court of law. Witnesses are sworn in and can be subpoenaed to appear by the arbitrator. After the hearing is closed, the arbitrator reads the briefs and notes from the hearing and examines the evidence, then makes a ruling binding on the union and management. Numerous court decisions have made it difficult for the losing side to overturn an arbitrator's ruling.

Unions should prepare for arbitration as they do for bargaining, involving the grievant or grievants at every step. The shop steward should carefully investigate the grievance and seek evidence that might buttress the case at arbitration. The employer is legally bound to give the union any information it has that might be relevant to the case, such as, for example, attendance and discipline records. If possible, witnesses should be secured who will corroborate the grievant's claims. Role-playing should be used to prepare workers to give testimony and to face what might be nasty cross-examination. The collective bargaining agreement should be scoured for provisions supportive of the union's arguments. In other words, the preparation for arbitration should be an exercise in solidarity-building.

The arbitrator normally goes into the hearing cold, with only a general idea of the nature of the grievance. Therefore, it is incumbent upon the union to make the issue as clear as possible, as soon as possible. The arbitrator's first obligation is to make a ruling faithful to the collective bargaining agreement, so the contract is often the most important piece of evidence presented. Crucial is any testimony telling the arbitrator what a particular provision means, what the parties intended it to mean, or how it has been interpreted in the past. If the contract is vague or silent on an issue, the past practices of the parties are important. And in some cases the arbitrator will just try to do what is fair; for example, an arbitrator may decide whether a work rule is fair to a rational person or may determine that the employer's discipline was too harsh for the offense. Knowledge of what arbitrators do when they make rulings is useful to the union in preparing its case.

Employers and outsiders often say that a union will take any case to arbitration, even that of a worker who deserves discharge, such as someone who is chronically drunk at work. Such an argument cannot be taken seriously. First of all, a grievance procedure is a due process clause, and, as in courts of law, every person has the right to due process, with a presumption of innocence. Second, a union has a legal obligation to investigate thoroughly every grievance, irrespective of the character of the grievant or the nature of the grievance. A union does not have to push every grievance to arbitration, but it could risk a lawsuit by the worker if it does not take a particular complaint to arbitration.[44] Finally, there may be times when it is wise, in terms of building solidarity, to take even a weak grievance to arbitration, to show the membership that the union is militantly fighting for their rights.

## POLITICS AND COLLECTIVE BARGAINING

Scholars of our labor movement have often argued that two tendencies have marked the struggle to build unions. On the one hand, there have been overtly political workers' groups, such as the Knights of Labor, the Socialists, and the Communists. The aim of these organizations has been to directly confront the economic system and the state that supports it, with the goal of establishing a more egalitarian society without a wage system. Such movements were not particularly interested in collective bargaining, or if they were, unions affiliated with such movements did not see it in the same way as more conservative unions. On the other hand, there were movements of working people that had no particular political platform and simply concentrated on organizing unions to bargain for better wages, hours, and terms and conditions of employment. The most important of these organizations was the American Federation of Labor, whose founder, Samuel Gompers, urged workers to reject radical politics and operate within the two-party system of Republicans and Democrats.

Some other scholars reject collective bargaining as inherently conservative (much as did the IWW), as essentially an ingenious device through which union bureaucrats and their managerial counterparts can contain and routinize worker-employer conflict.[45] Collective bargaining, by its nature, accepts the rights of the employers to run their businesses and relegates the workers to winning a slightly bigger share of the pie than they could without a union. In this view, collective bargaining, along with legislation like the NLRA which promotes it, is a trick played on workers to prevent them from taking more radical actions on their own behalf.

Recent studies by Maurice Zeitlin and Judith Stepan-Norris rebut both views.[46] What matters in collective bargaining (and by extension in union organizing and contract campaigns) is the context in which it occurs. Zeitlin and Stepan-Norris compared contracts secured by left-wing, centrist, and right-wing unions between the years 1937 and 1955 (1955 was the year of the merger of the AFL and the CIO). All of the unions were affiliated with the CIO. The left-wing unions, those most closely allied with the Communist Party and radical politics, won contracts that best enabled workers to protect their interests and build a basis for further victories against the employers.

Specifically, the left-led unions were more likely to have negotiated collective bargaining agreements with either no or weak management rights clauses, without no-strike agreements, with short durations (so that when contracts did include a no-strike agreement, workers would not be hamstrung for very long), and with worker-friendly grievance procedures (union representative present at the first step, relatively few steps, and strict time limits for each step). Unions that espoused a more conservative philosophy, such as labor-management cooperation, won weaker agreements in each of these areas. Unions that won better contracts also were usually the most democratic and subject to rank-and-file control. The lessons to be taken from these studies are that collective bargaining can make real improvements in workers' lives and that the most effective labor movement is one that has radical, democratic principles and acts upon them.

Through collective bargaining, workers have fought for and won impressive improvements in their standard of living, measured not just monetarily but in terms of human dignity. Mine workers have won both the right to be paid from the time they enter the mine until they leave it and washrooms to clean themselves in before they leave; steel workers have won generous early retirement benefits; teachers have gained some control over what they teach and the size of their classes; nurses have won limitations on the number of patients for whom they are responsible; janitors have won an end to the subcontracting of their work; and all union workers have won the right to stand up to the employer with dignity and without fear. While employers have condemned unions and collective bargaining as detrimental to managerial flexibility, workers have used them to deal creatively with disparate and rapidly changing circumstances. Today, some agreements provide childcare facilities in the workplace, flexible work schedules, transfer rights, limitations upon overtime, prohibitions against sexual harassment, sabbatical leaves, retraining and education funds, affirmative action, and a host of other innovative procedures and programs.

Yet it must be said that collective bargaining cannot alone emancipate working people from those aspects of life that are part and parcel of an economic system like ours. It cannot guarantee employment or meaningful work, or a clean environment, or an end to racism and sexism. Unions and collective bargaining are only a part of what working people must build on the way to a better society.

# chapter five

# UNIONS AND POLITICS

Unions are vehicles by which workers secure a voice in workplace decisions and, at the same time, obtain higher compensation for their
labors. However, there are some concerns that working people cannot
adequately address through struggles at their places of employment.
Our economic system seldom generates enough employment to go
around. Those few who own most of our workplaces have taken great
pains to economize on the use of labor and to maximize the number
of people who can do any given job. They have done this in a variety
of ways, from dividing up jobs, so that little skilled labor is needed, to
replacing workers with machines and investing capital around the
globe. The effect of these actions is to create a "reserve army of labor,"
a pool of potential workers whose function it is to reduce the wages
(lowering the price of labor by increasing the supply of labor) and
increase the insecurity of those who are currently employed. The
problem of unemployment, therefore, is systemic (brought about by
the nature of capitalism), and all but impossible to deal with in collective bargaining. It must be confronted at the level of society as a
whole.[1]

Social problems require social action. Many companies produce
products or use technologies that do great damage to workers' health
and the environment. Asbestos workers not only died a little each day
at work, but the product they produced harmed people around the

world.[2] These problems might be partially dealt with by a union, which can force a company to use safer equipment and reduce the exposure of the workers to toxic materials. But a union will be an inadequate vehicle for addressing widespread environmental destruction. What is more, there will be situations in which workers will be torn between their desire for a better environment and their need for adequate employment. Automobiles do harm to our health and safety (air pollution, acid rain, congestion, noise, accidents), but it would be foolish to expect the automobile workers' union to solve this problem, if doing so meant that their members would face unemployment. Likewise, consider health care. Unions have won health benefits for their members, but the level of benefits won varies considerably among different groups of workers. Most workers in the United States do not enjoy union representation and, therefore, they may have no health insurance at all.[3] Yet from a human rights standpoint, it is essential that all workers have adequate health care.

Consider finally what we might call the institutional framework in which unions are formed and bargaining takes place. All capitalist societies have complex legal systems, which have great bearing on the relationship between workers and their employers. For example, until the late 1950s, it was typically held in the United States that public employees (who now comprise nearly 20 percent of the workforce) could join unions, but they could not compel their employers to negotiate with them. In addition, it was illegal for them to strike, making it legal for their employers to fire them if they did. No public employees' union could change these circumstances. What was required was a change in the laws.[4]

Although employers are in competition with one another, they also join together to protect the interests of their entire class. Sometimes this takes the form of purely private actions, as when a group of employers agrees to provide money to a single employer in their industry to insure that this employer can withstand a strike. But much more common is the political collaboration of employers. While our government is formally independent of the economy, in practice it is intimately connected. Politicians need money to get elected, and governments need money to function. Those who own the wealth and have most of the income are in a pivotal position to influence what the government does, both by providing money for electoral campaigns and in taxes and by being major buyers of the bonds that governments often sell to pay their bills. Under circumstances in which workers are poorly organized, it is certain that the government will do the bidding of the employers.

It is often difficult to know where business stops and government begins.[5] Who hasn't heard the slogans, "The business of America is business" and "What's good for General Motors is good for the country"? There are scores of cases in which the federal government has used the armed forces to defeat strikes.[6] The federal government gave millions of dollars and millions of acres to the big railroad companies, and then sent Eugene V. Debs to jail for having the temerity to challenge their power. The entire legal machinery, from the laws to the courts, was stacked against working people from the earliest days of the republic until the 1930s. Individual labor unions sometimes achieved great things for their members, but they were powerless in the face of the collective power of business, expressed in the armed might of the government.

## WHY U.S. LABOR POLITICS ARE DIFFERENT

From the beginning, working men and women were not ignorant of the political power of the capitalist class. They sought ways to limit and challenge it. This was the case in Western Europe as well, but the situation there was somewhat different than in the United States. European nations had long had authoritarian political systems, with the central government firmly integrated into the economic system. When workers began to organize unions, they came into immediate conflict with the government, and it appeared to many labor leaders and intellectuals that the only way for working people to advance was to capture control of the state. During England's industrial revolution at the end of the eighteenth century, for example, not only did workers *not* have the right to vote, but they also faced time in prison if they formed a labor union. Therefore, workers were quick to form labor political organizations and parties that aimed to capture control of the government. These political parties were, generally speaking, hostile to capitalism itself. They set out to establish a cooperative economic system that would not rely on a labor market and wages.[7] The politics of these parties can, thus, be described as socialist or communist. Two of capitalism's greatest critics, Karl Marx and Friedrich Engels, were influential advisors and participants in the development of working-class political organizations and labor parties throughout their adult lives.[8]

In the United States, circumstances did not favor the formation of radical labor parties.[9] Here, white men and to some extent white women formed a nation by revolting against the English monarchy. They established what was, for its time, a radically democratic society. To the extent that most white working men saw the government as theirs as much as the merchants' and factory owners', they did not undertake to form a labor party.[10] When some of them did try, they found that the two-party system was so firmly entrenched and sanctioned by the laws that it was hard to mount a third-party challenge. The major parties often co-opted the workers' best leaders, further weakening labor's independent political efforts. The racist legacy of slavery propelled many workers into alliance with their white employers in politics, blocking common cause with the black working class.[11] Finally, the ideology of individualism and competition was stronger in the United States than anywhere else in the world, making workers skeptical of radical working-class politics and making it easy for employers to portray such politics as the work of foreigners.[12] This ideology was on every point supported by the police power of the government, which turned a wrathful eye on labor radicalism, whether in politics or the unions.

Despite these obstacles to independent labor politics, labor political organizations and parties did form, not much different from their counterparts in Europe and often led by recently arrived European immigrant workers. Parties, such as the Socialist Labor Party, the Socialist Party, and the Communist Party, developed as capitalism in the United States took on its modern form in the late nineteenth and early twentieth centuries. These all gained followings among workers, and at various times they had considerable influence within the labor unions, especially the Socialist Party before the First World War and the Communist Party during the Great Depression and the 1940s. However, none of them was able to challenge the political dominance of the Republican and Democratic parties, both dominated by big business interests. Radical parties were hounded and harassed by employers and by the government, and not a few of their leaders were sent to prison for upholding their beliefs.[13]

Some labor leaders, most notably Samuel Gompers and the other founders of the American Federation of Labor, argued that the best course for workers in the United States was to abandon labor politics and concentrate on building labor unions. Gompers observed that craft unions could take advantage of the employers' dependence upon the workers' skills to win admirable wages, hours, and working conditions. The labor parties wanted a legally mandated eight-hour day, but some craft unions had already won this through the economic pressures they could place upon recalcitrant employers. Craft unions were made up of white men, often of the same ethnicity, and this made it easier for them to act collectively. But even among them, Gompers observed, politics was often a divisive subject, which if placed at the forefront of the labor movement would make most collective struggles impossible to sustain.[14]

Gompers's solution to the problem of politics was to accept the status quo of the two-party system. The craft unions would use the strength of their economic pressure and their numbers to make politicians act in the interests of labor. As he put it, labor should "reward its friends and punish its enemies," whether they be Republicans or Democrats. Such a "pragmatic" politics would avoid the divisiveness of a labor politics and, at the same time, would not bring down the wrath of the government upon the house of labor. Unions would act as lobbying groups for pro-labor candidates and pro labor public policies. However, the AFL did not put very much faith in government. So often had the government betrayed labor that Gompers had little hope that the salvation of workers could be achieved politically. Instead, workers would organize into unions and through their unions get what they needed.

Over the years the AFL's "anti-politics" politics hardened into a conservative ideology.[15] Craft unions, in cities in which they had a strong presence, developed cozy relationships with the politicians who could throw work their members' way. This involved a great deal of corruption between union officials, business owners, and local public officials. These unions were never very democratic internally and occasionally some of them were taken over by criminal elements.[16] At the national level, the AFL did fight for protective federal laws, especially one law that would free unions from the grip of deadly labor injunctions. But bereft of a perspective that comprehended the basic conflict of interest between workers and employers, the AFL was unable to build a political movement that could compel the government to act in the interests of working people. By the early 1930s, the AFL had actually come out against much-needed government programs such as unemployment compensation, arguing that if workers got these things through the government they would lose interest in the unions and give up their independence.

## LABOR POLITICS IN THE 1930s

The upheaval that spawned the CIO during the 1930s also changed the politics of organized labor. Future CIO leaders like John L. Lewis fought hard for federal legislation, and these efforts paid off with the passage of the National Labor Relations Act in 1935, the year of the CIO's birth. In addition, this period marked the heyday of radical organizations like the Communist Party, which was to one degree or another in favor of an independent labor party (though, of course, the Communists wanted this party to be their party). The radical self-organization of workers in basic industries, and the alienation felt by many workers toward the economic system and the government, created the preconditions for a labor party.[17]

However, in the end, independent labor politics did not win out during the Great Depression. Most of the leaders of the CIO unions had come to maturity within the milieu of AFL pragmatism and could not, even in the crucible of Great Depression radicalism, bring themselves to champion a labor party. Lewis probably came the closest to a full break with the two-party status quo. In the 1936 presidential elections, Lewis practically emptied the treasury of the United Mine Workers to support Franklin Roosevelt's reelection and Democrats in Congress. When Roosevelt moved toward the right after the election, Lewis broke with him. But Lewis had been a lifelong Republican. He simply did not have the radical outlook required to see the necessity of forming a working class party.[18]

Furthermore, the national Democratic Party, under the leadership of Roosevelt, saw the new unions as the basis for the renewal and long-term power of the party. The working masses, many of them voting for the first time, swept the Democrats into office in 1932 and 1936. To insure that this continued to happen, Roosevelt began to curry favor with the more conservative and pliable CIO leaders. Roosevelt shunned the independent Lewis and had nothing to do with the radical CIO leaders, but he praised men like Sidney Hillman of the clothing workers and Philip Murray of the steel workers. The president's approval helped these leaders to strengthen their positions within the labor movement, and they then used their power to tie the unions to the Democratic Party.

The Second World War consolidated the union-Democrat alliance. The War Labor Board, established to deal with labor disputes, wage increases, and strikes, invited conservative labor leaders to join. Hillman and the other board members from labor began to meet with their capitalist counterparts to plan labor's role in the war effort, and this more or less completed the co-optation of labor into the Democratic Party. Labor leaders believed that they were sharing power with big business, and that they had great influence inside government. But this alliance was not based upon a mass movement of workers and democratic unionism. Instead, decisions were made at the top, and member apathy and obedience were encouraged. After the war, the CIO unions were split between those who had allied with the Democratic Party and the radicals who wanted greater political independence. The former, aided by the government and by their presumed class enemy, destroyed the radicals. This was made easier because some of these radicals were close to or members of the Communist Party, which became a target of repressive government policies when the Cold War began in the late 1940s. The consequence was that all of labor was weakened. Unions had some say within the Democratic Party, but they were junior partners to business, which, understanding that labor could not fight as strongly as before, began to lay the groundwork for the full-blown attack on organized labor that was to commence in the early 1970s.[19]

LABOR POLITICS TODAY

The AFL had always been more conservative than the CIO and had actually urged Congress to investigate the NLRB, which it alleged favored the CIO. This position put it firmly on the side of the employers, who had the same view. But the politics of the AFL and the CIO converged after the postwar defeat of the CIO's radicals. In 1955, the two organizations merged and continued to practice a modern version of the pragmatic politics of Samuel Gompers. Let us look at some examples of labor politics to see exactly how this has worked.

First, it is important to note that labor politics has operated at local, national, and international levels. Unions that depend upon local political decisions continue the tradition of maintaining close ties with local politicians. In Pittsburgh in the late 1990s, for example, powerful local construction unions worked out a labor-management accord through the offices of the county commissioners. They agreed not to strike during the construction of a new airport in return for an agreement that union labor would be used for the work. Municipal employees' unions naturally try to build alliances with local politicians, because these will ultimately set the budgets out of which wages will be paid. In most localities, the central labor councils (CLCs) act as the hub of local labor political activity. Traditionally, this has meant that the council will lobby local government on behalf of union programs and get out the vote for labor's candidates at election time. CLC unions will get members to circulate petitions for candidates, contribute money, do leafleting and door-to-door canvassing, and operate phone banks during the days preceding an election. In these ways, labor hopes to get its candidates elected and to get officials, once in office, to support labor's agenda. Usually, though not always, the closest ties are to Democrats.

Political policy is generally set by the AFL-CIO's national leadership and filters down to lower administrative levels. (In the Change to Win Federation, decisions appear to be made more by the member unions without much central oversight.) Of course, the AFL-CIO does not set the policies of the national unions, which, though affiliated with the AFL-CIO, are autonomous entities with their own policy-making structures. The United Auto Workers, for example, has its own political agenda, and it has not always accorded with that of the AFL-CIO. The UAW even has an international affairs department, reflecting the fact that the automobile industry operates on a global scale. National unions might have Political Action Committees (PACs), and these might support policies or politicians different from those supported by the AFL-CIO's PAC, the Committee on Political Education (COPE). Generalizations about labor's politics do not, therefore, necessarily describe the politics of all unions. This is especially true of some independent unions. The United Electrical Workers have maintained a political stance to the left of the AFL-CIO, for many years favoring the formation of an independent labor party.

The politics of the AFL-CIO are established by the federation's officers, none of whom are elected directly by union members. The chief officers are elected by delegates to the AFL-CIO's biennial convention, as are the members of the executive board, which typically consists of the presidents of the most powerful national unions. The delegates to the convention are selected by the national unions, which may or may not mean that they were elected by the memberships of the unions. To a considerable extent, the policies that the two national federations support and try to get made into law or public policy reflect the needs of working people. Thus, they champion such things as increases in the minimum wage and more comprehensive guarantees of health insurance for all workers.[20] And they support full civil rights for racial and ethnic minorities and women. Both strongly support better labor laws and strict enforcement of those now on the books, such as the Occupational Safety and Health Act. They favor, and have fought for, laws providing for union scale wages for workers on projects funded by the federal government, for pension reform so that workers cannot be arbitrarily stripped of their pension benefits, and for legislation extending the right to unionize and bargain collectively to public employees. The AFL-CIO struggled to win passage of a law prohibiting employers from permanently replacing strikers and for the defeat of the North American Free Trade Agreement. Both federations have opposed more recent trade agreements, arguing that these must include adequate protections for workers, and for the environment, in the trading nations. As this book goes to press, a trade deal with Colombia is on the table. Labor leaders in the United States have made the murder of union leaders in Colombia (by right-wing death squads with ties to the government) a key reason for their opposition to it.[21] The AFL-CIO actively rejected the Republican Party's Contract with America, which threatened vital social services. Its research department developed good materials that exposed the bogus statistics and analysis upon which the Contract was based.[22] The anti-labor polices implemented by the Bush administration after the terrorist attacks of September 11, 2001, were condemned by nearly all union spokespersons.

The problem is not so much the nature of the policies the AFL-CIO and Change to Win favor, although these could be more far-reaching. For example, neither federation has steadfastly championed a single-payer national health insurance program. The difficulty, however, has been in the political strategy and the structure of the organizations, which have made it increasingly difficult, perhaps impossible, for labor to get what it wants politically. The federations have relied far too heavily upon a staff of paid lobbyists in Washington, D.C. These lobbyists spend their time currying favor with Democratic Party politicians and operatives in the traditional "you scratch my back and I'll scratch yours" style. This has not worked especially well, both because the Democratic Party is not the party of labor and because the AFL-CIO and Change to Win seldom mobilize rank-and-file workers to put heat on the politicians. Consider some representative examples:

- In 1976, labor strongly endorsed the Carter/Mondale ticket. Jimmy Carter, from the right-to-work state of Georgia, had never shown much sympathy for organized labor, but Mondale was from a labor stronghold, Minnesota, and was a longtime friend of organized labor. During the first two years of this administration, the AFL-CIO pushed hard for some mild pro-labor reforms of the National Labor Relations Act. Among the reform bill's provisions were expedited certification election procedures, monetary penalties for employer refusal to bargain, and stronger penalties for certain other unfair labor practices. Both houses of Congress were controlled by Democrats, many of whom had been actively supported by labor, and the president was a Democrat and on record as supporting the bill.

Nevertheless, the bill did not get out of the Senate, the victim of a filibuster. President Carter never used his considerable arm-twisting powers to get the bill passed, and the same was true for many other powerful Democrats. In addition, the AFL-CIO failed both to educate its members about the bill's significance and to build a mobilization campaign to rally member support and action. Employers, on the other hand, went all-out to defeat the bill. Employer-funded organizations had members send millions of postcards and letters to Congressional representatives demanding that they vote against the reforms. Scores of plant managers were flown into Washington to meet with their representatives and senators and to testify before the relevant committees. Without counter-pressure from voting workers, the legislators simply did not see it in their career interests to rally around the bill.

- In 1996, the AFL-CIO once again warmly endorsed a Democrat for president, this time, Bill Clinton. Before he became the frontrunner for the Democratic Party nomination in 1992, Clinton had little labor support. He was the governor of one of the nation's poorest and most anti-union states, and was financed by the state's largest and worst employers, including chicken processors like Tyson, whose workers are among the country's most exploited.[23] I remember teaching a group of automobile workers at that time; they were uniformly hostile to Clinton. One man said that as you crossed the Mississippi River from Memphis into Arkansas, all that you saw were miles and miles of shacks. Yet, once Clinton was sure to be nominated, organized labor's officialdom gave him its unconditional support. His first term was a monumental disappointment to working people. Although he did appoint a relatively decent man, Robert Reich, to head the Department of Labor, all of his other appointees were drawn from the corporate elite and their hirelings. Clinton offered only the most tepid support for the banning of permanent striker replacements, forming instead a commission to promote labor-management cooperation and the elimination of the legal prohibition of company unions.

Not once did he mention raising the badly eroded minimum wage during the early part of his first term, when the Democrats still controlled the House of Representatives.

Clinton did, however, aggressively promote the interests of the wealthy. He embraced the anti-labor policies of Alan Greenspan, chairman of the Federal Reserve. And he pulled out all the stops to get the North American Free Trade Agreement (NAFTA) enacted into law. Most unions vehemently opposed NAFTA, understanding correctly that it threatened decent-paying jobs in the United States. NAFTA encourages companies to move operations to the low-wage Mexican economy, while at the same time it makes it very difficult for any of the three countries it covers (Mexico, the United States, and Canada) to legislate controls over the movement of capital and products across borders.[24] To their credit, the AFL-CIO and many member unions did mount a good campaign against NAFTA, with numerous grassroots actions, not only among U.S. workers but also among workers in all three countries. Despite massive corporate and government propaganda in favor of NAFTA, the general public continued to oppose it. Then Clinton went to work, putting maximum pressure on undecided Democrats and promising support for their pet projects. Tens of millions of dollars were promised in exchange for support of the treaty, and in the end, the politicians caved in and voted for NAFTA.[25]

You might think that Clinton's promotion of NAFTA would have chilled labor support for him. But such was not the case. The new leadership of the AFL-CIO endorsed Clinton well before the Democratic convention, and then spent more than $30 million to get him and other Democrats elected. This endorsement took place in the face of Clinton's support for the dismantling of the welfare system, which has meant the destitution of millions of working families, single women, and children. Neither the Democratic Party nor President Clinton made any commitments to labor in return for union campaign dollars. And after winning reelection, Clinton did nothing to champion labor's cause, even refusing to appoint anyone moderately pro-labor to chair the Department of Labor. (Secretary

Reich resigned, making some muted allusions to his boss's capitulation to the rich and powerful.)[26]

• In 2000, 2004, and 2008, organized labor "doubled down" on the Democrats, spending enormous sums of money on Al Gore, John Kerry, and Barack Obama. Gore and Kerry lost to George W. Bush, a man with no observable accomplishments and almost certainly one of the worst presidents in modern U.S. history. Gore and Kerry ran inept campaigns and rarely mentioned the support of organized labor in their speeches and television appearances. Unions did develop sophisticated methods of communicating with voters and getting out the vote, and they succeeded in getting many preferred candidates elected. But none of this translated into improved labor legislation or growing union membership. In fact, as we noted in the Preface, there appears to be a negative correlation between rising spending by labor in presidential campaigns and union certification victories. Although Barack Obama won in 2008, and labor was an important reason why, he has shown no greater proclivity to recognize union support or to suggest that his will be an administration that rewards workers for their loyalty. (Obama, to his credit, did say in the third debate with John McCain that he opposed the trade pact with Colombia because of the murders of so many union leaders. Too bad he didn't talk about the slow deaths meted out to union supporters by employers here, who routinely and vigorously violate labor laws and treat workers who would have the audacity to vote for a union like criminals.) Time will tell, of course, but think what a couple of hundred million dollars might have meant for organizing campaigns, support for worker centers, an all-out campaign for universal health care, new labor radio stations, and labor education programs inside and outside unions. Think too how likely it is Obama will be a friend of labor when his closest advisors are University of Chicago economists (this school is the ideological center of free market—read anti-worker—economics), Wall Street operatives like Robert Rubin, and former Federal Reserve chairman, Paul Volcker, who oversaw the employment and plant destroying economic policies of the early 1980s.

A second difficulty with the AFL-CIO's political structure and that of Change to Win, to date, is the failure to put forward a clearly working-class perspective. The employing class will make concessions to workers, but only if workers are organized enough to force the employers' hand. With the co-opting of much of the CIO's leadership and the eventual ejection of the more radical and independent elements from the labor movement, pragmatic politics became the handmaiden to those who really controlled the Democratic Party. No doubt, those co-opted began to feel that their credibility and respectability depended upon their acceptability to these same rulers. This meant that the AFL-CIO could not think of mobilizing the masses of workers for anything that the leaders of the Democratic Party found unacceptable. This capitulation was sometimes defended on the grounds that it was better to get a few crumbs than nothing at all, but all too often it has been nothing at all that workers have gotten. Under these circumstances, a politics of pragmatism was bound to degenerate into a politics of class collaboration. Both major political parties are dominated by money and the ultimate "special interest," corporate capital. Even the Democratic Party, which receives most union contributions, gets far more of its funding from corporations and corporate lawyers.[27]

Even those working people who lack a sophisticated understanding of politics know that the Democrats have failed to deliver much in the way of tangible improvements in working-class living standards or increased democracy. Seeing their union leaders cozying up to politicians who are far removed from the experiences of working people has often left members disgusted and unwilling to follow union endorsements at election time. Thus, we had the incredible irony of workers voting in large numbers for Ronald Reagan and George W. Bush, whose politics favored the rich, damaged unions, and drove down the wages of America's working-class majority. To those voters, the right wing at least seemed to stand for something, to be emotionally committed to core values. What is missing in the labor movement today is a philosophy for which people might be willing to make sacrifices in order to see it become a reality. Such a philosophy must be, without apology, a class philosophy, one that recognizes the position of workers in this system—a system which, by its nature, puts them in fundamental opposition to their employers. It must teach that the only real hope for working people lies in collective organization, not just to improve their circumstances within our economic system but also to create the conditions in which the things workers now have to fight for are taken for granted as basic human rights.

## THE MISSOURI VICTORY
## AGAINST RIGHT-TO-WORK[28]

A "right-to-work" law is a state statute that makes it illegal for a union and an employer to negotiate a "union security" clause. When a union organizes a shop in a right-to-work state, it cannot compel members of the bargaining unit to join the union (a union shop) pay dues or a dues equivalent (an agency shop), despite the fact that those who do not join the union receive the contract benefits that the union wins in bargaining. These laws allow the employer to play off those who are in the union against those who are not and to selectively hire union opponents with the hope of eventually getting them to decertify the union. There are twenty right-to-work states, mostly in the South. Studies have shown that workers in right-to-work states are worse off in terms of a variety of economic and social indicators, and that a right-to-work law causes union membership to be lower than it would otherwise be.[29]

In 1977, right-to-work supporters, led by the National Right to Work Committee (a right-wing organization founded in 1954 and funded mostly by corporations), successfully petitioned to get a proposed state constitutional amendment on the Missouri ballot. Just four months before the election, polls indicated that two-thirds of voters supported the right-to-work amendment, including 40 percent of all union voters. The state's labor movement, badly fragmented and reliant on the AFL-CIO lobbying model, seemed about to be dealt a terrible defeat. Yet labor managed in this short time to rally voters into opposition to right-to-work and

soundly defeated the amendment. The unions did this by organizing and mobilizing the members.

A three-pronged strategy was developed, and care was taken to
maximize the involvement of workers in each part. First, the
union launched a voter registration drive, with a focus on union
members and those identified as likely to vote against the amendment. Rank-and-file workers were energized to make multiple
contacts, through phone banks and home visits, and, in the end,
366,000 people were contacted, 24,000 volunteers were recruited,
and 190,000 new voters registered. One hundred thousand more
votes were cast on the amendment than in the political races.
Every group targeted, except college students, voted against right-
to-work. Second, a massive media campaign was launched, with
"Right to Work is a Ripoff" as the slogan. All told, the media group
put together by the campaign did one hundred separate jobs and
generated nearly nine million pieces of literature. Third, coalitions with other groups were built. It was discovered that most
groups had a stake in a high-wage economy, exactly what right-to-
work could not produce. Small farmers were contacted; they came
to oppose right-to-work because they hire few workers and
depend on decent wages to sell their crops locally. Similarly,
African Americans were solidly opposed, because more than any
other group, black workers depended on a high-wage labor market. Consumer, environmental, anti-nuclear, and religious groups
were also brought into the fold. All in all, it was a textbook campaign. It is too bad that labor nationally did not learn this
Missouri lesson: mobilize, build coalitions, and act decisively. If it
had, perhaps the political debacle of the 1980s would not have
happened.

## WORKERS OF THE WORLD SUPPRESSED

Labor politics in the United States also has an international dimen-
sion, one that has been the source of much controversy.[30] The early
AFL was strongly chauvinistic, even to the point of urging Congress to
legislate restrictions on the immigration of certain groups into the
United States. It is painful to read the vitriolic anti-Chinese comments

of Samuel Gompers and virtually every other AFL leader. To a great extent, this was but a reflection of the racism that marked much of American culture. Even many radical union leaders were racist in practice.

In its early years, the AFL maintained a position of pacifism, and in its 1898 and 1899 conventions it came out strongly against rising U.S. imperialism. This view was much contested during the so-called Spanish-American War, in which the United States annexed Cuba, Puerto Rico, and the Philippines, after suppressing their independence movements. But the AFL soon began to actively support U.S. imperialism. During and after the First World War, the AFL became fanatical in its support of U.S. foreign policy, especially its anticommunism. It supported the numerous U.S. interventions abroad before the Second World War, such as those in Cuba, Panama, Haiti, and Nicaragua. It seldom raised a complaint against the government's war on radical labor organizations such as the IWW and those with close ties to the Socialist and Communist parties. It accepted the government's argument that these organizations were anti-American and controlled by foreign powers.[31]

The radicals who were so important in the union drives of the Great Depression included many types: socialists, followers of the revolutionary Marxist Leon Trotsky, activists in A. J. Muste's American Workers Party, and idealistic adherents of various other currents. A high percentage were members of or close to the Communist Party. After the Second World War, these radicals were, as we have seen, driven out of the mainstream of the labor movement, accused of being dupes of the Soviet Union and tools of the Soviet dictator Joseph Stalin. As critics from the right and left have charged, the U.S. Communist Party was controlled in fundamental ways by the ruling Communist Party of the Soviet Union, a relationship that sometimes damaged its work in the labor movement. However, it did not follow from this that Communists in the labor movement were simply tools of Stalin, continually sacrificing American trade unionists' well-being on the altar of Communism. Despite their flaws, their expulsion from the labor movement was a tragedy with far-reaching consequences, detrimental to the whole of labor, not just the American left. It is no accident that after the purge of the radicals, the U.S. labor movement's international politics became increasingly indistinguishable from the politics of the U.S. State Department.

Globally, the period after the Second World War was one of revolutionary upheaval. In the immediate aftermath of the war, left-wing movements were poised to take power in Greece and Italy. The Communists were winning the civil war that had raged in China since 1926. The Vietnamese Communists were defeating the French colonialists and would deal them the decisive blow in 1954. The Soviet Union was establishing satellite states in Eastern Europe. A little later the spark of revolution ignited in Africa and Latin America.

The U.S. government had begun to formulate a strategy to defeat revolution before the war was over, and as soon as it was ended began to implement the policies summed up in the phrase "Cold War."[32] Significantly, one part of the Cold War was the use of the U.S. labor movement to block the formation of radical labor movements around the world. Much of the co-optation of labor was done through its close alliance with the Democratic Party. The International Affairs Department of the merged AFL-CIO became a haven for fanatical cold warriors, including a number of former Communists. Several unions became conduits for monies sent by the Central Intelligence Agency to foreign countries to subvert any labor movement that dared to defy the imperial policies of the U.S. government. Eventually entities affiliated with the AFL-CIO, but largely funded by the CIA and later by the State Department, were established to formalize and bureaucratize the collaboration between the U.S. government and the labor movement.

Despite the generally reactionary international position of the AFL and the AFL-CIO, many unions and union members have held and acted upon more progressive views. In addition to the AFL's early pacifism and the widespread labor opposition to the First World War, the CIO was originally hostile to U.S. imperialism and opposed the initiation of the Cold War. The left-led unions expelled from the CIO that were able to survive continued in their steadfast support of international worker solidarity. The Vietnam War eventually fostered renewed opposition to war (and sometimes also to empire) within labor, although the AFL-CIO leadership, especially Federation President George Meany, for the most part supported that immoral war to the end. Nixon's escalation of the war into Cambodia and the murder of students at Kent State and Jackson State brought millions of union members to support troop withdrawal, in conflict with labor's top leaders. In addition, the anti-war movement of the 1960s radicalized thousands of young people, some of whom found their way into the labor movement, where many have remained to this day.

The internal struggle of the labor movement over foreign policy intensified during the 1980s, as the U.S. government waged war against the workers and peasants of Central America. So too did the struggle within many unions and in the AFL-CIO over the decline of the labor movement and the lack of democracy in the house of labor. Meany's successor, Lane Kirkland, continued the Cold War program of the AFL-CIO, but the hold of knee-jerk anticommunism over the labor movement was weakening. Support for Central American police states seemed inexcusable, in light of the growing passivity of labor union leadership in the face of corporate warfare. The collapse of working-class living standards over a generation pointed more than ever to the need for unionization, but the labor movement was not rising to the task. As the Reagan/Bush years ended, the rumbling of dissidents in the labor movement grew louder, and in 1995, new and more progressive leaders wrested control from the old guard. Fortunately, the New Voice leadership in the AFL-CIO (see the Preface and Chapter Seven) dismantled the old International Affairs Department and began to reorient the new one toward solidarity with the world's millions of oppressed workers.

## THE AMERICAN INSTITUTE
## FOR FREE LABOR DEVELOPMENT[33]

For well over one hundred years, the United States has exploited the economies of Latin America and intervened in the internal affairs of the region whenever it desired. This policy, known as the Monroe Doctrine, has led to actions that have caused the death of hundreds of thousands of workers and peasants in countries from Mexico to Chile. Unfortunately, the AFL uniformly supported the Monroe Doctrine, typically under the guise of fighting communism—but in actual fact to promote U.S. business interests. Shortsightedly, Gompers believed that union members in the

United States would benefit because U.S. corporations would be more profitable and could afford to pay higher wages. Initially, the CIO was often in opposition to government foreign policy, but this changed dramatically during the early Cold War, and by the time of the merger, the two organizations were pretty much in synch in terms of international affairs.

Under the auspices of the State Department, the CIA, and business leaders such as the Rockefellers, organized labor in the United States became part of several ostensible labor organizations in Latin America, such as the Inter-American Regional Organization of Workers (ORIT) formed in 1951. But these proved inadequate to the task of promoting pro-American unions abroad, especially after the Cuban revolution threatened to unleash radical nationalism throughout the region. So in 1961, the American Institute for Free Labor Development (AIFLD) was established to promote "free" trade unionism (freed of communist influence) in Latin America. The AIFLD was part of the AFL-CIO, but received almost all of its funds from the U.S. State Department. It closely collaborated with American business interests, including some of the most notorious exploiters of Latin American resources, workers, and peasants, as well as the CIA and corrupt local governments. Its budget was a closely guarded secret, and its books have never been independently audited. Needless to say, it was a rare union member who knew anything about it.

The AIFLD was a disaster for the world's labor movements. It helped to plan the military coup against the democratic government of Brazil in 1964. It supported the coup that overthrew the Allende government in Chile. It seldom challenged ruthless military governments, even those that had AIFLD operatives killed. Among the governments with which it had cordial relationships were those of Guatemala, where more than one hundred thousand peasants and workers were murdered after the U.S.-sponsored coup of 1954; El Salvador, which waged a brutal war against peasants and workers throughout the 1980s; and Nicaragua under the authoritarian Somoza regime. After Somoza was overthrown by the Sandinista revolution in 1979, AIFLD began to foment strikes and sabotage against the new government. This made Nicaragua the only country in Central America in which the AIFLD urged actions that unions normally take. In other countries with governments more to Washington's liking, AIFLD concentrated on programs for small farmers, education, collaboration with employers, and the disruption and defeat of more militant unions. AIFLD leaders and most AFL-CIO leaders supported the criminal Contra war against the Sandinista government and very probably gave direct financial aid to the Contras. All of this damaged progressive trade unionism in countries among the poorest in the world, where strong, aggressive unions and political organizations are most needed. In the long run, these activities undermined the cause of U.S. workers as well by depressing competitive wage rates and making plant relocation profitable in coming decades.

It is to the credit of AFL-CIO president John Sweeney and the New Voice team that the AIFLD and the other similar international affairs departments have been abolished. However, as pointed out in the Preface, the U.S. labor movement may not have completely abandoned AIFLD-like interventions abroad.

## THE TIME IS RIPE

Unlike workers in most of the rest of the world, labor in the United States has been unable to form its own political parties. Unions have instead worked within the two-party structure, acting as a pressure group, mainly within the Democratic Party. This "pragmatic" politics has never worked especially well to promote the interests of the working class, and events over the past four decades indicate that if labor continues to pursue a pragmatic strategy, it will court disaster. The long postwar boom in the U.S. economy ended in the early 1970s. In response, employers began a massive restructuring of their workplaces. Plants were closed or moved overseas in search of cheap labor. Mergers and buyouts created huge conglomerates of capital prepared to move money around the globe irrespective of domestic consequences. Work arrangements were revolutionized to minimize the employers' dependence on any particular group of workers and to sharply intensify work effort. The attack upon unions escalated, with employers routinely refusing to bargain in good faith and committing numerous illegal acts whenever their workers tried to unionize.

Employers began to lobby relentlessly against any reforms of the labor laws. At the same time, they pushed for labor laws more attuned to their new strategies (for example, the abolition of the NLRA's prohibition of company unions, so that the new "teams" could not be legally challenged); for elimination of restrictions on international movement of capital (as in NAFTA and similar trade agreements); for the drastic curtailment of environmental, health, and safety regulations and anti-trust provisions; and for the shredding of the social safety net, including slashes to public assistance, medical care, unemployment compensation, and Social Security. Employers were nonpartisan in their efforts, enlisting the support of sympathetic Republicans and Democrats alike. A sophisticated propaganda campaign was engineered to win public support for their agenda. Americans were told that the world had become increasingly competitive and that the United States could not survive this competition unless it did what business wanted. With market forces "inevitably" changing the world economy, American workers were warned to get in tune with what the markets dictated or sink into an economic swamp of low growth and falling living standards. Business funded a host of think tanks and propagandists to promote its agenda. Today essays and media appearances by ideologues from the Heritage Foundation, the American Enterprise Institute, and the Cato Institute proliferate in newspapers and magazines. An entire television network, Fox, spreads pro-business and anti-labor propaganda twenty-four hours a day, seven days a week.

Since the mid-1970s, politicians of both parties have bent over backwards to implement what amounts to a full-scale assault on working people. By any measure, working-class living standards began to plummet, shored up only by borrowing and excessive workdays. The rich have gotten richer, while workers have gotten progressively poorer. What should the labor movement do in the face of all of this? Until the election of new leadership in the AFL-CIO in 1995, organized labor did very little to combat capital's war on the working class. Fighting back was left to various grassroots groups, including some within the ranks of labor, but their valiant efforts were too localized and piecemeal to reverse labor's decline.

Let us make a logical argument. First, the Republican and the Democratic parties are obviously allied with and subservient to the most powerful employers in the nation. The Republicans may seem to be more ruthless and transparent in their willingness to obey the dictates of capital, but the Democrats, in practice, are no different. In fact, the Democrats are often more dangerous to workers, because they have a reputation for being the friend of labor. Democrats usually campaign on a worker-friendly program, but this is largely hype. Once in office, they do the bidding of employers, just as surely as the Republicans. And since they are perceived to be more liberal than they are, they are able to get away with more vicious attacks on workers than the Republicans. They gut welfare and support NAFTA while giving lip service to liberal social causes like a clean environment and abortion rights. In a pinch, they say that they are helpless to do anything of benefit to workers because of the overwhelming power of the Republicans. But look at who funds both parties and who serves in the administrations of both parties—Wall Street financiers, corporate lawyers, corporate executives, and other assorted wealthy individuals, almost without exception.

Second, labor's natural constituency is comprised of those hurt by the policies of both political parties. A labor movement is made up of nonsupervisory workers, together with the unemployed and the poor who are not in the labor force. A labor movement must ally itself with groups that support the interests of these people, including community, religious, environmental, and civil rights organizations, both here and abroad. In other words, a labor movement is, by definition, a movement of those opposed to employers. Therefore, labor's politics should be a politics of opposition to capital and support of workers and their allies. The Democratic Party has long since abandoned any allegiance to working people (indeed, its alliance with labor during the Great Depression must be considered an exceptional result of its own self-interest and the open revolt of workers). It is now a party of capital, every bit as much as the Republican Party. If organized labor ties its star to the Democratic Party, it is tying itself to its class enemy.

Third, if labor continues to conduct its politics within the Democratic Party, it cannot hope to be fully accepted by its natural constituency, because it will not be able to fully champion the causes of that constituency. When Democratic politicians must promote the interests of employers, as a consequence of who they are and who pays their bills, labor will be forced to knuckle under or risk its own status in the party. Thus, union officials will not offend the Democrats by rejecting their open ravaging of the social safety net. Thus, unions will give support to an anti-labor foreign policy— for example, the wars in Vietnam and Afghanistan, and the draconian trampling on human rights of the Bush administration after September 11, 2001—that usually pits the United States against working people worldwide. Thus, unions will support any Democratic candidate for president or other high office, irrespective of that candidate's labor record. Labor officials will argue that the Democrats are the lesser evil or that they do not want to risk Democratic support for certain labor objectives. But today the Democratic Party's main interests are not those of working people, and when push comes to shove, Democrats will show up in capital's corner. In such a circumstance, labor may win an occasional battle, as when Clinton finally supported an increase in the minimum wage, but it will lose the war.

Labor needs to develop a politics of its own, an independent politics, one to which it holds no matter what policies are promoted by the two parties of capital. If it fails to do so, it may as well give up hope of revitalizing its cause.

## THE EMPLOYEE FREE CHOICE ACT[34]

**The AFL-CIO, the CTW, and most member unions poured more than one hundred million dollars combined into the presidential campaign of Barack Obama and millions more into efforts to get Democratic senators and representatives elected. One important reason for this support is that Obama and many Democratic politicians are on record in favor of passage by Congress of the Employee Free Choice Act (EFCA). This act, which most of organized labor believes critical to union survival, would amend the NLRA in several important respects:**

- **It would compel employers to recognize a union, if a majority of the members of the bargaining unit sign union**

authorization cards (called card check recognition). Some
unions have won through negotiations with an employer
in one location a commitment from that employer to recognize the union in another place on the basis of a card
check. However, no employer is bound to agree to such a
thing, and the George W. Bush appointees who control the
NLRB have ruled that if the NLRB certifies a union on the
bases of card check, workers in the unit have forty-five
days to petition for a secret-ballot decertification election,
which can be triggered if 30 percent of the unit sign a
decertification petition or card. The EFCA would overturn
the NLRB decision and, given that employers routinely,
grossly, and successfully violate the labor laws in organizing campaigns that end in a certification election, would
make it easier for unions to organize employees.

- Employers could be ordered to pay "treble damages" to
workers illegally fired for engaging in activities protected
by the NLRA.

- Employers deemed to be repeat labor law offenders could
be made to pay a $20,000 fine in addition to other penalties.

- To avoid the long, drawn-out, and often futile bargaining
for a first agreement, a union (or an employer) could
invoke binding interest arbitration. An arbitrator would
then, after a hearing, establish the terms of the first collective bargaining agreement, and these would be in effect for
two years, after which traditional bargaining would take
place.

Organized labor is pinning its hopes on the EFCA. Obama
said this about the act, while campaigning in Ohio during the
Democratic primary:

If a majority of workers want a union, they should get a
union. It's that simple. We need to stand up to the business

lobby and pass the Employee Free Choice Act. That's why
I've been fighting for it in the Senate and that's why I'll
make it the law of the land when I'm president of the
United States.[35]

Unions are pouring money into the campaigns of EFCA-
friendly politicians and sending members around the country to
bear witness to the need for the new law. Labor is also tying labor
law reform and the EFCA to national economic problems.
Economist Dean Baker said that

> While suppression of workers' right to organize may
> appear to have little direct relationship to the collapsing
> housing bubble that is the cause of this recession, on clos-
> er examination they are closely linked. . . . If workers are
> able to form unions and get their share of productivity
> growth, it can again put the country on the path of wage-
> driven consumption growth, instead of growth driven by
> unsustainable borrowing. . . . Restoring a wage-driven
> growth path will provide workers and businesses with
> much more stability than the current bubble economy.[36]

Not surprisingly, corporate America is spending gobs of
money opposing the EFCA and preparing to lobby hard against it.
The act made it through the House of Representatives in 2007, but
it never got to a Senate vote. In any case, there were not then
enough votes to overcome a certain Bush veto. But a Democratic
sweep in 2010 could make passage much more likely.

There is no doubt that the EFCA would benefit workers. But
there is reason to be skeptical. As we have seen, past efforts at labor
law reform have failed even when Congress and the White House
were controlled by Democrats. In the face of massive business lobbying, how, short of a mass mobilization of workers, will skittish
politicians vote for the EFCA? When there will be so many excus-
es not to, will a Democratic president make the EFCA a priority?
And how, given the top-down nature of so many unions, will
workers be mobilized? And even if the EFCA becomes law, how

will it change things? What does it do to guarantee the rank-and-file organizing campaigns that alone ensure long-term union survival? Even if a union is certified on the basis of a card check and even if an arbitrator gives the parties a two-year agreement, what ensures that the union will be able to negotiate on its own after the first contract expires?

A few labor scholars and activists argue that the entire EFCA strategy is flawed. It represents one more piecemeal attempt to change the law, each attempt unconnected to the last and unconnected to a coherent long-term strategy to rebuild the labor movement. These critics point out that "free choice" is not the central issue for workers. Instead, they say that labor needs to embark upon a full-fledged "rights" campaign, modeled on the great civil rights and labor movements of the past. This must involve three practices: a long-term struggle for fundamental principles; the promotion of fundamental principles (such as full freedom of association and an unrestricted right to strike and show solidarity with other workers by any nonviolent means); and reliance on rank-and-file activity (including civil disobedience any time fundamental principles are restricted). History teaches us that revolutionary changes in rights occur only when a mass mobilization of ordinary people, led by men and women who refuse to compromise, forces the powers that be to respect them. For changes in labor law to effect progress for workers, organization must precede not follow them.

It is easier to talk about political independence than to achieve it. In 1996, unions representing hundreds of thousands of workers helped to organize the Labor Party. Spirited and well attended conventions in Cleveland and Pittsburgh had hopes running high that at last working people in the United States would have a party of their own. The Labor Party's "A Call for Economic Justice" offered a rallying cry for all workers:[37]

> We are the people who build and maintain the nation but rarely enjoy the fruits of our labor. We are the employed and the unemployed. We are the people who make the country run but have little say in running

the country. We come together to create this Labor Party to defend our interests and aspirations from the greed of multinational corporate interests. Decades of concessions to corporations by both political parties have not produced the full employment economy we have been promised. Instead income and wealth disparities have widened to shameful extents. We offer an alternative vision of a just society that values working people, their families, and communities.

We, the members of this Labor Party, see ourselves as keepers of the American Dream of opportunity, fairness, and justice.

In our American Dream, we all have the right:

To a decent paying job and a decent place to live.

To join a union freely without fear of being fired or other retribution.

To strike without fear of losing our job.

Not to be discriminated against because of our race, gender, ethnicity, disability, national origin, or sexual orientation, at work or in our communities. To free, quality public education for ourselves and our children.

To universal access to publicly-funded, comprehensive, quality health care for all residents.

To retire at a decent standard of living, after a lifetime of work.

To quality of life in our communities, enhanced by a fully funded public sector.

The Democratic and Republican parties serve the corporate interests that finance them. We oppose corporate power that undermines democratic institutions and governments. We oppose corporate politicians and parties that provide billions in corporate tax breaks and subsidies to the rich, selling themselves to the highest bidder. We reject the false choice of jobs versus environmental responsibility. We will not be held hostage by corporate polluters who poison our workplaces and our communities. We reject the redistribution of billions of dollars of wealth from poor and working people to the rich. And we reject every opportunist who plays the race, gender, or immigrant card to keep us from addressing our real needs, and the needs of our families and communities.

Our Labor Party understands that our struggle for democracy pits us against a corporate elite that will fight hard to retain its powers and privileges. This is the struggle of our generation. The future of our children and their children hangs in the balance. It is a struggle we cannot afford to lose.

Member recruitment began in earnest, after the 1998 convention in Pittsburgh, and chapters were begun throughout the country. A lively newspaper was created. However, party-building stalled within a few years and has never recovered. Two problems were that the party decided not to run candidates for political office and that the sponsoring unions and their officers, with some exceptions, maintained their ties with the Democratic Party. The decision to stay on the electoral sidelines left some supporters wondering why the party was formed. The good efforts made by members to secure national health insurance were swamped by the failure of the party to act like one. Candidates have been fielded more recently, and the party is active in a few states, notably South Carolina, but valuable momentum was lost. The refusal by the unions to declare their independence from the Democratic Party meant that they had their feet in both camps, and it proved easier for most to drift away from the new party and continue their old allegiances. Perhaps the economic crises now enveloping the whole world will create conditions in which the Labor Party can gain traction again. I hope that this happens.

# chapter six

# RACE, GENDER, ETHNICITY, AND SEXUAL ORIENTATION

The U.S. working class has always been a diverse mix, in part because of the continuous transformation of the labor process. As capitalism develops, new skills are created and old ones destroyed, with each change bringing forth new diversity in the labor force.[1] At the beginning of capitalist production, employers were forced to rely upon skilled workers, because work in pre-capitalist society was not yet subdivided and deskilled. Once capitalists began to employ a detailed division of labor, a split was created between skilled and unskilled workers. Skilled workers were the first to form labor unions because they could see that the employer needed them and would pay them more if they stuck together. These unions did not see a need to organize their unskilled brothers and sisters; it was not uncommon for them to look down upon the unskilled. Some occupations require specialized formal training and this has created categories of professional employees. Professionals, too, sometimes look with disdain upon other types of workers. Needless to say, employers find it in their interest to exacerbate feelings of difference that reduce the likelihood of groups joining together against them. Thus, my old employer argued during a union drive that unions were fine for coal miners and steel workers but not for professors. Sometimes skilled workers embrace this argument on their own: during the 1930s, for example, the craft workers in the AFL butchers' union showed no interest in organizing their less skilled counterparts in the stockyards.[2]

The establishment of a privileged tier of workers is only one of many divisions in the working class, some of which predate capitalism. Both men and women have always done work, but gender differences take on specific characteristics in capitalist economies. Throughout our history, women have been concentrated in certain types of work, typically extensions of the unpaid household labor they traditionally have been expected to perform. Domestic employment, primary school teaching, secretarial work, and nursing are occupations that have been and still are overwhelmingly female.[3] The skilled trades, such as carpentry, plumbing, and construction labor, have been reserved for men. Men have resisted, sometimes with violence, the entry of women into "male" jobs. Naturally, this impedes the development of common collective actions by men and women.

Religion, ethnicity, race, and sexual orientation have also divided workers at one time or another in our history. Irish immigrants suffered terribly at the hands of native workers and were confined to the worst jobs for many years. Employment ads appeared in newspapers that stated, "Irish need not apply." Similar discrimination has been the lot of nearly every non-Anglo-Saxon group that came to the United States, as well as some religious communities, especially Jews.[4] Gay and lesbian workers have endured brutal discrimination and, unlike the other groups discussed in this chapter, still do not enjoy protection under our civil rights laws.

The sharpest divide has been racial. The great majority of African Americans spent their first 250 years here as slaves, and the racism spawned by that inhumane system is still with us.[5] After the Civil War, black workers were systematically excluded from skilled labor and most unskilled industrial jobs. It was not until the 1920s that appreciable numbers of black workers gained employment in our mass production industries, and it was not until the 1960s that they made inroads into skilled and professional work. It has not been uncommon for employers to play the "race card" to keep employees disorganized and weak, although white workers often needed no encouragement to act out of racism. Employers have sometimes recruited black workers as strikebreakers, inflaming racial tensions and bringing down the wrath of white strikers upon blacks.[6] Some black workers used as strikebreakers in the meatpacking plants in the early 1920s were kept on by the companies for the purpose of fomenting antagonisms within the workforce.

While the U.S. workforce has always been characterized by diversity, its nature has undergone significant changes between the early years of capitalist industrialization and the present. In 1890, only 17 percent of the labor force was female, and of all women in the labor force, just 13 percent were married. Women in the labor force were more likely to be poor; white married women were unlikely to be working for wages unless their families needed the money. The occupations open to women were limited. Of the 5.3 million women in the labor force in 1900, nearly 30 percent worked as servants in private households. For certain women, especially blacks, private household labor was all that was available. At the turn of the century, most African Americans worked in agriculture, although few owned farms. Still, African Americans also worked for wages in industries outside of agriculture, as did immigrants from Mexico, Japan, China, and the Philippines, in mining, laundries, restaurants, railroad construction, and the garment industry.[7]

TABLE 3[8]
Union Members by Gender and Race, 2007

| Group | Members | As % of All Members | Union Density |
|---|---|---|---|
| Total | 15,670,000 | 100.0% | 12.1% |
| Men | 8,767,000 | 55.9 | 13.0 |
| Women | 6,903,000 | 44.1 | 11.1 |
| White | 12,487,000 | 79.0 | 11.8 |
| Black | 2,165,000 | 13.8 | 14.3 |
| Hispanic | 1,837,000 | 11.7 | 10.8 |
| Asian | 654,000 | 4.2 | 10.9 |

Note: Hispanics may declare themselves to be white or black or other in the racial breakdown.

Three trends stand out since the Second World War, which had a tremendous impact on the composition of the labor force, opening up new sectors to women and people of color. First, the participation of women in the labor force has risen rapidly. In September 2008, 60.8 percent of women over twenty years of age were in the labor force, still less than the 75.8 percent for men, but getting closer. It is conceivable that in the not too distant future, women will comprise half of the entire labor force. Furthermore, the participation of married women with children in the labor force has been increasing more rapidly than that of women as a whole. The notion that married women should not work for wages was never completely applicable to the poorest families; now it has been discarded by nearly all families. Second, there has been a massive shift of minority workers out of agriculture and personal services into other types of work. This is not to say that African Americans, for example, are represented proportionally in all occupations. Quite the contrary, they are still more likely to be in the worst paying, most difficult, and dirtiest jobs. Within a given workplace, moreover, jobs are still highly segregated, so that whites and nonwhites do not usually work together. Yet black workers make up significant proportions in many manufacturing industries and in a range of services. Minority workers have made significant inroads into the public sector, largely as a result of the civil rights movement and decades of litigation.[9] Third, new entrants into our labor force are increasingly likely to be black, Hispanic, and Asian. The Bureau of Labor Statistics estimates that the participation of these groups in the labor force will continue to rise more rapidly than that of non-Hispanic whites. Therefore, the share of whites in the labor force will continue to fall, while that of nonwhites and Hispanics will keep rising.[10]

Table 3 provides a breakdown of union membership in 2007 by gender, race, and ethnicity. Just as the labor force is heterogeneous and changing, so too is union membership. This has important implications for organizing. If unions are to grow, if they are to meet the challenge of a multiracial and gendered economy, they must organize more women and more people of color. The prospects are good here, because a higher percentage of women and minorities consistently tell pollsters that they would vote for a union than do white men. And win rates for unions in certification elections rise dramatically, when a majority of the workers in a bargaining unit are women. They are highest of all, when the workers are predominantly women of color.[11]

We will refer to Table 3 later in this chapter. Note here that, although not marked in the table, the share of union members who are women, Hispanics, and black women has been rising. For example, Hispanics comprised 8.3 percent of all union members in 1995 but 11.7 percent in 2007. The share of women rose from 39.3 to 44.1 percent. Between 1985 and 2002, the share of black women rose from 8 to 10 percent.[12]

## UNIONS AND RACE

Racism has cast a long shadow in the United States, from the slaughter of Native Americans and the theft of their lands to the enslavement of Africans and the brutal treatment of their descendants to the routine cruelties meted out to Hispanics, Asians, and other people of color. White workers have not been immune to this racism, nor have unions.[13] Under slavery, African Americans did most of the work, from backbreaking labor in the fields to highly skilled crafts. After the Civil War, they hoped to pursue whatever employment they were capable of doing, but this was not to be. White workers, employers, and public officials drove them out of the skilled trades and denied them work in many unskilled occupations as well. The craft unions of the AFL systematically barred black workers. Most of the early craft unions and all of the railroad brotherhoods had race restrictions in their constitutions, and some of these remained in effect into the 1960s. Even left-wing labor organizations sometimes excluded African Americans, including Eugene V. Debs's American Railway Union, although this was done against Debs's wishes. Chinese workers were the victims of special wrath; even some unions formed by black workers excluded them from membership. Samuel Gompers wrote a pamphlet in which he condemned Chinese immigrants for bringing "nothing but filth, vice, and disease." Gompers must not have remembered the railroads and the many Chinese laborers who were worked to death building them for employers who were, in fact, responsible for the "filth, vice, and disease." A few early labor organizations were notable for their racial egalitarianism, for example, the Knights of Labor and the IWW, but these were a distinct minority. And occasionally workers of different races joined in struggle against employers. In the 1890s, for example, black and white dockworkers at the port of New Orleans came together in a general strike. Events of this type, however, were anomalies.[14]

As industrialization sped up during the first decades of this century, the composition of the labor force began to change. Change came first to the South, where in 1900 90 percent of all African Americans still lived. African Americans became more numerous in industries such as coal and ore mining, iron and steel production, dockworking, railroads, tobacco, food processing, textiles, and lumbering. When economic and political forces began to drive blacks out of southern agriculture, they migrated north, where they performed largely unskilled labor in the automobile factories, packinghouses, rubber plants, and other mass production workplaces that would be the centers of the union upsurge of the 1930s. Other minorities followed similar trajectories, albeit with different timing and sometimes in different industries.[15] Thus, at the time when workers began to organize industrial unions, minority workers sometimes comprised significant fractions of the workforce and occupied strategic jobs. Successful unionization, therefore, required multiracial organizations.

The CIO unions and leadership differed sharply from the racist AFL, and this was especially the case when socialists and communists led the new unions.[16] Some scholars have argued that the CIO's attitude toward race was strictly pragmatic; it was not possible to build strong unions in mass-production industries (unlike the crafts) unless minority workers, usually African American, supported the unions. However, this view overlooks the interracial egalitarianism of many union leaders, at both local and national levels, which reflected a deeply held worldview. For example, the UMW had a long history of organizing black miners, insisting upon their equal treatment by the companies, and it did this in the South, where the risks were high.[17] The egalitarianism of the UMW changed the attitudes of many white miners, making them willing to defend their black brothers and to socialize with them at union functions. The same was true for many other unions during the 1930s and 1940s. The anti-racism of the early

CIO was obvious enough to lead the great black scholar and activist, W. E. B. Du Bois, to say this:

> Probably the greatest and most effective effort toward interracial understanding among the working masses has come about through the trade unions. . . . As a result [of the organization of the CIO in 1935], numbers of men like those in the steel and automotive industries have been thrown together, black and white, as fellow workers striving for the same objects. There has been on this account an astonishing spread of interracial tolerance and understanding. Probably no movement in the last 30 years has been so successful in softening race prejudice among the masses.[18]

The extent to which unions attacked racism and continued to extend the rights of minority workers varied greatly from union to union. Some unions had few minority workers but aggressively fought for them and for civil rights in the larger society: the Fur and Leather Workers Union, the Farm Equipment Workers, and the National Maritime Union. Some, like the Food, Tobacco, and Agricultural Workers, the Mine, Mill, and Smelter Workers Union, and the United Packinghouse Workers Union, with substantial or majority black memberships, not only built their unions upon a foundation of anti-racism but also continued to deepen their members' commitment to this throughout their existence. And these unions achieved black-white solidarity not just in the cities of the North but in the South as well, disproving the all but universal belief that white workers in the South would never accept blacks as equals. It is true that there were some left-wing unions that did not always live up to their anti-racist ideology.[19] But it can be said with some certainty that the unions with strong left-wing leadership set the standard by which unions could be (and, for the most part, can still be) judged in terms of racial equality.

Against these examples of racial solidarity can be set the actions of other CIO unions—and nearly all of the AFL unions and the railroad brotherhoods. The United Steelworkers abandoned the theme of racial unity soon after the industry was organized. Under the leadership of Philip Murray, the union purged the radicals who helped organize the workers and established a top-down method of leadership with little

respect for rank-and-file initiative. Not surprisingly, the union negotiated agreements that, through the rule of departmental seniority,
excluded black workers from the better jobs, condemning them to life-
times in the hottest, dirtiest, and most dangerous departments. Under
departmental seniority, a black worker who transferred out of a low-
paying and dirty department, like the coke plant, and into a better
department would have zero seniority in the new department. If there
was a layoff in the new department, he would be the first worker let go,
despite the fact that he might have had more plant seniority than every
white worker in the department.[20] Similar conditions prevailed in the
more liberal United Auto Workers, where the skilled jobs in the plants
were reserved for white workers. Both unions participated fully in the
anticommunist witch hunts at the start of the Cold War, ridding themselves of many leaders committed to racial equality. This period also
coincided with the CIO's abandonment of its "Operation Dixie" drive
to organize the South, in which unions like the United Packinghouse
Workers of America and the left-led unions purged from the CIO had
shown that it was possible, even in the face of legally enforced Jim
Crow segregation, to form interracial unions and begin the difficult
task of breaking down white worker racism.

## THE UNITED PACKINGHOUSE WORKERS[21]

**Working in a packinghouse, preparing animals for our supermar-
kets, is, by all accounts, a little like laboring in hell. Imagine
extremes of hot and cold, vile smells, blood all over the place,
sharp knives, slippery floors, and a killing pace, and you might
begin to get the idea. Just the names of the jobs are chilling: stock-
handlers, knockers, shacklers, stickers, beheaders, hide removers,
skinners, leg-breakers, foot-skinners, backers, rumpers, hide-
droppers, butchers, gut-snatchers, gutters, splitters, and luggers.
No wonder black workers made early inroads in the packinghouses; white workers went elsewhere if they had the chance. By the
1930s, African Americans made up an important share of the
workers in the nation's stockyards, especially in Chicago. When
the union bug bit stockyard workers, these black workers could
not be ignored, especially since they often worked the "killing**

floors," the first stage of work in the slaughtering of animals and the operation upon which the rest depended.

Out of these industrial madhouses in Chicago, Kansas City, Sioux City, and Austin, Minnesota, there arose a remarkable union: the United Packinghouse Workers of America (UPWA). In this radical, rank-and-file controlled union, black and white workers came together, not just to better their working conditions and wage rates—which they did—but also to fight for civil rights in the factories and in their communities. Led by radicals of various stripes (Wobblies, socialists, and Communists), packinghouse workers moved from the lowest rung of industrial workers to among the highest. At every level of the union, black workers were leaders, and they helped to build a union in the 1940s and 1950s that was one of the most interracial organizations in the nation. Unlike many other CIO unions, the UPWA made racial issues a central focus of union efforts, and it did not purge its radical leaders. Furthermore, the union maintained local control over the national union and never gave up the local unions' right to strike; nor did it shy away from actions of dubious legality when struggling for control over the pace of work.

Concretely, the UPWA achieved the following contractual provisions that were instrumental in winning equality for black workers: (1) equal pay for equal work; (2) an end to lower wages for southern workers, many of whom were black; (3) open access to the highest paying jobs; (4) the continuation of seniority during layoffs, so that black men and women who entered meatpacking during the Second World War could get their jobs back when employment levels regained their wartime highs; and (5) an anti-discrimination clause that not only prohibited discrimination against employees but also against "applicants," so that the union could attack discrimination in hiring. In connection with this last provision, historian Roger Horowitz writes:

In 1950 the Swift union arranged for both black and white women to apply for jobs and carefully monitored the employment office to determine the company's response to the applicants. While white women were courteously ushered into a back room, interviewed, and then hired, company officials brusquely turned black women away with the excuse that there were no openings. The local filed a grievance against Swift and won a landmark ruling requiring the company to hire the black women with back pay from the date they had initially applied. The international union widely publicized the Chicago victory and pressed other local unions to follow a similar strategy.[22]

Largely because the rest of the labor movement failed to follow the lead of the UPWA, the union was not able to resist the radical restructuring of the industry in the 1960s, 1970s, and 1980s. Plants in union strongholds were closed and moved to nonunion rural areas, a move made possible, in part, by technological changes in both the packing of meat and its distribution. The union simply did not have the resources to organize the new plants, and the rest of labor did not see fit to help. Today, the gains won by the UPWA have been largely reversed, and the Latino, Asian, and poor white workers who prepare our meat work under conditions not unlike those which prevailed before the UPWA waged its heroic struggles. However, as we will see later in this chapter, the new meatpacking workers are trying valiantly to follow in the footsteps of their UPWA brothers and sisters.

## THE BROTHERHOOD OF SLEEPING CAR PORTERS

Some unions have had overwhelmingly minority memberships, and in these unions the connections between issues of race and class were always clear. One example is the Brotherhood of Sleeping Car Porters.[23] The Brotherhood of Sleeping Car Porters was founded in 1925 by black socialist A. Philip Randolph. The Pullman Company, which had helped to destroy Debs's American Railway Union in the 1890s, employed some 15,000 black porters on its railroad sleeping cars, making it the largest employer of black workers in the country. For white Americans, the subservience that porters were obliged to show passengers made this fitting work for African Americans. The average porter worked four hundred hours a month and traveled eleven thousand miles. Nevertheless, given the job segregation faced by black workers, this was good employment and attracted many talented and well-educated men. Porters flocked to the union banner despite their cool reception from the AFL, which refused to charter a national union of porters. When the union was not able to force the Pullman Company to recognize it and bargain a contract, many porters quit the union in disgust. But the union revived itself during the Great Depression, winning membership in the AFL in 1936, a year after a federal mediation board certified it as the official representative of the porters. In 1937 it finally won an agreement with Pullman, with significant benefits for the workers.

At the same time, Randolph became a major spokesman for African American workers, and, in alliance with other black groups, including some with Communist ties, formed the National Negro Congress. Among many other civil rights activities, the congress urged the CIO to organize black working people. Randolph worked tirelessly against racism within the AFL, but his efforts had only moderate success. In 1941, he called for a march on Washington to pressure the government to end discrimination in the plants producing goods for the war. In response, President Roosevelt issued Executive Order 8802, which prohibited such discrimination and established the Fair Employment Practices Committee; Randolph declared victory and called off the march. Again, these legal gains had mixed results and did not end segregation, but they showed employers, the government, and organized labor that black unionists were a force to be reckoned with.

## UNIONS AND WOMEN

Our nation's first industrial workers were the rural New England women recruited by the owners of the region's textile mills. Ever since, women have been wage laborers. Today, women's participation in the labor force is rapidly approaching that of men. The experiences of women with labor unions are, to some degree, akin to the experiences of racial minorities. That is, women workers have faced deep discrimination within the labor movement, but there have been examples of successful unionization, as well as solidarity between male and female workers.[24]

There are, however, at least three significant differences between the labor union experiences of women and those of minority workers. First, gender segregation in wage labor has often been even more profound than racial segregation between workers of the same sex. Women have been concentrated in certain occupations in which there have sometimes been no male co-workers. This meant that the male-dominated AFL and CIO usually saw no need to make serious efforts to organize women. There were exceptions, such as female textile and garment workers, who by the force of their self-organization compelled organized labor to take notice. Yet even in cases of successful unionization, unions in which women were a significant proportion of the members, or even most of the members, have usually been run by men. Table 4 provides some interesting data. Each of the unions listed has a significant female membership (columns 3 and 4). And most have made progress in promoting women to leadership positions (column 5). Yet women are underrepresented in each union (though, for most, less so in 2000 than in 1978). This is shown in the last column. The AFT, for example, had a 60 percent female membership in 2000 but just a 39 percent female leadership. Dividing 39 into 60 gives us the 65 percent number in the last column. The closer the number in the last column is to 100, the closer is the female leadership percentage to the female membership percentage. So a number of 100 would mean that women were represented in leadership in exact proportion to the female membership. A number less means that women are underrepresented in leadership positions. In 2000, AFSCME had the best match between female membership and leadership (column 5 equals 73, the highest number in the column for 2000).[25]

Second, even in racially progressive unions, women have been second-class citizens. In the meatpacking industry, women were concentrated in certain jobs, most of which paid less than those performed by men. The United Packinghouse Workers, although, as we have seen, one of the labor movement's most egalitarian unions, did not fight for an abolition of male-female job distinctions. The UPWA did demand and get equal pay for equal work; that is, if a woman did a job ordinarily done by a man, she got the same pay. The trouble was that women

TABLE 4[26]

Female Membership and Leadership in Select U.S. Unions,
1978 and 2000

| | | FEMALE MEMBERS | | FEMALE LEADERS | |
| --- | --- | --- | --- | --- | --- |
| *Union* | *Year* | *Number* | *%* | *Top Leaders(%)* | *Col. 5/Col. 4 (%)* |
| AFSCME | 1978 | 408,000 | 40 | 3 | 8 |
| | 2000 | 728,000 | 52 | 38 | 73 |
| AFT | 1978 | 300,000 | 60 | 25 | 42 |
| | 2000 | 600,000 | 60 | 39 | 65 |
| SEIU | 1978 | 312,000 | 50 | 15 | 30 |
| | 2000 | 650,000 | 50 | 32 | 64 |
| NEA | 1978 | 1,240,000 | 75 | 55 | 73 |
| | 2000 | 1,500,000 | 61 | 33 | 54 |
| UNITE | 1978 | 610,000 | 72 | 11 | 15 |
| | 2000 | 330,000 | 66 | 30 | 45 |
| HERE | 1978 | 181,000 | 42 | 4 | 10 |
| | 2000 | 185,000 | 48 | 18 | 38 |
| CWA | 1978 | 259,000 | 51 | 0 | 0 |
| | 2000 | 320,000 | 51 | 12 | 24 |
| UFCW | 1978 | 480,000 | 39 | 3 | 8 |
| | 2000 | 700,000 | 50 | 11 | 22 |
| IBT | 1978 | 481,000 | 25 | 0 | 0 |
| | 2000 | 450,000 | 30 | 4 | 13 |

AFSCME is American Federation of State, County and Municipal Employees; AFT is American Federation of Teachers; SEIU is Service Employees International union; NEA is National Education Association; UNITE is Union of Needletrades, Industrial and Textile Employees; HERE is Hotel Employees, Restaurant Employees; CWA is communication Workers of America; UFCW is United Food and Commercial Workers; and IBT is International Brotherhood of Teamsters.

almost never did get such jobs. The UPWA did force the packinghouses to honor the seniority that female workers accumulated during the
Second World War. It did not discourage women from taking leadership roles, especially within the locals, and it held special meetings and
conferences dedicated to issues important to women workers. But it
was not until women filed suits against both the employers and the
union, under the 1964 Civil Rights Act, that the segregated job classi-
fication system was eliminated. Unfortunately, the corporate destruction of the unionized sector of the meat packing industry meant that
few women got to enjoy the fruits of their efforts.[27]

Third, unlike male workers of all races and ethnic backgrounds,
women have borne and still bear the primary responsibility for raising
children and holding families together. An ideological underpinning
of the early labor movement was that it was the duty of a man to support his family financially and the duty of a woman to keep the home
fires burning. The unions pressed employers to pay a "family wage,"
one large enough for the husband to support the family without the
wife working for wages. This ideology generated resentment on the
part of men who thought that women workers would take jobs that
would otherwise go to male breadwinners, thereby undermining the
family. In addition, it helped to foster the belief that there must be
something wrong with a woman who worked: a woman "outside the
home" was suspected of being morally "loose" or just not "good
enough" to land a man. While the realities of working-class life dictated that women work for wages, the ideology militated against taking
their work seriously. After the Second World War, for example, most
men and even many women saw it as the duty of women to leave the
labor force and give the jobs back to the returning male ex-soldiers
who were their legitimate "owners."

Throughout the great postwar economic expansion, women continued to increase their presence in the labor market and in union
workplaces. But just as the labor movement was not in the front lines
of the black and Latino civil rights struggles, so too was it dragged,
often kicking and screaming, into the fight for gender equality. The
collapse of working-class standards of living that began in the early
1970s and coincided with a rapid decline in union membership has
forced families to send more members into the workforce. Women's

hours of wage work have risen dramatically as a consequence, and unions have been forced to address women's concerns, both to accommodate increasingly stressed female union members and to rebuild the labor movement to reflect the influx of women into the labor force. As we saw, unions, mostly those with large female memberships, have placed more women in leadership positions. They have also relied more heavily on women organizers, including women of color. This is because organizing success in workplaces that are mostly female is positively correlated with the proportion of the union's organizers who are women. Researcher Kate Bronfenbrenner tells us that "in the late 1980s, only 12 percent of lead organizers were women and 15 percent were people of color. Today [2005], 21 percent of lead organizers are women, 22 percent are workers of color (primarily African Americans and Hispanics), and 7 percent are women of color." She goes on to say that win rates in certification elections in units, in which women predominate, rise significantly as the union uses a woman as lead organizer and win rates are still higher in units in which women of color are a majority and the organizer is a woman of color.[28]

Unions have promoted the interests of women beyond collective bargaining.[29] The AFL-CIO has long been on record as strongly supportive of public policies, such as the Equal Rights Amendment, which benefit women. They have supported the Equal Pay Act, as well as the Family and Medical Leave Act. However, today there is a move to better match rhetoric with concrete actions. Unions have always been strong proponents of an increased minimum wage, and this disproportionately benefits women and people of color since they are more likely than white men to earn the minimum wage or one just above it.

## WOMEN IN STRUGGLE

**Despite the barriers placed in front of them, working women have been the stuff of labor legend. One of the most famous women unionists was Mary "Mother" Jones, who worked to organize coal miners throughout her long life. When the miners went out on strike, she led brigades of women and children, marching and banging pots and pans, in the coal towns of Pennsylvania to sup-**

port the men.[30] Here are a few other examples given to me by labor
historian and educator Priscilla Murolo:

- After the Civil War, African American women were forced,
  out of necessity, to seek wage labor. The only jobs available
  to them were in domestic service, although the hatred of
  slavery made them unwilling, unless absolutely necessary,
  to live in the homes of former masters. They, therefore,
  preferred a job such as washerwoman, in which they could
  do the work in their own homes and return the cleaned
  clothes to the employer, thereby maintaining some autonomy and the ability to care for their families. Employers
  hated this and tried repeatedly to force the washerwomen
  back into a slave-like servility. In response to employer
  antagonism, Atlanta's washerwomen conducted a massive
  strike in the summer of 1891, building large-scale community support despite threats of taxation from public officials, arrests, and violence. This strike encouraged other
  black workers to take collective actions against the multiple repressions that they faced.[31]

- In 1909, more than twenty thousand female garment
  workers in some five hundred New York City shops struck
  against the deplorable conditions in which they labored
  and lived. They worked eleven to fourteen hours per day
  in hot or cold, dangerous, cramped sweatshops, without
  decent drinking water, under the direction of brutal fore-
  men. At home, conditions were similar: large families
  crowded into dirty and dangerous tenements. When several women workers at the Triangle Shirtwaist Company
  admitted that they were members of the new
  International Ladies' Garment Workers' Union (ILGWU),
  their employer told them that no more work was available for them. They picketed the shop and were beaten by
  company-hired thugs and arrested by the police. It
  looked like they were defeated, but the Women's Trade
  Union League, established in 1903 by workers and liberal

sympathizers to help women workers, entered the dispute. The League publicized the horrible working conditions and helped build solidarity to the point that the garment workers organized a general strike. Over the next few months, thousands of strikers were beaten and arrested, but in the end, with help from workers around the country, they prevailed and made the ILGWU into a powerful union.[32]

- In Lawrence, Massachusetts, in 1912, textile employers responded to a state law restricting the hours of work for women and children by cutting their workers' pay. Years of abuse, which resulted in extremely high rates of infant mortality, childhood diseases, rampant child labor, and crippling and disease-causing work conditions, pushed the women laborers to respond with a spontaneous strike at the American Woolen Company. The strike spread throughout the city, and was soon aided by the IWW, which sent its best organizers to Lawrence, including the famous firebrand Elizabeth Gurley Flynn. Met with fierce repression, including the police beating of pregnant women, the strikers responded with mass picketing: thousands of workers circled the factory, arm in arm, around the clock. Faced with starvation, strikers sent their children to towns and cities in New York and Vermont to stay with sympathizers, a move which was met with police clubbings at the train station. Finally, the U.S. Congress investigated the strike and held hearings at which mill children gave moving testimony. The strength and endurance of the strikers, along with the bad publicity generated by police and corporate brutality, forced the companies to settle. Lawrence became known as the "Bread and Roses" strike, because the strikers fought not just for more pay but also for a chance to enjoy some of life's pleasures. "Yes, it is bread we fight for," they sang, "but we fight for roses too."[33]

- In the late 1930s, packing and canning workers, most of them Chicanas and Mexicanas, formed a remarkable union: the United Cannery, Agricultural, Packing, and Allied Workers of America (UCAPAWA).[34] Building upon close social relationships in their communities and work-places, these women succeeded in challenging the power of California's growers and packers, winning strong collective bargaining agreements that not only protected them as workers but as women as well. The national union was developed from the ground up (similar to the UPWA) and was a model of democracy, with women participating at every level of the union's governance. Over the next decade, the union organized packers and canners, migrant farm workers, pecan shellers, and southern tobacco workers. Led by a band of radicals, including its president, Donald Henderson, UCAPAWA faced down vigilantes, sheriffs, and police to organize some of society's most exploited workers. Membership grew under the boom conditions of the Second World War, and the union took advantage of labor shortages to improve the wages and conditions of the workers. The union also operated labor schools and held social events to unify and educate the members. Eventually, it changed its name to the Food, Tobacco, Agricultural, and Allied Workers of America (FTA) to reflect its changing membership, but its policies remained steadfastly militant and inclusive.

  Sadly, this wonderful union was destroyed after the war by a combination of redbaiting, legal persecution, and raiding by the Teamsters. But its legacy lives on. Between 1985 and 1987, hundreds of workers, mostly Chicanas, struck for eighteen months and defeated Watsonville Cannery and, at the same time, returned their Teamster-led union back to the strategies and tactics of their old union, UCAPAWA.[35]

- In 1984 and 1985, female clerical workers brought mighty Yale University to a halt when it refused to negotiate with their union. The union was formed through patient grass roots organizing that focused directly on the lower pay of women (and especially women of color) who did work directly comparable, although not the same, to the work male workers did in the university. The Ivy League school responded by hiring well-paid union busters to defeat the union organizing drive and to stall the bargaining after the union's election victory. The women fought back by organizing students, teachers, the male union of custodians and maintenance employees, and townspeople in support of their efforts to win decent wages from one of the richest schools in the world and New Haven's biggest employer. Picketing, street demonstrations and blockades, and innovative strike tactics (the women returned to work at one point in the bargaining to recoup lost wages) conquered Yale's administrators and built a formidable union.[36]

## THE INTERSECTION OF RACE AND GENDER

Historically, women of color have had higher rates of participation in the labor force than white women. Many of the new entrants into the labor force today are also women of color, often newly-arrived immigrants from Asia and Latin America. Some unions are making special efforts to organize women of color.[37]

Take the garment industry. Just as at the beginning of the twentieth century, when the unions of garment workers were formed, most garment workers today are immigrant women, although primarily women of color. As in the earlier period, women work for low wages under deplorable conditions. Large clothing companies like Levi's and The Gap, as well as purveyors of designer clothing, use contractors to get the actual work done. The contractors, in turn, farm work out to subcontractors, of which there are many thousands. In small shops in cities like Los Angeles and New York, women make dresses, pants, and jeans, often taking work home with them. Their employers flagrantly violate the labor laws, paying them below minimum wage (or not paying them at all), denying them overtime wages, and ignoring health and safety laws and codes.[38] So it was nothing out of the ordinary when twelve Asian women from a Bay Area sweatshop came to the Asian Immigrant Women Advocates (AIWA) to complain that their boss had not paid them. AIWA is a community organization formed in 1983 to address the myriad problems faced by Asian immigrant women. The twelve women, acting with the AIWA, developed a campaign to recover lost wages.

Their immediate employer had declared bankruptcy. This is a common tactic among subcontractors. The subcontractor then turns around and opens another shop under a new name. However, this employer supplied clothing for a number of well-known designers, including fashion designer Jessica McClintock. The women and the AIWA decided to go after McClintock, arguing that the manufacturers were ultimately responsible for what the contractors did and should not contract out work to those who violated the laws. McClintock refused to take responsibility for the contractors, declaring that she simply had a market relationship with them; what they did was not her concern. But the women thought otherwise. They put pressure on McClintock with newspaper ads—which brought in thousands of dollars in contributions, along with letters of protest to the designer from consumers outraged to learn that the workers got about $5 for making a $175 dress—and direct actions such as boycotts and picketing of stores that sold McClintock clothing. With support from the ILGWU, now merged with the Amalgamated Clothing and Textile Workers Union to form a new union called the Union of Needletrades, Industrial, and Textile Employees (UNITE), other unions, and central labor councils, a national campaign of justice for garment workers was initiated. Local governments and the U.S. Department of Labor were brought into the conflict, as workers demanded that illegal sweatshop practices be prosecuted. Ultimately, the workers prevailed, not only recovering lost wages but also winning a garment workers' education fund and a hotline monitored by the Department of Labor.

Another important example of new organizing is home health care workers.[39] These women, again nearly all of color, provide home care for disabled people, usually elderly and always in poor health. The workers are hired and discharged directly by the consumers, but their pay comes from public Social Security funds. Pay is low, benefits nonexistent, and the work extremely dangerous. Home health care workers suffer very high rates of back injuries from lifting patients; when injured, ironically, they usually have no health insurance of their own.

Given the isolation in which home health care workers labor, it would seem impossible for them to organize. But the SEIU, working closely with community groups, succeeded in forming a union of these workers in Alameda County in California. First, the union began to research the industry, and discovered that a critical problem was the absence of a traditional employer. So the union pressured the local government to create a public authority with which it could negotiate, along with a central place at which workers could register for work. Through dedication and coalition-building, the union visited thousands of workers in their homes and began to collect authorization cards. The diverse cultures of the workers necessitated the development of union sensitivity to complex family, ethnic, and community issues. Literature had to be published in several languages, a throwback to the days of CIO organizing in the 1930s.

In July 1994, the union won a certification election and then faced the equally difficult problem of collective bargaining for a large group of isolated and dissimilar workers. One of the achievements of the organizing has been the establishment of centers for home care workers under the direction of SEIU and the nonprofit Labor Project for Working Women. Longtime union leader Ruth Needleman describes the working of the center as follows:

> The workers' centers will be run by home care workers. Designed as neighborhood union centers, they will sponsor social as well as work and union-oriented activities. A "job co-op" will match workers to jobs at a local level to enhance the referrals of the job registry. A health clinic in East Oakland will volunteer monthly health screenings at the centers. The plan includes dances, bingo, immigration and legal advice, and a day each week when union members can meet with a union steward at the center. To take advantage of the "job co-op" or other services, workers will have to volunteer time, for which they will receive points. Points are needed for services. The idea for this exchange came from the United Farm Workers (UFW) centers that required workers to contribute time for assistance.[40]

SEIU has used the Alameda campaign as a template to organize more than 100,000 home health care workers in California, including in Los Angeles and the Bay Area, and in other states as well. It has also used its growing political influence, won through lobbying, its growing membership, and campaign contributions, to help it organize other groups of workers. It helped nursing homes get more public reimbursements in return for union recognition agreements. This strategy has met with criticism, including some from within the union itself. Critics argue that SEIU is obsessed with membership growth regardless of the compromises needed to achieve it.[41]

## GAY, LESBIAN, BISEXUAL, AND TRANSGENDER/TRANSSEXUAL WORKERS

Despite stereotypes to the contrary, most gays and lesbians are working people who face intense discrimination, irrespective of their race or gender. Because they are not protected by our civil rights laws, it is legal for employers to fire them simply because they are gay or lesbian. To avoid this, as well as to avoid harassment by coworkers, many gay and lesbian workers feel compelled to keep their sexual orientation secret. Unions, historically, have not taken the lead in creating work environments in which gay and lesbian workers could feel secure enough to come out.

The great Stonewall uprising of 1969, in which gay bar patrons in New York City fought back against police harassment, helped to change this. Gays and lesbians began to organize openly, and some of this activity spilled over into workplaces. Lesbian, gay, bisexual, and transgender/transsexual (LGBT) caucuses have been formed within some unions, and organizations specifically devoted to LGBT workplace issues have been started. Gay rights groups have also begun to agitate for workplace reforms. Some victories have been won. It is much more common now for collective bargaining agreements to include "sexual orientation" as one of the worker characteristics against which the employer cannot discriminate, thus conferring to unionized gay and lesbian workers the same protection that the civil rights laws give to other workers. Some employers have begun to grant bereavement leave to gays and lesbians, of special importance to those who have lost friends and lovers to AIDS. Health benefits are now sometimes available to domestic partners, not just spouses. Openly gay and lesbian workers have begun to run for or seek appointment to union office and have won in a few cases. In 2004, Mary Kay Henry, an open lesbian, became an SEIU International Executive Vice President, and in 2005, Nancy Wohlforth became the first LGBT person elected to the AFL-CIO Executive Board. Many unions and the two federations are on record as opposing all discrimination against LGBT people, and they have also gone on record against state laws banning gay marriage.[42]

The more activity spearheaded by gay and lesbian workers within the labor movement, the more sensitive will labor become and the more allies they will win. In the late 1990s, the AFL-CIO welcomed a gay and lesbian organization, "Pride at Work," as an officially affiliated organization. Of course, this does not mean that the labor movement has fully embraced its gay and lesbian brothers and sisters. But it is a step in the right direction, one upon which future victories can be built. When former AFL-CIO vice president Linda Chavez-Thompson gave a speech, she routinely greeted her audience by including all workers—black, white, and Hispanic, men and women, gay and straight. This may be small and symbolic, but it is impossible to imagine George Meany or Lane Kirkland doing it.[43] I have taught union staff persons and officers in labor education classes since 1980, and I can say that sensitivity to LGBT issues has grown markedly over the years, especially since the election of the New Voice team in the AFL-CIO in 1995.

## WHAT COLLECTIVE BARGAINING HAS WON

Collective bargaining has been an important vehicle through which minority and female workers can win justice. As former ILGWU officer Susan Cowell said in connection with female workers who must balance the demands of both job and family:

> Labor's long-held goals are truly pro-family because they demand that the workplace and society accommodate workers as people—as members of families and communities, not merely as factors of production.

Thus, while the marketplace rewards productivity, unions insist on protecting workers during nonproductive periods. Union contracts provide sick leave, disability, health insurance, pensions, seniority, and job security, which are intended to protect the incomes of individuals and their families throughout the life cycle, particularly in periods of vulnerability. This principle is just as important for women who are trying to combine work and family obligations as it always has been for the traditional male breadwinner.[44]

What Cowell says can also be applied to labor's fight to shorten the hours of work. The fact that women still face a "double day" of both wage and household labor makes the struggle for shorter hours (for the same level of take-home pay) especially important for them.

In addition to the general advantages of collective bargaining, there are many ways in which collective bargaining can address the unique needs of minority and female workers. Unions can themselves practice affirmative action to insure that minorities and women are encouraged to fill union offices at all levels.[45] Affirmative action can take the form of mandatory appointments to some shop steward positions or rules for the composition of national executive boards.[46] Collective bargaining agreements can contain "no discrimination" clauses that go beyond the civil rights laws to protect workers from discrimination because of sexual orientation and marital status. As was the case for the United Packinghouse Workers, these clauses can specify that employers must hire in a nondiscriminatory way, and the union can set up special committees to see to it that antidiscrimination clauses are enforced. The idea is, in effect, to read the civil rights laws into the agreement. An arbitrator may, then, be inclined to use the way in which the laws have been interpreted as a guide. For example, if a black worker discharged for fighting could show that white workers caught fighting were not as likely to be fired, the discharged worker could use a *disparate impact* argument to win the case.

Affirmative action, including quotas, can be mandated for all training and apprenticeship programs run by the union or jointly with the employer. Unions also have education departments that can make the issues of racism and sexism central to their efforts, again following the lead of unions like the UPWA. Shop stewards can be trained to enforce the antidiscrimination clause by making the appropriate information requests from the employer (hirings, promotions, etc., by race and by gender) and educating the members so they are encouraged to file grievances.

Unions have negotiated many provisions that are of special interest to women, including, of course, women of color.[47] These include:

- Parental leave: This gives a parent the right to take a leave upon the birth (or adoption) of a child. Unlike the rights guaranteed parents under contracts and laws in Europe, these leaves are usually unpaid, but they do allow the parent to return to work with no loss of seniority, wage rate, and so forth. Some unions have extended these leaves to cover care for sick family members, and some contracts continue health benefits during the leave.

- Child care: Some agreements provide for affordable daycare in facilities on the employer's premises or in a nearby facility. In the early 1980s, ILGWU garment workers in New York City's Chinatown won daycare after a protracted struggle with employers and the city, with the latter providing a building.[48] Other contracts subsidize some of the employees' daycare expenses, while still others allow employees to contribute money to a tax-exempt account, which is used to pay for daycare.

- Alternative work schedules: These arrangements give employees some control over their hours and days of work and also include provisions that allow two people to, in effect, share a job. Unions have been somewhat leery of these because, in the case of four ten-hour instead of five eight-hour days, for example, the gains have to be weighed against the dangers of long days and the erosion of overtime clauses.

- Sexual harassment: We know now, without a doubt, that women are routinely harassed in their workplaces, either through direct touching, threats of job loss unless sexual favors are granted, or through the creation of a sexually intimidating working environment. Contracts are more likely now to include clauses that make sexual harassment a contract violation. Some have provisions that allow for special handling of any resulting grievance, and some provide for regular training of employers and bargaining unit members.[49]

- Health and safety: Women's jobs subject them to a variety of health hazards, and collective bargaining agreements are beginning to address these. For example, women clerical workers must sit in front of video display terminals (VDTs) for hours every day and in doing so risk serious health problems. A contract between the Ontario Public Service Employee Union and the provincial government devotes an entire page to VDT health issues.[50]

## POLITICS OF LIBERATION

Because the nature of our economic system makes it impossible for working people to liberate themselves through labor unions alone, political action is also necessary, especially for female and minority workers. Here, the peculiar political trajectory of the U.S. labor movement, namely its rejection of a labor party and purging of its leftist members, has been most damaging. Sexism and racism are so deeply rooted in our society that nothing short of mass political movements, complete with civil disobedience and direct confrontations with authority, have any chance of victory in eradicating them. Such movements did develop, but organized labor was not in the forefront of them. As a consequence, the civil rights and women's movements have not had a strong enough labor component to deal a decisive blow against sexism and racism in the workplace. The absence of organized labor from the early struggles weakened the civil rights victories, and middle-class women are often blind to the issues facing working-class women.[51] No labor movement in this nation can succeed unless it challenges racial and gender inequality consistently. Had the labor movement made opposition to racism and sexism paramount many years ago, it is doubtful that the dismantling of the welfare state that we have witnessed for the past thirty years could have occurred.

What workers of all sexes, races, religions, and ethnicities have in common is that they are workers—by definition subordinate to their employers, which see them as the source of profits, status, and power. If working people are to have good lives, the power of their employers must be directly confronted and weakened. For this to happen, workers must act collectively. Differences of sex and race must be set aside and ultimately seen for what they really are—artificial barriers to collective action. Where else are such differences as likely to be dealt with and overcome but in a labor movement? What other movements have the egalitarian potential of the labor movement? Despite its historical racism and sexism, the labor movement still offers the best hope of achieving a society without the subordination of one group to another, precisely because it aims to abolish the exploitation of the vast majority of people, those in the working class. The goal must be to remake the labor movement to represent what W. E. B. Du Bois said about the early CIO: "the greatest and most effective effort toward interracial understanding among the working masses."

# chapter seven

# IMMIGRANT WORKERS

## A NATION OF IMMIGRANTS

More so than perhaps any other country, employers in the United States have relied upon, and indeed actively encouraged, periodic waves of immigration to provide them with easily exploited pools of cheap labor. For the past three decades, millions of immigrants, primarily from Mexico, Latin America, and East Asia, have come to this country seeking work, in what Kim Moody calls our third historical influx of immigrants.[1] While some of the new arrivals are highly educated, with technical skills that give them access to special visas, most are poor men (men typically come first and their families follow) displaced by both political upheavals aided and abetted by U.S. foreign policy and the deregulated international trade and capital flows that have made it impossible for them to make a living as peasant farmers. In 2007, the Bureau of Labor Statistics estimated 15.7 percent of the U.S. labor force—about twenty-four million people—to be foreign-born. Not all of these workers have proper immigration documents, although we do not know precisely how many. There are probably, at least, twelve million undocumented persons in the United States today, but not all of these are in the labor force. The Pew Hispanic Center estimates that undocumented workers make up about 5 percent of the labor force, so if this is true, there are about 7.6 million undocumented workers here or a little less than one-third of all foreign-born workers. The number of immigrant laborers, both with and without documents, has risen dramatically (though unevenly), especially since the early 1990s. In 1970, foreign-born workers comprised only 5.2 percent of the labor force; in 1990, the figure was 8.8 percent.[2]

By far, the largest group of recent arrivals has come from Mexico. In 2005, a little under one-third of all immigrant workers were from Mexico. Given that most of these have limited formal education and given the near impossibility of poorly educated and unskilled persons entering the United States legally, there is no doubt that a significant proportion of Mexican workers are here without documents. Other countries that have sent significant numbers of immigrants are the Philippines, India, China, Dominican Republic, Vietnam, and El Salvador.[3]

There has always been anti-immigrant sentiment in the United States, and today is no exception. Radio and television talk shows broadcast the most horrible kinds of immigrant-bashing vitriol everyday. They say: immigrants, especially those who are undocumented, cost taxpayers billions of dollars every year in public benefits such as health care; immigrants take American jobs; immigrants engage in multifarious criminal activities; and immigrants dilute the culture. None of these things happen to be true. Immigrants pay their own way and then some. Undocumented workers, for example, contribute billions of dollars to our Social Security trust funds but will never receive a dime of benefits. They pay sales taxes and property taxes. And they do work that is valuable to the society, work that it is unlikely native-born men and women would do. What often happens is that immigrants fill job slots that native-born workers have abandoned as they move into better employment. As a *Boston Globe* columnist put it with respect to those here without documents:

> They perform jobs that are inseparable from our standard of living. Undocumented workers are about 5 percent of our overall labor force but—according to the Pew Hispanic Center's analysis of Census data—are between 22 and 36 percent of America's insulation workers, miscellaneous agricultural workers, meat-processing workers, construction workers, dishwashers, and maids. The American Farm Bureau, the lobbying group for agricultural interests, says that without

guest workers, the United States would lose $5 billion to $9 billion a year in fruit, vegetable, and flower production and up to 20 percent of production would go overseas.[4]

Mexican immigrants, many undocumented, do most of the dry-walling in southern California. They are independent truck drivers at the ports in Los Angeles and Long Beach. They toil in the basements of Korean-American–owned greengroceries in New York City. They are the major part of the manufacturing workforce in Los Angeles. They do the arduous garment work in sweatshops and homes that their Eastern European counterparts did one hundred years ago in the Lower East Side of Manhattan. They take care of the children of the well-to-do. They manicure lawns, work in nurseries, break their backs in midwestern meatpacking and southern chicken and hog processing plants. They clean our motel and hotel rooms. Indian and Pakistani immigrants drive cabs and the limousines that take corporate executives to and from work in our large cities. Along with Chinese, Vietnamese, and Thai immigrants, they slave away in restaurant kitchens. So do Salvadorans, Nicaraguans, and Hondurans. West Africans labor as grocery delivery men and sell items of all kinds from sidewalk carts. They do the hard work of the United States, the work the native-born are no longer willing—and with good reason—to do.

Of course, it is inevitable that there is some competition between the two groups, some cases where undocumented workers replace those either born in the country or are here through legal channels. Through special visa programs, the United States allows domestic companies and public entities to hire skilled workers such as computer programmers, engineers, nurses, and teachers from countries like India for a fraction of what it was paying its native employees. Here, the domestic workers are clearly hurt by immigrant competition, although the foreign workers are also badly exploited, forced to pay large fees to job recruiters, and subject to visa revocation if they make waves at work. Since there are ample reserves of domestic employees in these cases, the competition could be ended if the special visa programs were eliminated or at least altered to demand that employers show, with real proof, that they cannot hire domestic workers for these jobs. On the whole, though, recent immigrants do not compete directly with native labor. They do work that natives won't do any more, making possible in some cases, such as manufacturing around Los Angeles, the continued existence and expansion of businesses that either would have died or moved abroad. In addition, as immigrants work and earn and spend money, they generate new businesses and employment.[5]

## THE UNITED FARM WORKERS UNION

The United Farm Workers (UFW) was founded in the early 1960s out of a merger of unions formed by Filipino and Chicano work-ers in the Southwest.[6] The leader of the UFW was César Chávez, who labored as a farm worker after his parents lost their small farm in Arizona during the Great Depression. Chávez built the union into a formidable social movement, utilizing nation wide consumer boycotts and strikes, and attracting hundreds of ideal-istic young people as volunteers to make these direct actions work. During the 1960s, Mexican-Americans forged a civil rights move-ment to demand a place at the American table. Chávez was an extraordinary, charismatic leader, adept at using a combination of civil rights rhetoric and religious symbolism to electrify migrant farm workers. His famous grape boycott helped to bring some of California's growers and wineries to the bargaining table to win for farm workers more of the fruits of their backbreaking labor. As the UFW grew into a social movement, it was able to secure pas-sage of state legislation guaranteeing farm workers the rights that most private sector workers enjoyed under the NLRA. (The feder-al labor laws do not cover agricultural workers.) The California Agricultural Labor Relations Act of 1970 even went beyond the NLRA in providing monetary penalties against employers refus-ing to bargain. After 1970, the UFW won hundreds of union repre-sentation elections and secured hundreds of collective bargaining agreements.

The growers never accepted this union of their social "inferi-ors," and they waged ceaseless war against it. Many of the victories of the early years were undone in the late 1970s and the 1980s. The growers got the Teamsters Union to challenge the UFW and began to sign "sweetheart" contracts with it. Then they used their enormous political power to undermine the collective bargaining law. Beset by these external forces and racked by internal tensions that led to the firing and resignation of most of the union's best organizers and staff, the union had sunk into impotence by the time of Chávez's death in 1993. Under the leadership of Chávez's son-in-law, Arturo Rodriquez, the union has tried to regain its former luster. It mounted a campaign, with strong support from the new AFL-CIO leadership, to organize workers for California's 270 strawberry growers. Combining job actions, boycotts, and community organizing, the union hoped to regain its lost glory and help the thousands of farm laborers who are no better off today than they were when John Steinbeck published *The Grapes of Wrath* in 1939. Unfortunately, the campaign failed, in part because the union was no longer a movement of the poor. It has become a top-down, undemocratic organization, and there is considerable evidence that it has become infected with corruption.[7]

UFW headquarters is in a former sanitarium in Keene, California, which is located in the Tehachapi Mountains, about thirty miles east of Bakersfield. It is called "La Paz." I lived there during the winter and spring of 1977, when I served as the union's research director. I was one of the scores of union volunteers who lived there more or less communally, serving the union. It was one of the most memorable experiences of my life. I will never forget my first union meeting in a small town down the mountain, not far from the former location of the government camp made famous in *The Grapes of Wrath*. Hundreds of men and women, most speaking little English and not one of them yet under contract, met, discussed their union and problems with the growers, and sang songs. Dirt poor and excluded from the mainstream of American life, they had banded together in this wonderful union, ready to risk their lives for the cause. I was overwhelmed by their friendliness and gratitude that I had come to work for them. Scenes like this were repeated many times during my stay in California, at the bargaining table with farm workers, at court hearings, at demonstrations, and in door-to-door electoral campaigning. Mexicans, Chicanos, Filipinos, and Palestinians found

power in the simple idea of a union, of a movement greater than
themselves.

As we have seen, organized labor, especially the AFL and then the
AFL-CIO, has been, with some notable exceptions such as the IWW
and the United Electrical Workers Union, part and parcel of the problem of nativism. In 2000, however, the AFL-CIO reversed course and
demanded amnesty for undocumented workers. Since then, the relationship between groups trying to improve the life circumstances of all
immigrants and the union movement has been much warmer and
closer. The 2003 "Immigrant Workers' Freedom Ride," in which immigrants traveled across the country holding rallies and educating working people about their conditions, and the May 1, 2006, "A Day without Immigrants" strikes and demonstrations, in which five to six million immigrants and their supporters participated, were strongly
championed by the labor movement.

Some of the change in attitudes and policies within the house of
labor has come from the realization that immigrants hold command-
ing positions in occupations and industries that unions would like to
organize and they are willing, indeed eager, to organize. The workers
who remove asbestos from buildings in New York and New Jersey are
overwhelmingly from other countries, many here without documents.
The Laborers Union has had great success in organizing these workers.
They have stood up firmly in the face of strong employer antagonism,
even under the risk of deportation. In their homelands, they may well
have experienced themselves or known those who have experienced
brutal repression for struggling for trade union rights. So employer
resistance here is not something of which they are afraid. Similar stories can be told about packinghouse workers, who are trying to build
a labor movement in what was once a union stronghold, or hotel and
restaurant workers in San Francisco, who have waged multi-year battles to secure union recognition and better wages, hours, and working
conditions. Greengrocery store workers, black car (limousine) drivers,
and grocery deliverers have all made heroic efforts to unionize. Name
a recent labor struggle and it is likely that immigrants have been in the
forefront of it. Here is how Kim Moody describes the organization of
the "black car" drivers in New York City:

The city's 12,000 "Black Car" drivers work for fleets that serve corporate customers who want the elegant cars for their executives and clients. But, like the taxi drivers, they are independent contractors who must lease their cars. After paying their lease fees and other expenses they make between $4.00 and $6.00 an hour. Most are South Asians, but there are also East Asians and Central Americans. In 1995, they began organizing themselves. In this case, through an acquaintance they approached District 15 of the Machinists. Unlike many unions in this sort of situation, the Machinists allowed the drivers to organize and lead their own local, Machinists' Lodge 340. In an unusual turn of events . . . the Machinists won an NLRB case in 1997 declaring the drivers employees. In 1999, Lodge 340 won its first contract with one of the major companies. Resistance from employers was intense, and because many drivers were Muslims they were frequently harassed by the Federal Government after 9/11. Nevertheless, by 2005, Lodge 340 had 1,000 dues-paying members. The effort to organize the whole industry continues.[8]

There are data on the number of immigrants in unions, and it is encouraging. Between 1996 and 2004, the number of immigrants who are union members rose by nearly 25 percent. During this same period, the number of native-born union members fell. The percentage of all union members who are foreign-born also rose, from 9 to more than 11 percent. We do not know how many immigrant union members are undocumented, but given how many they are and where they are working, the number must be considerable.[9]

The growing desire for unions among immigrants and the threat that union support for them poses can be seen in the increasingly aggressive actions of the Immigration and Customs Enforcement (ICE), which has been raiding plants where it believes undocumented workers have been hired. In meatpacking plants in Iowa, Nebraska, and elsewhere, for example, ICE has arrested and railroaded into quick trials thousands of immigrants, who are either deported or put in prison. Not coincidentally, these raids have disrupted union organizing campaigns. In one case, employers hired Somali immigrants from a nearby state, here with documents because they have been declared political refugees. This, of course, created tensions between the new and older arrivals, much to the benefit of the employers, who love a divide-and-conquer strategy. In a Mississippi electrical equipment factory, ICE raids conveniently helped employers and their right-wing political allies, who are fearful of an alliance between immigrant and black workers that could challenge their power. These raids, which have occurred across the country, are a boon to employers. As Marielena Hincapié of the National Immigration Law Center tells us, "raids drive down wages because they intimidate workers, even citizens and legal residents. The employer brings in another batch of employees and continues business as usual, while people who protest get targeted and workers get deported. Raids really demonstrate the employer's power."[10]

## THE IMMOKALEE FARM WORKERS
## TAKE ON THE FAST FOOD COMPANIES
### With thanks to Elly Leary

In the United States today, nearly all of the men and women who plant, tend, and harvest our crops are immigrants. Despite many valiant attempts, most notably by the United Farm Workers under César Chávez, farm workers are largely unorganized. A large labor supply, trade agreements, such as NAFTA, which uproot peasants, and rapid labor-saving technological change have made the wages and working conditions of these workers among the lowest in the nation. Working conditions are deplorable and dangerous, and child labor is common. As I noted in another book, "the life expectancy of a farm worker in California is still forty-nine years, the same as it was in 1960 when Edward R. Murrow narrated the famous documentary, 'Harvest of Shame'."[11]

Florida is a major agricultural producer, and among its major crops are tomatoes. An important center of tomato production is the area around the dusty town of Immokalee in southwest Florida, not far from Fort Myers and Naples. In the tomato fields of growers, large and small, several thousand Mexicans, Guatemalans, Haitians, and African Americans labor in the hot sun for meager pay. To give readers an idea of just how bad Florida farm work can be, there have been several documented cases of growers forcing employees into indentured servitude.

As was true for previous immigrants, the new arrivals soon began to demand their rights. In Florida, they formed or helped to initiate worker centers. The farm laborers in Immokalee organized the Coalition of Immokalee Workers (CIW) in 1993.[12] CIW defines itself as a "community-based worker organization." Its members are "largely Latino, Haitian, and Mayan Indian immigrants working in low-wage jobs throughout the state of Florida." CIW says:

> We strive to build our strength as a community on a basis of reflection and analysis, constant attention to coalition building across ethnic divisions, and an ongoing investment in leadership development to help our members continually develop their skills in community education and organization.
>
> From this basis we fight for, among other things: a fair wage for the work we do, more respect on the part of our bosses and the industries where we work, better and cheaper housing, stronger laws and stronger enforcement against those who would violate workers' rights, the right to organize on our jobs without fear of retaliation, and an end to indentured servitude in the fields.[13]

The basic principle as well as the main strategy of the CIW is summed up with a simple but powerful phrase: "Consciousness + Commitment = Change." Today, the CIW has a core of activists, comprised of nearly one hundred workers, and a membership of nearly twenty-five hundred.

Once the CIW had succeeded in making workers aware of their rights and cognizant of the structure of the industry in which they worked, it was able to engage in local struggles to begin to achieve its goals. Between 1995 and 2000, the CIW conducted three community-wide strikes, a thirty-day hunger strike by six members, and a long march across Florida to publicize their working conditions and to improve them. While these actions resulted in some wage increases, they could not produce more widespread and permanent gains. There are many relatively small growers, so it would be difficult, even under the best of circumstances, to win union recognition from all of them. Workforces are often transient, so it would also be hard to build permanent local unions. The National Labor Relations Act does not cover farm workers, so employers are free to intimidate, even fire, anyone who supports unionization. For uncovered workers, there is no such thing as an unfair labor practice. If a grower did agree to recognize a union, that employer would be under no legal obligation to negotiate a collective bargaining agreement. If it signed a contract, it would not be legally bound to abide by it.

When some tactics fail or are capable of winning only partial and temporary victories, a creative organization reexamines its position and develops new tactics. The CIW studied the chain of production from the planting and harvesting of tomatoes to their final sale. They saw that the end buyers were often fast food chains like Burger King, McDonald's, and Taco Bell. These corporations, themselves often part of still larger conglomerates, wield enormous power over the growers who actually hired Immokalee's farm workers. Any single grower depends a lot more on Taco Bell, for example, than Taco Bell depends on the grower. And while it might seem that a small organization like the CIW could not possibly take on a mega-corporation like YUM Brands—Taco Bell's parent company, which also owns KFC, Long John Silver's, and Pizza Hut—analysis suggested that this might be easier and more effective than waging war against hundreds of small growers that were in direct and brutal competition with each other and could not contemplate absorbing a wage increase not paid by all of their rivals. In addition, farm employers operate under the radar as far as the consuming public is concerned. If a grower's behavior is especially egregious, it might be possible to shed some light on it and even get some public entity like a state legislature to take notice. However, the effort necessary to accomplish this might not be worth whatever prizes were won. Taco Bell, on the other hand, was a near universally recognized chain of fast food restaurants, with stores in thousands of towns and cities and ubiquitous television commercials. High profile companies like this do not want their reputations tarnished. Taco Bell wants to be seen as a purveyor of cheap but delicious Mexican food, not as a ruthless, if indirect, exploiter of workers mired in poverty and sometimes forced into what amounts to slavery. When people think of Taco Bell, they are supposed to remember clever advertising slogans ("Think outside the bun") or smile at the memory of that cute Chihuahua dog saying, "¡Yo quiero Taco Bell!" If a way could be found to blacken Taco Bell's carefully packaged image, perhaps it could be forced to compel its suppliers to pay their workers more money. One such way was found: a consumer boycott.

Since the CIW is not a union, it is not bound by the NLRA's prohibition against secondary boycotts. That is, urging, by picketing or other means, companies to cease doing business with Taco Bell. The CIW sent members around the country—to give witness, to participate in marches and hunger strikes, to attend stockholders' meetings. However, the CIW could not get consumers to stop patronizing Taco Bell or persuade other companies and entities to stop dealing with Taco Bell by its own actions. In order to bring Taco Bell to its knees, it needed allies. From its beginning, the CIW had actively sought and built alliances with unions, church groups, students, globalization activists, human rights advocates, and groups concerned with our food and the way we eat. Now these efforts bore fruit, as allies offered support for the boycott. An interesting and important aspect of the CIW alliances is that, while the CIW planned the overall campaign and supplied research and other materials to its supporters, it gave its allies complete autonomy to plan and implement their own boycott support work.

Taco Bell could be attacked on many fronts. As union activist Elly Leary notes, the idea was to use "what Taco Bell considers its strengths and assets against them." Behind the smiling faces of the young workers in the Taco Bell commercials was the reality of "sweatshops in the fields." This was a slogan that working people and unions could get behind, and they did. CIW got support from the United Farm Workers, SEIU, the Los Angeles Central Labor Council, various IWW unions, and many others. John Sweeney and the AFL-CIO endorsed the boycott, and Jobs with Justice helped touring CIW members galvanize local support. Latino workers in unions, especially in California, allied themselves with the boycott. Taco Bell implies in its ads that it is a Latino-friendly company, but its Mexican employees in California understood that its main interest was in buying their labor cheaply, while gulling the public into buying ersatz Mexican food.

Taco Bell and other fast-food restaurants are now the main purveyors of food on our college campuses and in many high schools, too. College social justice groups, like those protesting the sale of sweatshop-made logo clothing on campus, as well as Chicano/Mexicano student organizations, were natural friends of the boycott. A Student-Farmworker Alliance was formed, and it began a "Boot the Bell" campaign that succeeded in forcing Taco Bell from twenty-two high school and college campuses. If Taco Bell wanted to maintain its image as a supplier of cheap food to grateful young students, it was going to have to do something for those who harvested the tons of tomatoes it used each week.

Fast-food restaurants are international enterprises and proud of it. But the deregulated global economy that they have championed has a seamy underbelly. The boycott provided a good opportunity for the CIW to tell the nation how its members came to the Florida fields in the first place. Trade agreements, such as NAFTA, permitted cheap U.S. corn to flow into Mexico untaxed. This made it impossible for Mexican peasants to sell their corn and thereby made it impossible for them to survive. They were consequently forced from their lands and driven into exile, inside Mexico and in the United States. Here, they have been treated as aliens, good only for cheap hard labor. What they want is justice; what they have is the opposite. This argument resonated especially strongly with communities of faith, whose steadfast support—providing housing and food for workers and allies across the country, making demands at shareholder meetings, sermonizing from pulpits—was critical to the boycott's success. The CIW also made friends of other worker centers around the issue of global justice and with foreign organizations like Brazil's Landless Rural Workers' Movement.

Taco Bell, like other similar restaurants, claims that its food is nutritious. This is hardly the case, as many food activists have shown. The fight against Taco Bell naturally made sense to those demanding healthier, safer, and less environmentally damaging food. Eric Schlosser, author of *Fast Food Nation*, endorsed the boycott, one more indication of the wide range of activists and movements drawn to the plight of Immokalee's workers, and perhaps a harbinger for a future revival of the labor movement.

In 2005, after more than fours years, the boycott campaign achieved victory. Yum Brands and Taco Bell capitulated. Taco Bell would deal only with tomato suppliers who agreed to pay workers one penny a pound more for tomatoes picked, giving the farm workers a raise of 75 percent. Taco Bell would provide detailed purchasing records, so that CIW could monitor the agreement. Taco Bell would make sure that indentured servitude did not exist and would help with efforts to get better worker protection laws enacted in Florida for all tomato workers.

After the Taco Bell victory, the CIW began campaigns against McDonald's, Burger King, and Whole Foods, all of which replicated the initial victory. With Burger King, the CIW had to overcome a black bag of sleazy tactics, including using its lobbying group to impose fines on growers who granted the penny a pound raise, the threatening of RICO suits against the CIW, using provocateurs to spy on and discredit the CIW, and faking emails to discredit the boycott and the CIW. However, after Eric Schlosser wrote an op-ed in the *New York Times* describing Burger King's tactics, the company retreated and eventually agreed to the CIW's terms.

The achievements of this small group of impoverished immigrant farm laborers serve as a reminder that workers who are conscious and committed can act to do great things. Unions should take heed.

Today, there is a growing realization by labor that employers and their allies in governments around the world have succeeded in creating a global economy, one in which both production and workers are constantly on the move, the former in search of profits and the latter in search of employment. In other words, we now have a global labor force, one that moves among nations, back and forth, working for the same employers and often in the same conditions. A full understanding of this might give rise to a serious internationalism on the part of organized labor. Immigrants have their feet in at least two nations. They could be powerful bridge-builders between unions in different nations; they could spearhead cross-border organizing; they could help promote the formation of international unions (for example, a union uniting the workers of different countries who have the same employer). Such an understanding would also show that employers and governments are natural allies, and that both must be combated by workers—all workers. Trade agreements, the wars in Iraq and Afghanistan, the outsourcing and offshoring of work, are all part of the same system, and it is this system that must be opposed. It really is "us" against "them"—all of us. Unions must support immigrant workers, irrespective of how they got here, with whatever resources they can muster and as a matter of principle. Labor must support full and unconditional amnesty for undocumented workers and fight to change the laws to make our borders more open and friendly to the world's workers. The ICE raids, described above, must be vigorously opposed, and the affected immigrants helped in all ways possible.

An important catalyst of organization among immigrants has been the hundreds of worker centers that have arisen wherever there are large numbers of foreign-born men and women. Many different groups, including community organizations, labor unions, and the new arrivals themselves, have initiated these centers. Janice Fine, one of the most authoritative scholars of worker centers, says:

> These centers have emerged as central components of the immigrant community infrastructure and are now playing an indispensable role in helping immigrants navigate the world of work in the United States. They are gateway organizations that provide information and training in workers' rights, employment, labor and immigration law, legal services, the English language, and many other programs. They represent a new generation of mediating institutions that are integrating low-wage workers into American civic life and facilitating collective deliberation, education, and action. Worker centers provide low-

wage workers a range of opportunities for expressing their "collective voice," as well as for taking collective action.[14]

Fine has identified 139 worker centers, of which 122 were immigrant based. They could be and, in some cases, have been an extraordinary component of the labor movement. Coalitions of traditional unions and worker centers could galvanize a new labor as the story of the Immokalee workers shows.

# chapter eight

# THE TASKS AHEAD

What has this book established?

- Unions have been permanent features of capitalist economies. Given the inherent conflict between workers and their employers, workers in most workplaces band together informally to improve their circumstances. However, unions provide workers with a more permanent and formal power at work.

- Unions benefit workers in many ways. Unionization has a positive independent effect on the wages and benefits of employees. Unions also give workers a voice in workplace decisions. Unions benefit all workers and not just those who are organized. Higher wages stimulate spending in the overall economy and this leads to more employment. Unions reduce inequality in incomes and fight for things beneficial to all workers, such as unemployment compensation and universal health care. Nonunion employers frequently raise wages and provide workers with some voice just to avoid unionization.

- Unions in the United States usually operate under the provisions of the National Labor Relations Act (or some similar federal or state statute). As amended and interpreted by the NLRB and the courts, the act makes it difficult to organize workers. However, unions that utilize aggressive organizing models can succeed in organizing workers and build strong unions despite the law. Unions can also be organized without using the act, and unions have begun to do so.

- In the United States, workers are organized in numerous national (or international) unions. These unions charter local affiliates and most member activity occurs within these locals. The relationship between the locals and the national union can vary a great deal. Locals within a certain geographical area may form a central labor council, the activities of which also vary widely; some engage in organizing and coalition building, while others confine themselves to participating in local charities and getting the labor vote out at election time. Most, but by no means all, of the national unions in the United States belong to one of two federations of unions, the AFL-CIO and Change to Win (CTW). They lobby nationally, help fund central labor councils, train labor organizers, do labor-related research, help to coordinate relationships between the national unions, and so forth. The extent of democracy at all levels of the labor movement varies considerably, from the autocracy of some construction unions to the rank-and-file control of the UE.

- Collective bargaining is one primary function of a union. Bargaining should be viewed as an extension of organizing and conducted as a militant and democratic campaign utilizing escalating pressure tactics, including work-to-rule, strikes, picketing, corporate campaigns, and civil disobedience. Collective bargaining agreements represent truces in the war between capital and labor. These agreements are diverse, but any agreement can be analyzed in terms of its provisions for union security and management rights, the wage and effort bargain, individual security, and contract administration.

- Unions alone can achieve many things for their members, but there are some aspects of working life that must be addressed politically. Unlike their counterparts in most of the rest of the world, unions in the United States have adopted a narrowly defined politics. Instead of rooting themselves in an independent political movement with working-class goals, U.S. unions have practiced what labor leaders call a "pragmatic" politics. In practice, this has meant limiting their role to that of a pressure group within the Democratic Party, trying to get pro-labor politicians elected, and lobbying to get pro-worker legislation enacted. The international politics of organized labor, in the United States, has often been little different from that of the U.S. State Department. The AFL-CIO has not shown solidarity with most of the world's labor movements and has strongly supported U.S. economic and military dominance—in short, imperialism.

- The U.S. labor movement, at its best, has shown that it is possible to overcome the deepest divisions within the working class, most notably those of race and gender. Unfortunately, it has not always been at its best, and U.S. history is filled with examples of worker and union racism and sexism, which have badly weakened the labor movement. Despite this checkered record, unions and the labor movement may offer the majority of minority and women workers their best opportunity for liberation from their oppressive work lives and demeaned social and political circumstances.

## THE DIFFICULTIES LABOR FACES

The United States has offered mixed blessings to its working men and women. On the one hand, workers have considerable political freedom, though for African Americans, gays and lesbians, and women, this was gained only after protracted, sometimes violent, struggle. But, "rags to riches" stories to the contrary, working people have seldom enjoyed sustained periods of prosperity. U.S. workers face the ups and downs of the business cycle, constantly buffeted by recessions and depressions, some of the greatest severity. In very few other countries have employers enjoyed such a free hand in their drive to accumulate wealth. From the 1830s to 1930s, for example, the nation's labor laws put workers completely at the mercy of their employers. During these same one hundred years, virtually no social safety net existed, so if a person could not work and had no wealth, he or she faced starvation. Further, the prevailing ideology glorified the same individualism and selfishness that led to such distressing working-class conditions in the first place. To fail in the competitive struggle marked one as unfit for survival; you had only yourself to blame for your conditions, whatever they might be. Compounding this exploitation was the great diversity of the working class. Employers used these differences to divide workers. So English workers might hate their Irish brethren; Protestants might despise Catholics; men might feel threatened by women and brutalize and harass them; most white workers defined themselves in part by the fact that they were not black; and gays and lesbians were stigmatized and persecuted almost universally.

Yet despite the tremendous odds against them, workers did fight back, building up their unions in good times, losing ground in hard times, but keeping the memory of their successes alive to inspire their children. Periodically, in times of deep economic depression, workers rebelled against their employers and demanded radical changes. Out of these patient efforts and sporadic upheavals arose the two preeminent U.S. labor organizations: the AFL and the CIO. The AFL was rooted in the culture of skilled laborers, who formed narrow craft unions and used the skills and the homogeneity of the members' race (white), gender (male), and culture (collective and democratic) to organize themselves and extract from their employers higher wages, shorter hours, and respect for their power. To avoid political factionalism, the AFL espoused Samuel Gompers's "reward our friends and punish our enemies" political philosophy, rejecting a more radical politics and opposition to the wage labor system.

The CIO, emerging out of the mass upheavals of the Great Depression—and built on the organizing legacy of the Knights of Labor, the Wobblies, the Socialists, and the Communists—had its base in the heterogeneous mass-production workers who toiled in our mines, mills, and factories. By the end of the Second World War, the CIO unions were a force to be reckoned with, and over the next thirty years, they helped industrial workers to achieve a level of economic security unprecedented in the nation's history. I grew up in a union household during this period and can attest to the benefits that industrial unionism brought: a house, a car, occasional vacations, family stability, and college educations for some of the children. The unions also brought profound changes in relationships inside factories where management once held arbitrary power. At the same time, the industrial unions helped to break down some of the differences between men and women and white and black workers—if not always in social life, then at least in terms of wages, benefits, and jobs. Finally, the CIO unions helped to democratize the larger society by providing workers with a vehicle through which they could influence the politics of the nation. The recognition of universal economic rights, such as health care, Social Security, and unemployment insurance, owes a great deal to the labor movement.

Unfortunately, the hopes and promises engendered in the heady days of the 1930s and early 1940s were aborted. In 1955 the CIO merged with the unrepentantly exclusionary and conservative AFL to form the AFL-CIO, under the leadership of a former plumber from an all-white local, George Meany. Perhaps the future looked bright because union density was close to its highest level ever and the economy was near the beginning of a long wave of growth. But we can see now that labor's optimism at the time of the merger was unwarranted. First, union density, the fraction of those employed who are in unions, began to fall in the mid-1950s, declining from 35 percent in 1955 to 23 percent in 1980. The Reagan years brought more precipitous and lasting declines. By 2007, density had declined to about 12 percent. In the private sector, density is a mere 7.5 percent, lower than at the beginning of the Great Depression. In the public sector, density is a more robust 35.9 percent, so it is clear that without tremendous growth in public sector unionization, the labor movement would be much weaker. Declining densities have become so marked that absolute union membership has fallen as well; while in 1983 union membership was 17.7 million, in 2007 it was only 15.7 million. Once proud unions have witnessed catastrophic losses of members and have begun to merge with one another to stop the bleeding. Between the year in which each union's membership was at its peak and the year 1995, the UAW lost 509,000 members, the Carpenters 372,000, and the Steelworkers

659,000.[1] A few unions have gained members, but this has sometimes been wholly or partly the result of mergers with other unions.

Second, the low and declining union densities in the United States are all the more troubling when they are compared with those in other advanced capitalist economies. The following data are from 2003, when density was 12.4 percent in the United States. In Scandinavia, densities were between 50 and 80 percent. In the rest of Europe, they were not as high, but for the most part they were much higher than in the United States—29 percent in Great Britain and 22 percent in Germany, for example. In France, density was only 8.3 percent, but unions have a much stronger position there than here, as demonstrated by the ability of a few public sector unions to shut down much of the economy. In Canada, density was 28.4 percent and had not fallen as precipitously as here. Even in New Zealand, which has undergone a profoundly anti-labor political restructuring, density was at 22.[1] percent. It would be misleading to imply that the United States is unique in suffering union density losses, because organized labor has been losing ground nearly everywhere in the world. However, the situation in the United States is certainly among the worst.[2]

Third, the political achievements of our labor movement have been pretty meager, especially if measured against those of many other movements. The AFL-CIO was unable to stop or even slow down the reactionary policies of the Reagan-Bush era, policies which were, incredibly, supported by the largest U.S. union, the Teamsters (before its corrupt regime was swept aside by union reformers). Matters got still worse during the administration of George W. Bush, which was universally hostile to unions. The U.S. social welfare system has always paled in comparison to those in Western Europe and Scandinavia. Americans do not have universal health care. The U.S. unemployment compensation system is extremely porous, covering less than one-half of the unemployed. The United States does not have comprehensive training and retraining programs for its young people or those displaced by corporate restructuring, and it has the highest level of inequality of wealth and income of any advanced capitalist country. Visitors from abroad are shocked at the extent and depth of the poverty that marks U.S. inner cities.[3] The social welfare system was dismantled, not just at the insistence of Republicans, but at the initiative of President Clinton and other Democrats supported by organized labor.

## LABOR'S DECLINE: EXTERNAL FORCES

Analysts, both inside and outside of organized labor, have offered many reasons for the decline of the U.S. labor movement. Much of the discussion portrays unions as victims of external forces over which they have had little control.[4] It is instructive to look at these arguments, because, while each contains some truth, taken as a whole they are not compelling.

First, it is argued that the shift away from production of goods and toward services has inevitably led to a reduction in union density. This is because a higher fraction of workers are unionized in the goods-producing industries than in those producing services. Other things equal, this shift lowers the union density. Of course, there must be some truth to this because the shift has, in fact, occurred, although not to the degree commonly consumed.[5] Yet it cannot be the whole truth because densities have also fallen within the goods-producing industries, for example, in coal mining, steel, and the automobile industry. Furthermore, this argument begs the question: why is density so low in the service sector? There is nothing inevitable about this. Service workers are highly organized in the Scandinavian countries. If bank tellers, clerks in stores, secretaries, janitors, and building guards can be organized there, why not here? Unions, such as SEIU, have organized hundreds of thousands of service sector workers, so we know that it can be done.

Second, the proposition is advanced that workers in the United States have a low and declining demand for the services that labor unions provide. This may be because U.S. workers still believe that they can move into a higher economic class through their own efforts. Or it may be because employers have provided workers with enough voice and good enough wages and benefits to make workers believe that a union would not do them much good. There are many problems with this argument. Polls indicate that a much higher number of employees would like to have a union at their place of employment than are currently in unions. The gap between desire and reality is

greatest for minority workers, who overwhelmingly favor unionization, and these are the very workers whose share of future employment
has been increasing. There have been recent periods in which the willingness of workers to vote for a union has declined, but this could just
as well be a consequence of labor's decline as a cause of it. That is,
workers might choose to join strong and democratic unions, if given
the option, but when they express disinterest to pollsters, they have in
mind the weak and often bureaucratic unions that now exist.

Third, it is claimed that capital is now so mobile, especially internationally, that employers can easily subvert unionization attempts by
moving their plants to places like Mexico, China, and Vietnam, where
wage rates are a fraction of what they are here. This mobility is largely
the product of the electronics revolution, the tendency of employers to
use unskilled labor whenever possible, and the deregulation of trade
and money capital flows. Capital is now so "global" that, barring the
immediate development of an international labor movement, labor
unions in any one place are doomed to fail. Insurance companies in the
United States can have their paperwork done in Central America and
transmitted back home by computer. General Motors can open a plant
in Mexico, and because of its advanced electronic technology, suffer no
loss of worker productivity. All companies, it seems, are moving to
China. Such arguments have been made so often, by persons of all
political persuasions, that they are taken as articles of faith. Yet reality is
more complicated. Many service-sector operations cannot be moved at
all; a McDonald's or a nursing home cannot be moved to Mexico City
and still serve customers in L.A. Further, capital in most industries is
not instantly mobile, and, in many industries, capital prefers to locate
close to major markets. Since most sales are still in the advanced capitalist countries, business typically prefers to be located in them. Thus, a
good deal of manufacturing, presumably the sector most likely to move
to poor, low-wage nations, is still located in advanced capitalist
economies. In the United States, the UAW lost members at the same
time that U.S. companies and foreign manufacturers were moving to
southern states like Tennessee, Georgia, and Mississippi. The problem
was that the union was unable to organize these workers, a factor that
might have been due to what had happened inside the union as much
as to the fact that it is more difficult to organize in the South.[6]

It also needs to be kept in mind that increasing capital mobility—capital in the form of money and in physical equipment—is partly the result of political decisions made by governments influenced (if not ruled) by the owners of capital, and not the result of inevitable and inexorable technological change. Governments make trade agreements and tax laws that encourage corporations to locate just across the border in Mexico. Governments are responsible for the lack of environmental protection laws that lower the cost of production and encourage capital export. Governments have eliminated the controls that they once had over the flow of money across national borders; there is no reason why such controls cannot be resurrected.

A fourth suspect in labor's decline is the harsh legal climate in which unions must function. There is no doubt that our labor laws favor the employer in both union organizing campaigns and collective bargaining. Employers are free to campaign aggressively against unions, and can disseminate anti-union messages even if they are false. Employers can hold mandatory captive audience meetings in the workplace, but unions have no right to respond in the workplace. Union organizers who are not employees have no right to be on the employer's property, but an employer is free to hire a union-busting consultant and have its staff on the premises every day. Supervisors have no legal protection if they refuse to participate in the employer's anti-union campaign. Many employers engage in illegal practices, such as firing or otherwise discriminating against union supporters, because they know that the penalties for doing so are pitifully small. In collective bargaining, the penalty for an employer bargaining in bad faith is most often an order from the NLRB to return to the bargaining table. An employer suffers no monetary penalty for bad-faith bargaining, so is it any wonder that employers routinely refuse to reach agreement with the unions representing their employees? Nor is it any wonder that they would declare an impasse and implement their last offers, daring the union to file an unfair labor practice or to strike. But if the workers strike, it is legal for the employer to hire permanent replacements, and many companies have done so.

The original National Labor Relations Act, enacted in 1935, was more protective of workers' rights than is now the case. The original law has been amended several times, and each amendment has strengthened the hand of employers. The Taft-Hartley amendments of 1947, for example, prohibited the use of most "secondary" actions by labor unions. Thus, it is now illegal for workers to picket the sites of employers other than their own. This, however, is a tactic that is often necessary to pressure an unfair employer's weak points. Taft-Hartley also prohibits one group of workers from striking in sympathy with another. Similarly, the early National Labor Relations Board was much more inclined to see its job as enforcing the rights of workers to form and join labor unions and to engage in concerted struggles against their employers. But for the last thirty years—with some exceptions—the NLRB has been more sympathetic to employers. The board, under Reagan and both of the Bush administrations, pretty much abdicated its legal responsibilities to workers. The consequences have been a rapid increase in unfair labor practices, a sharp reduction in the rate at which unions win certification elections, and a decline in union ability to win a first contract.

Changes in the labor laws and weak enforcement have thus been responsible for some of labor's collapse since the peak period of union density in the mid-1950s. However, two points need to be kept in mind. First, it is possible to win union certification elections despite the law, provided that unions use the tactics described in this book. It is also possible to force an employer to recognize a union without using the NLRB at all, again employing the same weapons combined with direct actions. In Las Vegas, for example, unions have used mass picketing, demonstrations, boycotts, strikes, and civil disobedience to force the big hotels to recognize their employees' unions. Similar tactics were used by West Coast janitors, in their famous "Justice for Janitors" campaign, to win recognition from the owners of the big office buildings which they clean.[7] Additionally, one must ask why the labor laws were changed in the first place, and why they are so weakly enforced. Could it be that organized labor's own weakness is itself responsible? If so, the effect has been confused with the cause.

A final, and very common, explanation offered for the union movement's growing weakness is the initiation of an anti-union "corporate agenda" sometime in the early 1970s. According to one version of this argument, a "labor-management accord" was reached after the Second World War.[8] Top corporate leadership came to accept the inevitability of unions and agreed to bargain collectively with them over a range of wages, hours, and terms and conditions of employment. In return, the unions agreed not to interfere in the management of the businesses (which is reflected in the "management rights" clauses in nearly all agreements) and to refrain from striking during the contract period. (Thus, the "no strike" clauses found in nearly all contracts.) Both parties benefited greatly from this "accord," as corporations prospered and workers enjoyed rising real wages and improved benefits. When the long postwar boom ended, sometime in the early 1970s, what once seemed inevitable began to seem dispensable. As corporate profit rates fell, employers found the "accord" too onerous and began to look for a way out. This took the form of the "corporate agenda": an all-out offensive against organized labor, including plant closings, the creation of anti-labor lobbying groups, a greater willingness to endure (or even encourage) strikes and hire permanent replacements for strikers, and a thorough propaganda campaign against organized labor. The agenda reached fruition with the election of Ronald Reagan as president in 1980. Reagan fired the air traffic controllers and appointed corporate lackeys to the NLRB, the Occupational Safety and Health Administration (OSHA), and many other agencies whose job, presumably, was to protect workers' rights.

The AFL-CIO has endorsed the "corporate agenda" argument, portraying itself as a victim of corporate irresponsibility and greed. In the AFL-CIO pamphlet "America Needs a Raise," one goal for renewal is to "persuade employers to practice corporate responsibility for their employees and the communities they serve as well as for their stockholders and executives. . . ."[9] In other words, labor is urging capital to return to the "accord," ending the "corporate agenda."

This last explanation for labor's demise is also unconvincing. The fall in union density began before the early 1970s. What accounts for this earlier decline? Capital was busy undermining the "accord" long before the 1970s. Throughout the postwar boom, employers were busy introducing labor-saving machinery, greatly reducing their reliance on union labor. They continuously used the time-management principles of Frederick Taylor to deskill work, making union workers more easily replaceable.[10] They expanded and moved their operations to nonunion parts of the United States and to foreign countries. In other words, corporations were violating the "accord" even its heyday. In my hometown, the critical year was 1958, when the Pittsburgh Plate Glass Company (now PPG Industries) defeated the union in a long strike and began to open plants in low-wage, rural, and nonunion areas, introducing a new method of making plate glass that doomed the union plants. The end of the long postwar boom merely culminated in the "corporate agenda," the makings of which had existed all along. In other words, the "accord" was already frayed when economic troubles began.

REASONS FOR LABOR'S DECLINE:
INTERNAL FORCES

When the labor-corporate "accord" ended in the early 1970s, officers who were not elected by the democratic vote of the rank and file ran most unions, and people appointed by these officers staffed them. The top officers were well paid, lived and associated with people in similar circumstances, and seldom faced the risk of being unseated by insurgent forces. Collective bargaining was a centralized affair, far removed from the control of the workers, who seldom participated in negotiations or even grievance processing. Few unions contained organized oppositions, and it was a rare union that afforded its members a formal democratic system of due process, when the incumbent leaders decided that a member had behaved in a manner critical of the leadership. Even the best unions, such as the United Auto Workers, could be described as "one-party states" with new leaders chosen (anointed might be a better word) by the old. The worst unions, such as the Teamsters and many construction unions, were run as dictatorships, complete with violence against anyone who dared to complain. They were also infiltrated by criminal elements, who raided union treasuries to finance casinos and other underworld ventures. When Joseph "Jock" Yablonski, a former officer of the United Mine Workers, organized a reformist challenge, the union's president, Tony Boyle, had Yablonski murdered.[11]

Still, at the local level thousands of unions operated democratically, negotiating contracts, enforcing agreements, and investigating grievances. National unions won many good things for their members, including decent pensions and longer vacations. Central labor councils helped to elect many decently liberal members of Congress. The AFL-CIO continued to support policies that were in the interest of the working class. But even at their best, unions practiced what Kim Moody calls the "servicing model" of unionism.[12] That is, each union saw its main function as servicing its existing membership: getting the members more money and benefits and policing the collective bargaining agreements. This approach, in turn, meant that unions spent little money and used minimal personnel to organize new locals. In the late 1990s, the average union spent a scant 3 percent of its budget on organizing; in some cases more money was spent on the union's annual convention than on organizing. In 2006, when the forces that were to become the CTW were trying to reform the AFL-CIO, they demanded that each union in the federation spend at least 10 percent of its revenues on organizing. Not many unions met this threshold, nearly a decade after new leadership in the federation had made organizing a priority.[13] Notwithstanding the external forces working against them, how did unions expect to defend their members when they devoted almost no attention to organizing the unorganized? Some union leaders, including former AFL-CIO president George Meany, professed a lack of interest in nonunion workers, implying that these people were somehow responsible for their lack of union representation.[14]

There were other serious problems with organized labor during the years of the "accord." By ceding control over workplaces to the employers, unions ignored the fact that, though workers wanted and enjoyed the higher wages won during this period, working conditions are also critical to workers' well-being. Employers continued to intensify the pace of work and to deny workers a meaningful say in how the work was done. Autoworkers may have earned high wages, but they were physically and emotionally tested by the numbing monotony of work along a high-speed assembly line.[15] Unions hesitated to deal with immediate workplace problems directly, as they had often done in the past, and instead told workers to file grievances. The union's job was to enforce the contract, including the "no-strike" agreement. On another level, the labor movement was thoroughly enmeshed in the politics of the Democratic Party, which is beholden to corporate funding. It would take a remarkably naive person to believe that this is the party of the working man and woman. Yet labor did the Democrats' bidding, and internationally served the interests of U.S. corporations by allying itself with the CIA and State Department. How could a labor movement serve the interests of the working class if it was integrated into the politics of the very "corporate agenda" that many now blame for the woeful state of working America?

The labor-management "accord" began during the same period in which the left-wing unions and radical unionists responsible for the birth and growth of the CIO were being systematically purged from the labor movement. The severing of the labor movement from the left had disastrous consequences, because labor radicalism has always been essential for workers to advance. Would employers have been so willing to recognize and bargain with the AFL unions had not Debs and the rest of the militants nearly brought the house of capital to its knees? Would the CIO unions have survived without the efforts of the radicals who confronted the employers everywhere in the nation?

The success of the radicals in mobilizing workers during these periods did not come from "service" unionism or an alliance with the Democratic Party. It came from the ability of radicals to infuse workers with a vision of a better society—where workers had rights and some control over their lives where they were more than factors of production. In this vision, people stuck together as a matter of principle, irrespective of their gender or race. Furthermore, for the labor left, organizing workers was only the beginning. Once organized, their unions would be democratic and militant. Collective bargaining agreements would not be ends in themselves but one of many means, including direct actions, to deepen and strengthen worker power on the job. Politically, the left-led unions would fight for those things that would make workers more powerful: full employment, progressive taxes, an end to militarism and empire, support for public investment in health, education, and welfare, and solidarity with workers around the world.

We saw in Chapter Four that the radical unions of the CIO, whatever their weaknesses (and often a knee-jerk reverence for the Communist states was one of them), won better contracts than most of their competitors, contracts that gave more power to the rank and file. Furthermore, these unions were among the most democratic in the labor movement, and they were the biggest thorn in the side of the employers. In those unions controlled by more conservative elements, the radicals, sometimes organized as formal caucuses, provided a constant challenge to the leaders to take stronger positions than they otherwise might have taken. Most remarkably, the left prompted the unions to make more progress toward ending racial (and to some extent gender) discrimination than any other organizations in the history of the country. After the Second World War, the CIO began "Operation Dixie" to organize workers in the low-wage and racist South. Unfortunately, the war against the left had already begun, dooming this critical movement to failure. Had the left been allowed to lead this movement, and had it been supported as strongly as, say, the UMW supported the CIO in the late 1930s, the entire postwar history of the United States might have been dramatically altered.[16] Had the CIO retained its radical core, it might have at least won something akin to the enviable social welfare state achieved by the Scandinavian unions during the same era. To its shame, the CIO ended up in bed with the AFL. Instead of standing up to the cold warriors of both political parties and the AFL, and instead of fighting McCarthyism and the witch hunts of the 1950s, the CIO threw out its best and brightest and doomed the labor movement to the "corporate agenda." Some workers got more money and moved to the suburbs, but the labor movement as a movement for social justice died, and with that death came the opportunity to roll back working-class living standards.

## THE "NEW VOICE"

George Meany, with his ubiquitous cigar and rough New York accent, was at least colorful. His successor, Lane Kirkland, like Meany a career labor functionary, was dull and incapable of developing a strategy to confront the "corporate agenda." While business was beating up on workers, the AFL-CIO, in the 1970s and 1980s, preached labor-management cooperation, trying to resurrect the "accord." But the latter was the product of special circumstances. Workers prospered during the postwar boom because the economy grew rapidly, and enough of them were organized to make it worthwhile for employers to bargain with their unions rather than go on the offensive. By the time Kirkland took office, corporations were preaching cooperation but engaging in a no-holds-barred class war. As union density plummeted and total membership also began to fall, it became clear to some within the AFL-CIO that fundamental changes were needed. In many unions, rank-and-file groups, sometimes led by radicals who had come of age during the tumultuous 1960s, formed and pushed sclerotic leadership bodies to do something to stop the assault on working-class living standards. The Teamsters for a Democratic Union (TDU) is perhaps the most famous of these organizations, and deservedly so.

The reform movement in the national unions eventually reached the AFL-CIO itself. In the early 1990s, pressure was put on Kirkland to resign. At first he refused, and when he ultimately did resign, he hoped that his anointed successor and interim president, Tom Donahue, would be able to stave off the reformers and keep power in the hands of the old guard. But it was too late. A reform slate, the "New Voice," contested the election of officers at the 1995 AFL-CIO convention in New York City. It was the first contested election in one hundred years. The New Voice candidates were John Sweeney, president of the grow-ing and innovative Service Employees International Union (creator of the Contract Campaign Manual), Richard Trumka, militant president of the United Mine Workers, and Linda Chávez-Thompson, a dynam-ic Chicana local leader from the American Federation of State, County, and Municipal Employees (AFSCME). The New Voice slate convincingly defeated the Donahue forces and began to implement their programs, which, they said, would build a new social movement to challenge the "corporate agenda."

The New Voice leaders did some remarkable things. Sweeney tried to make organizing the prime focus of the AFL-CIO. The AFL-CIO's Organizing Institute trained new organizers and encouraged the use of the confrontational tactics described in this book. Former director of organizing Richard Bensinger refreshingly stated, "we will be success-ful only to the degree that we recognize our own responsibility for our own failures."[17] The AFL-CIO has conducted "Union Summers" in which young people, mostly college students, are trained to participate in organizing campaigns. The success of this program led to the start of a "Union Senior" counterpart.[18] Sweeney encouraged member unions to devote 30 percent of their budgets to organizing, and while not many unions did this, some did take organizing seriously. The AFL-CIO created a Working Women's Department, headed by Karen Nussbaum, the former director of the women's organizing group, 9 to 5. Women workers were polled throughout the country to help unions get a better handle on women's issues. Sweeney hoped to build bridges with women's organizations as well as many other interest groups who might be labor's natural allies. Cities across the country were declared "union cities," and plans were made to rejuvenate and support their central labor councils in spearheading the organizing of new unions.

The AFL-CIO sponsored a study of the nation's central labor councils, and it discovered that some of these were already organizing, some even helping to build broad-based social movements. Since central labor councils are tied directly to the AFL-CIO, they could become good vehicles for funding and organizing somewhat independently of the national unions, over which the AFL-CIO has no immediate control. These bodies could also encourage their member unions to cooperate in organizing. If one union does exceptional organizing in an area, it could help to organize any group of workers, even if another union would typically organize them. Or unions could develop joint organizing campaigns. If it seemed best to organize all of the workers in a town or region at once and together, the central labor council could lead the organizing drive itself. Labor councils could also be important focal points for the creation of broader social movement groups, such as the one built in Atlanta to secure high-paying jobs at the last Olympics. As we have seen, there are already many worker centers, such as Black Workers for Justice, which have done good work in organizing, and the central labor councils could join with these and perhaps provide, via the AFL-CIO, critical funding.[19]

To their great credit, the New Voice officers dismantled the AFL-CIO's International Affairs Department. In some ways, this marked the beginning of a new era in international solidarity (see the Preface for a caveat). Some member unions, and the independent UE, have participated in cross-border organizing to help Mexican workers confront the transnational corporations located along the U.S.-Mexico border and to build independent unions. The AFL-CIO hosted, for the first time, representatives of the world's International Trade

Secretariats, organizations that represent unions worldwide in various economic sectors, such as metals, construction, and communications. These secretariats help to coordinate the actions of unions in each particular sector around the world. When the United Steel Workers went after the union-busting Ravenswood Aluminum Corporation, it asked for and got tremendous help from the secretariats and European labor unions.[20]

In 1980, the AFL-CIO stood by while Reagan fired the air traffic controllers. New Voice took an active and sometimes aggressive stance in connection with particular labor disputes. Sweeney, Trumka, and Chavez actually went to labor hot spots and offered support. They did this for strawberry workers in Watsonville, California, apple harvesters in the state of Washington, and the newspaper strikers in Detroit. The AFL-CIO offered strong support to the Teamsters in the UPS strike. Such solidarity is important, because it encourages member unions to show solidarity, too. On a more symbolic level, the federation has begun to hold its conventions in places where there is a strong working-class presence rather than in the Florida resort town of Bal Harbor.

The AFL-CIO also made overtures to intellectuals. During the 1930s many progressive intellectuals supported and worked for the labor movement. The labor movement was the center of action for anyone interested in fundamental social change. In 1996, a teach-in on labor and intellectuals held at Columbia University in New York City attracted thousands of participants, including many prominent scholars and writers. A similar event was held at UCLA in February 1997, and a third at the University of Pittsburgh in September 1997. Such events are important because they give organized labor good publicity and lay the groundwork for recruiting college students into the labor movement. The labor movement is more open to intellectuals, even those who are openly left-wing, than it has been at any time since the 1930s and early 1940s, creating an opportunity to transcend the split between labor and the left. There are many leftists in the unions and in AFL-CIO staff positions, and they now can be a lot more open about their political views. In turn, the unions and the AFL-CIO are more open to the left intellectuals' analyses of their unions and of the larger society and to their suggestions for more successful organizing and bargaining. The AFL-CIO contracted with the left-leaning Center for

Popular Economics in Amherst, Massachusetts, for a package of materials for worker study groups in economics. The eight-week course,
titled *Common Sense Economics*, represented a real step forward in
economic education for the AFL-CIO. Of course, the federation cannot force member unions to use the materials, and the materials themselves were not without problems, but labor educators used the course,
and the workers who took it encountered a more accurate view of the
capitalist economic system than most institutions in this society provide.

## AN INTERNATIONAL LABOR MOVEMENT?

As capital has become more mobile, ceaselessly moving around
the globe in search of new markets and lower costs, and as national governments have become more helpless to control this, some
analysts have argued that it is no longer possible for workers in
any one country to successfully challenge employers. The threat of
plant closings and capital flight is indeed too great for any particular country's government or workers to challenge employers. The
only hope for workers is to forge an international labor movement
to challenge employers globally.

Workers can and must organize whenever and wherever they
can. Yet while employers are increasingly flexible and mobile,
most production is still domestic and much of it cannot be moved.
National governments could place controls upon capital mobility,
but they will not, unless there is a well-organized labor movement
to force them to do so. It is rather foolish to believe that an international labor movement is going to suddenly emerge, when
unions have not been able to organize more than a tiny minority
of workers here. So, for now, the main task of the U.S. labor movement must be to organize as many workers as it can and to develop an independent labor politics to build a comprehensive labor
movement.

However, labor in the United States must ally itself with workers in the rest of the world and do what it can to support workers'
struggles everywhere. Workers around the world are becoming
more alike in that they face the same attacks from employers and

governments. So there is a real basis for cooperation and support. It is in the interests of U.S. workers to help to raise the living standards of workers worldwide, because this reduces the ability of employers to pit one group of workers against another. And with the end of the Cold War, it is now possible to imagine that the U.S. labor movement will take off its ideological blinders and support workers' struggles in other countries, irrespective of the politics of these struggles. Already we have witnessed many hopeful signs: some U.S. unions helping Mexican workers to organize; the use of electronic communications to facilitate worldwide support for various strikes, including boycotts of employer products; international coordination of collective bargaining and so forth. American workers need to learn about efforts elsewhere in the world. For example, Korean workers have engaged in mass agitations to win representation, as well as to assert themselves politically. Throughout Europe and in Argentina, the unemployed have taken to the streets, often with the support of the labor movements. Confronting employers and confronting the government more and more amount to the same thing; workers' struggles are increasingly political struggles. Further, international labor needs to coordinate its goals. For example, if workers in all countries were fighting hard for a reduction in the working day, it would be much easier for labor movements to cooperate with one another and show solidarity.[21]

In the past, internationalism has meant that U.S. unions have supported unions in the rest of the world because there was some specific self-interested reason to do so. This has left a bad taste in the mouths of potential allies abroad. Instead, it would be better to show solidarity with the workers of the world out of principle, all the time and in any way possible. Bill Fletcher, Jr., and Fernando Gapasin suggest that labor in the United States show "social justice solidarity" by addressing things like the rights of immigrant workers, political repression, human rights, and opposition to imperial wars.[22] It is also well past time for organized labor to make public its past collaboration with U.S. foreign policy and to insist that the government end its embargo against Cuba and its machinations against the Chávez government in Venezuela.

STILL TO COME

I have described in the preface the record of New Voice and the decision by several unions to leave the AFL-CIO and form a new federation, Change to Win. So I will not repeat labor's most recent history here. Instead, let me elaborate a point made in the preface, namely that U.S. labor needs to develop a coherent ideological focus, one aimed at giving working people a compass to find where they stand in the larger society and a vision of what might be if workers demanded that it be so.

What do the labor federations see as a good society? It is difficult to know. A close inspection of *America Needs a Raise* or *Common Sense Economics* or SEIU president Andy Stern's *A Country that Works: Getting America Back on Track*[23] reveals little in terms of what the labor movement stands for in principle. There are a lot of words devoted to what it is against: low wages, growing inequality in income and wealth, unregulated free trade, the destruction of our social safety net, the privatization of public services, high interest rates, exorbitant CEO pay, excessive overtime, bad labor laws, a flat tax, cuts in the capital gains tax, corporate tax breaks, and the "corporate agenda." But the AFL-CIO shies away from saying forthrightly what it stands *for*. It does not as a matter of course demand things that should be human rights. Brief mention is sometimes made of these things, but they are not at the center of the labor movement's program.

What organized labor lacks is a working-class ideology, a labor-centered way of thinking and acting based upon the understanding that a capitalist society is not and cannot be a just one. What might motivate workers to become part of a movement is the possibility that the current system can be transcended and a new, democratic, egalitarian society built.

A list of labor-centered principles that would respond to this need might look like this:

1.  Employment as a right. Unemployment not only wastes the output that the unemployed could have produced, it also wastes human beings and leads to a large number of social problems from arrest and imprisonment to murder and suicide.

2. Meaningful work. Human beings have the unique ability to conceptualize work tasks and then perform them. Yet most jobs utilize only a fraction of human ability. This leads to profound alienation and a hatred of work. Instead of seeing labor as the fulfillment of our humanity, we see it as a necessary evil to be avoided if at all possible.

3. Socialization of consumption. We waste enormous effort to purchase goods and services that ought to be provided by society. Examples include education at all levels, health care (including care of the aged), child care, transportation, and recreation (parks, libraries, playgrounds, and gyms). It would be far more efficient to share responsibility for such public needs.

4. Democratic control of production. We pride ourselves on having a free society, yet nearly all workplaces are run as dictatorships. Shouldn't we have control over the production of the outputs that we depend upon for survival? Why should the glass factory that dominated my hometown for nearly a century be able to pack up and leave without the will of the people being considered, much less being decisive?

5. Shorter hours of work. At the same time that hundreds of millions of people worldwide cannot find enough work, millions of others are working hours comparable to those worked during the industrial revolution. People are working too much to enjoy life. Why should this be so?

6. An end to discrimination. What possible justification can there be for the gross inequalities in jobs, incomes, housing, and wealth that exist between those who are white and male and just about everyone else? No just society can be built on a foundation of racial, ethnic, and gender discrimination.

7. Wage and income equality. I can think of no good reason why I earned four times as much as the men and women who clean

the buildings in which I labored and taught. Would I have refused to work if they had earned the same as I did? How can it be justified that a CEO or a hedge fund manager makes hundreds of millions of dollars per year? For what? Does anyone believe that no one would do these jobs for a lot less?

8. A clean and healthy environment. I have never been an economic catastrophist, one who thinks that a capitalist economy will inevitably sink into such a depression that it will collapse of its own weight. However, there is good reason today to be an environmental catastrophist. Global warming, the destruction of species, the killing effect of pollution, all should give us pause and all should be of concern to the labor movement.

What prevents our labor leaders from openly advocating these things? An anecdote will provide a proximate answer. A friend of mine was hired by an international agency to investigate how employer threats to shut down plants affect workers' ability to unionize. The AFL-CIO, largely, funded this study. The report showed that employer shutdown threats had increased markedly since the passage of NAFTA. When it appeared that the Clinton administration was putting pressure on the Department of Labor not to publish the report, my friend turned to the AFL-CIO for help. Such help was not forthcoming. It appeared that powerful forces within the AFL-CIO did not want to embarrass their good friend, Bill Clinton. Eventually the AFL-CIO apologized to the author, but not before she received a lot of heavy fire, especially after she decided to inform the press of her findings. This is a curious situation. The AFL-CIO went all out to prevent the passage of NAFTA, and only massive payoffs from President Clinton got NAFTA through Congress. Yet, when a report showed NAFTA doing the things that opponents had predicted, some AFL-CIO leaders opposed making it public.

What is going on here? In a nutshell, business as usual for the labor movement: stay in line with the Democratic Party come hell or high water. When the CIO was formed and its unions were taking on the bosses, there was a strong left-wing component in the labor movement. The left wingers helped to build unions that were among the most democratic in the country, unions that confronted employers and won some of the best contracts. What is more, the left-wingers held fast to a vision of a better society, one more democratic and egalitarian, without discrimination or wars, and founded upon community and solidarity. They knew that such a society could only be brought about through an independent politics, even though provisional alliances with the traditional parties might be necessary, as was the case during the New Deal. Class-conscious and democratic unions, combined with progressive politics, would provide a framework within which rank-and-file workers could improve their lot in life and at the same time think about larger issues. Through these unions, it was possible for black and white workers to forcibly integrate their neighborhood bars and restaurants and for women to sometimes play leading roles. They were by no means perfect, yet these CIO unions held out promise of a great social transformation. Sadly, this was not to be. Too many labor leaders, almost all of those in the AFL unions and quite a few from CIO unions, joined hands with the cold warriors and crushed the progressive unionists. At the same time, the remaining CIO unions became firmly entrenched as junior partners in the Democratic Party. The "accord" was about to begin, except from this perspective it looks a lot more like labor-management collaboration.

New Voice was a hopeful sign, but much more was and is needed. If the AFL-CIO and the CTW are to become the center of a new social movement, they will have to proclaim a more radical vision of the future than it has done so far. This cannot be done unless labor embraces an independent, working-class politics. How this could happen remains to be seen. One possibility is that a statement of principles could be used as a basis for winning as many allies as possible. Perhaps local, regional, and national meetings could be convened at which these groups could debate the principles and refine them, leading to a national umbrella group. The resulting organization could have the short-term goal of redefining the agenda of the major political parties, much as right-wing coalitions have done for the past thirty years.

For any of this to happen, thoughtful, effective radicals must play a part in every part of the labor movement. But the kind of labor radicalization that will do the job is most dependent on the workers in locals across the country fighting to make their unions democratic. In grassroots organizing, based as it must be on rank-and-file control, in struggles for the hearts and souls of our national unions, in alliances with organizations and individuals committed to building the kind of society that is within our grasp, in battles with the employers and politicians, whose usefulness becomes less apparent each day, a new labor movement and a new social movement might be born. That is the hope for the future.

As this new edition goes to press, the economy is in a deep recession. The situation is so bad that the Big Three U.S. automobile corporations face bankruptcy, and workers, once proud members of a union that brought high wages and benefits to millions of people, may now lose their jobs and benefits. As much as any union, the UAW today exemplifies what happens when unions abandon a class-centered ideology and embrace one of class partnership. First the union abandoned its duties to the entire working class, settling instead for winning things for its members alone. Not national health care for all workers but cradle to grave protection for its members and their families alone. Then it became a cheerleader for the auto industry, ignoring the poor management decisions that have driven the companies into the ground. If GM did not want to meet fuel efficiency standards, the union agreed. If Ford wanted to produce gas-guzzling and dangerous SUVs, why should the UAW object? If management wanted to make workplaces into what Ben Hamper called "gulags," well, at least the pay was good. Now that the top managers of the Big Three have gone to Washington hat in hand (by private plane) begging for money, the union supports them and will no doubt agree to more bargaining concessions. Perhaps this recession will be so bad that the union's rank and file will revolt and the leadership will take notice (or be replaced). Perhaps the time will finally be right for workers everywhere to say "enough is enough." To say to political leaders that if you're going to nationalize the financial sector, maybe it's time to do the same for the auto industry and others. Run them in the public's interest: by the people and for the people with full concern for the environment, in conjunction with national health care, with the full participation of workers and their unions, including a revitalized UAW.[24]

# USEFUL RESOURCES

In the age of the Internet, it is not difficult to find useful labor union resources. However, as websites and organizations disappear, any comprehensive list of resources can quickly become obsolete. So I will offer some tried and true sources and let readers go from there.

Both the AFL-CIO and Change to Win have good websites, as do all national labor unions. Even local unions now have an online presence. The AFL-CIO website is at **http://www.aflcio.org**. Here, there is a list of all member unions, with contact information, at **http://www.aflcio.org/aboutus/unions**. The AFL-CIO's various allied organizations, such as Pride at Work and the Coalition of Labor Union Women, can be found at **http://www.aflcio.org/aboutus/allies**. The CTW website is at **http://www.changetowin.org**. Contact information for its member unions is at **http://www.changetowin.org/about-us.html**. The independent union most discussed in this book, the United Electrical Workers (UE), has a site at **http://www.ueunion.org**. UE has an international solidarity website at **http://www.ueinternational.org**. It has much useful information about international workers' campaigns. The IWW's website is **http://www.iww.org**. At this site you can read Staughton Lynd's classic *Labor Law for the Rank and Filer*, at **http://www.iww.org/organize/laborlaw/Lynd/**.

The primary source for data on employment, wages, working conditions, union membership, and the like is the U.S. Bureau of Labor

Statistics (BLS). Its website, at **http://www.bls.gov**, is a treasure trove of information. From this site, there is also access to the *Monthly Labor Review*, at **http://www.bls.gov/opub/mlr/**, which contains many accessible articles on labor unions and working people. A book that should be in every union library is *The State of Working America*. This is the best book available for labor data, including the economic impact of unions. It is written by economists at the Economic Policy Institute (EPI) and published by Cornell University Press every other year. It can be ordered from the EPI website, which also contains many good studies of interest to unions and workers. The site is at **http://www.epinet.org**.

The National Labor Relations Board (NLRB) provides essential information (on certification elections, unfair labor practices, etc.) for unions and union officers, staff, and stewards at **http://www.nlrb.gov**. The Bureau of National Affairs (BNA) publishes many books on unions, labor law, and collective bargaining, which can be purchased at their website: **http://www.bna.com/products/ books.htm**. The books of labor lawyer Robert W. Schwartz have become so popular that he started a publishing company to market them. From classic works like *The Legal Rights of Union Stewards* and *How to Win Past Practice Grievances*, union members can get invaluable practical information. These and other works are available for purchase at **http://www.workrightspress.com**.

There are several other important resources that union activists should become familiar with. The Association for Union Democracy has been a staunch ally of rank-and-file union movements for many years. Its website, **http://www.uniondemocracy.org**, contains "must reading" for union reformers. Another valuable resource is *Labor Notes*. This magazine and organization has kept the union fires burning for many years. Articles from the magazine and much more can be found at **http://www.labornotes.org**. Be sure to check out the many good books available at the site, as well. The Center for Labor Renewal, founded by union activists and dissidents, is a good place to find provocative articles on union struggles and important topics such as immigration; go to **http://www.centerforlaborrenewal.org**. The website of the finest labor journalist in the United States, David Bacon, has many of his articles: **http://dbacon.igc.org**. A good bibliography of contemporary labor issues has been compiled by Kim Scipes at **http://faculty.pnc.edu/ kscipes/LaborBib.htm**.

Two general interest labor magazines are *New Labor Forum*, which is available at **http://www.newlaborforum.org**, and *WorkingUSA*, available at **http://www.blackwellpublishing.com/journal.asp? ref=1089-7011**. A more scholarly publication is the *Journal of Labor Studies*: **http://muse.jhu.edu/journals/labor_studies_journal**.

For a list of all worker centers, see **http://www.epi.org/content. cfm/bp159**.

The Chinese Staff and Workers' Association has a website at **http://www.cswa.org**. The Black Workers for Justice site is at **http://blackworkersforjustice.org**. Jobs With Justice is at **http:// www.jwj.org**.

# NOTES

PREFACE

1. The best source for data on the economic conditions of the working class and one that corroborates my remarks in this preface is Lawrence Mishel, Jared Bernstein, and Heidi Shierholz, *The State of Working America, 2008–2009* (Ithaca, Cornell University Press, 2009). Another invaluable source is the website of the Bureau of Labor Statistics: http//www.bls.gov. This is the source for the union membership data given in the next paragraphs.

2. Kim Moody, *US Labor in Trouble and Transition* (London: Verso, 2007), especially chapter 8.

3. Moody, p. 136.

4. Bill Fletcher, Jr., and Fernando Gapasin, *Solidarity Divided: the Crisis in Organized Labor and a New Path toward Social Justice* (Berkeley, University of California Press, 2008), chapters 14 and 15. Moody also analyzes Change to Win, in chapter 9.

5. Moody, p. 172.

6. Fernando Gapasin and Michael Yates, "Labor Movements: Is There Hope?," *Monthly Review* 57 (June 2005).

7. Janice Fine, "Worker Centers: Organizing Communities at the Edge of the Dream," Economic Policy Institute Briefing Paper, available at <http://www.epi.org/content.cfm/bp159>.

8. Daniel Clawson, *The Next Upsurge: Labor and the New Social Movements* (Ithaca, NY: Cornell University Press, 2003).

9. Nicole C. Wong, *Boston Globe*, 30 August 2008.

10. Ruth Milkman and Bongoh Kye, *The State of the Unions in 2008: A Profile of Union Membership in Los Angeles, California, and the United*

*States* (Los Angeles: UCLA Institute for Research on Labor and Employment, 2008).

INTRODUCTION

1.  For a now slightly dated but still useful labor-friendly guide to labor law, see Bruce Feldacker, *Labor Guide to Labor Law*, 4th ed. (Englewood Cliff, NJ, 1999). Also, Douglas L. Leslie, *Labor Law in a Nutshell*, 5th ed. (New York: Thompson West, 2008). For an interesting analysis of U.S. labor law and how unions should use it, see Ellen Dannin, *Taking Back the Workers' Law: How to Fight the Assault on Labor Rights* (Ithaca, NY: Cornell University Press, 2008).

2.  An excellent critical examination of teams can be found in Mike Parker and Jane Slaughter, *Working Smart: A Union Guide to Participation Programs and Reengineering* (Detroit: Labor Education and Research Project, 1994).

3.  Frank Elkouri and Edna A. Elkouri, *How Arbitration Works*, 6th ed. (Washington, D.C.: Bureau of National Affairs, 2003).

4.  Mishel, Bernstein, and Shierholz, *The State of Working America, 2008/2009*, chap. 5.

5.  Ibid., especially chapters 2, 3, 4, and 7. Also, Michael D. Yates, *Naming the System: Inequality and Work in the Global Economy* (New York: Monthly Review Press, 2003).

6.  Mishel, Bernstein, and Shierholz, chap. 4.

7.  See Keith Gushard, "Local PPG Plant to Be Part of $500M Deal," *The Meadville Tribune*, 14 Sept. 2007, and Joe Napsha, "PPG Completes Sale of Auto Glass Unit," *Pittsburgh Tribune-Review*, 1 Oct. 2008.

1. WHY UNIONS?

1.  See Michael D. Yates, *Naming the System: Inequality and Work in the Global Economy*, chap. 6.

2.  Joan Roemer, *Two to Four from Nine to Five: The Adventures of a Daycare Provider* (New York: Harper & Row, 1989); Alison Clarke-Stewart, *Daycare* (Cambridge, Mass.: Harvard University Press, 1993). The United States Department of Labor publishes an Occupational Outlook Handbook that examines a large number of jobs. For what it says about daycare workers, see <http://www.bls.gov/oco/ocos170.htm>.

3.  On this tendency of workers to form unions, see, among many others, Sidney and Beatrice Webb, *The History of Trade Unionism* (Clifton, N.J.: Augustus M. Kelley, 1970); John R. Commons, *History of Labor in the United States*, 4 vols. (New York: Macmillan, 1918–1935); Selig Perlman, *The Theory of the Labor Movement* (New York: Augustus M. Kelley, 1973); A. Lozovsky, *Marx and the Trade Unions* (New York: International Publishers, 1942); John Anthony Moses, *Trade Union*

*Theory from Marx to Walesa* (New York: Berg, 1990).

4.  For examples of how formal groups form out of more spontaneous actions, see the essays in John Anner, ed., *Beyond Identity Politics* (Boston: South End Press, 1996).

5.  Again, among many others, see Commons, *History of Labor in the United States*; Philip S. Foner, *History of the Labor Movement in the United States*, 9 vols. (New York: International Publishers, 1947–91); American Social History Project, *Who Built America?*, 2 vols. (New York: Pantheon Books, 1989–1992); Paul LeBlanc, *A Short History of the U.S. Working Class: From Colonial Times to the Twenty-First Century* (Atlantic Highlands, NJ: Humanities Press, 1999).

6.  American Social History Project, *Who Built America?*, 1: 337.

7.  The Philadelphia cordwainers were prosecuted and convicted of criminal "conspiracy" in the first famous labor law case in the United States. The case is *Commonwealth v. Pullis*, cited in John R. Commons et al., *Documentary History of the United States* (New York: Russell & Russell, 1958). See also William E. Forbath, *Law and the Shaping of the American Labor Movement* (Cambridge, Mass.: Harvard University Press, 1991).

8.  American Social History Project, *Who Built America?* 1: 336.

9.  The American Federation of Labor was founded by skilled craftsmen in 1886. See Philip S. Foner, *History of the Labor Movement in the United States*, vol. 2: *From the Founding of the AFL to the Emergence of American Imperialism* (New York: International Publishers, 1955).

10. *Cafe Tartuffo, Inc.*, 261 NLRB 281 (1982). For other relevant legal material, see Michael D. Yates, *Power on the Job: The Legal Rights of Working People* (Boston: South End Press, 1994), chap. 4. For information on reading legal citations, see ibid., 279–81.

11. See the classic account of labor violence, Louis Adamic, *Dynamite: The Story of Class Violence in America* (1931; reprint New York: Chelsea House Publishers, 1968).

12. William J. Puette, *Through Jaundiced Eyes: How the Media Views Organized Labor* (Ithaca, N.Y.: ILR Press, 1992); Tom Zaniello, *Working Stiffs, Union Maids, Reds, and Riffraff: An Expanded Guide to Films about Labor* (Ithaca: ILR Press, 2003).

13. Edward S. Herman and Noam Chomsky, *The Political Economy of Human Rights*, 2 vols. (Boston: South End Press, 1979); Noam Chomsky and Edward S. Herman, *Manufacturing Consent: The Political Economy of the Mass Media* (New York: Pantheon Books, 1988); William W. McChesney, *The Political Economy of Media: Enduring Issues, Emerging Dilemmas* (New York: Monthly Review Press, 2008).

14. Lawrence Mishel, Jared Bernstein, and Sylvia Allegretto, *The State of Working America, 2006/2007* (Ithaca, NY: Cornell University Press, 2007), Table 3.33.

15. Mishel, Bernstein, and Shierholz, *The State of Working America, 2008/2009*, Table 3.33.
16. Ibid., Table 3.36.
17. Ibid., Table 3.35.
18. See, for example, Andreas Jorgenson, "Efficiency and Welfare Under Capitalism: Denmark v. The United States; A Short Comparison," *Monthly Review* 48 (February 1997): 34–42.
19. On conditions in the early auto factories, see Sidney Fine, *Sit-Down: The General Motors Strike of 1936–37* (Ann Arbor: University of Michigan Press, 1969).
20. See the interesting films, *Taylor Chain, Part One*, 33 min., New Day Films, Hohokus, N.J., 1980, videocassette; and *Taylor Chain, Part Two*, 33 min., New Day Films, 1984, videocassette. It is in *Part Two* that one of the workers mentioned the whistling. These films are available at < http://www.newday.com/films/index.html>.
21. Mishel, Bernstein, and Shierholz, *The State of Working America, 2008/2009*, Table 3.32.
22. The classic account is Richard B. Freeman and James L. Medoff, *What Do Unions Do?* (New York: Basic Books, 1984), 94–110.

2. HOW UNIONS FORM

1. William Forbath, "The Shaping of the American Labor Movement," *Harvard Law Review* 102 (January 1987): appendix B.
2. See the following books by a great labor historian, David Montgomery: *Beyond Equality: Labor and the Radical Republicans, 1862–1872* (New York: Knopf, 1967); *The Fall of the House of Labor: The Workplace, the State, and American Labor Activism, 1865–1925* (New York: Cambridge University Press, 1987); and *Citizen Worker: The Experience of Workers in the United States with Democracy and the Free Market during the Nineteenth Century* (New York: Cambridge University Press, 1993).
3. Haggai Hurvitz, "American Labor Law and the Doctrine of Entrepreneurial Property Rights: Boycotts, Courts, and the Juridical Reorientation of 1886–1895," *Industrial Relations Law Journal* 8 (1986): 307-61.
4. Melvyn Dubofsky and Warren Van Tine, *John 1. Lewis* (New York: Quadrangle/The New York Times Book Co., 1977); Herbert G. Gutman, 'The Negro and the United Mine Workers of America: The Career and Letters of Richard L. Davis and Something of Their Meaning," in Julius Jacobson, ed., *The Negro and the American Labor Movement* (Garden City, N.J.: Anchor Books, 1968); American Social History Project, *Who Built America?* (New York: Pantheon Books, 1989–1992) 75–77.
5. Michael Rogin, "Volunteerism: The Political Functions of an Anti-

Political Doctrine," *Industrial and Labor Relations Review* 15 (July 1962): 521–35. See also Paul Buhle, *Taking Care of Business: Samuel Gompers, George Meany, Lane Kirkland, and the Tragedy of American Labor* (New York: Monthly Review Press, 1999).

6.     "The Great Uprising" and many other labor revolts are described in Jeremy Brecher, *Strike* (Boston: South End Press, 1972). See also Philip S. Foner, *The Great Labor Uprising of 1877* (New York: Monad Press, 1977). See also the fine documentary film, *The Grand Army of Starvation*, available on DVD at <http://www.ashp.cuny.edu/order1.html#order>.

7.     Brecher, *Strike*; Adamic, *Dynamite*; Paul Avrich, *The Haymarket Tragedy* (Princeton, N.J.: Princeton University Press, 1984).

8.     Paul Krause, *The Battle for Homestead, 1880–1892: Politics, Culture, and Steel* (Pittsburgh: University of Pittsburgh Press, 1992). See also Leon Wolff, "Battle at Homestead," available at <http://www.americanheritage.com/articles/magazine/ah/1965/3/1965_3_64.shtml>.

9.     Brecher, *Strike*; Rev. William H. Carwardine, *The Pullman Strike* (Chicago: Charles H. Kerr, 1973); Nick Salvatore, *Eugene V. Debs: Citizen and Socialist* (Urbana: University of Illinois Press, 1982).

10.    Foner, *History of the Labor Movement in the United States*, vol. 8: *Post-War Struggles, 1918–1919* (New York: International Publishers, 1988), xi; David Brody, *Steelworkers in America: The Nonunion Era.*(New York: Harper Torchbooks, 1969).

11.    A good introduction to labor struggles in the Depression years is Irving Bernstein, *Turbulent Years: A History of the American Worker, 1933–1941* (Boston: Houghton Mifflin, 1969). This period is also covered in the excellent general history by Nelson Lichtenstein, *State of the Union: A Century of American Labor* (Princeton, NJ: Princeton University Press, 2002).

12.    Read the interesting books by Farrell Dobbs: *Teamster Rebellion* (New York: Monad Press, 1972) and *Teamster Bureaucracy* (New York: Monad Press, 1977).

13.    Michael Goldfield, *The Color of Politics* (New York: The New Press, 1997).

14.    Michael D. Yates, *Power on the Job: The Legal Rights of Working People* (Boston: South End Press, 1994); Charles O. Gregory and Harold A. Katz, *Labor and the Law* (New York: W. W. Norton, 1979).

15.    Yates, *Power on the Job*, chaps. 4, 5, and 6.

16.    Mike Parker, "Are Industrial Unions Better than Craft? Not Always," available at <http://mrzine.monthlyreview.org/parker300808p.html>.

17.    See James Parks, "Labor Board Ruling May Bar Millions of Workers from Forming Unions," available at <http://blog.aflcio.org/2006/10/03/labor-board-ruling-may-bar-millions-of-workers-from-forming-unions/>.

18. For the inside story, check out the book by former union buster, Martin J. Levitt, *Confessions of a Union Buster* (New York: Crown Publishers, 1993).

19. Kate Bronfenbrenner, "Organizing in the NAFTA Environment: How Companies Use 'Free Trade' to Stop Unions," *New Labor Forum*, no. 1 (Fall 1997): 50–60.

20. See Fernando Gapasin and Michael Yates, "Organizing the Unorganized: Will Promises Become Practices?," *Monthly Review* 49 (July-August 1997): 46–62; Kate Bronfenbrenner and Tom Juravich, "The Impact of Employer Opposition on Union Certification Win Rates: A Private/Public Comparison," working paper no. 113, Economic Policy Institute, February 1995; and Kim Moody, *U.S. Labor in Trouble and Transition*, 137–142.

21. See Joe Crump, "The Pressure's On: Organizing Without the NLRB," *Labor Research Review* no. 18: 33; "Labor's Corporate Campaign," *Labor Research Review* no. 21 (Fall Winter 1993); Ashley Adams, "Winning Union Recognition Without the NLRB," *Labor Notes*, February 1993: 12.

22. Ellen Dannin, *Taking Back the Workers' Law*.

23. For some information on the California Nurses Association, see http://www.calnurse.org; http://en.wikipedia.org/wiki/California_Nurses _Association. For an article about the growing power of organized nurses, see http://articles.latimes.com/2007/sep/11/business/fi-nurses11. For an essay on the growing degradation of nursing work by employers, see http://mrzine.monthlyreview.org/yates280705.html.  For more on this as well as evidence on why union hospitals are better for patients, see Gordon Lafer, "Hospital Speedups and the Fiction of a Nursing Shortage," *Labor Studies Journal* 30 (Spring 2005), pp. 27–46. Also, see an article in the *Las Vegas Sun*, "If a Hospital Is Unionized, Might Care Be Better?" available at <http://www.lasvegassun.com/news/2008/ oct/10/if-hospital-unionized-might-care-be-better/>.

24. See http://labornotes.org/node/20.

25. Employers are nervous about some neutrality agreements.  See http://www.laborlawyers.com/shownews.aspx?Houston-Nurses-Vote-for-Unionization&Ref=list&Type=1122&Show=10502.

26. Kate Bronfenbrenner and Tom Juravich, "Union Tactics Matter: The Impact of Union Tactics on Certification Elections, First Contracts, and Membership Rates," working paper, Institute for the Study of Labor Organizations, no date.  Also Kate Bronfenbrenner et. al. (eds.), *Organizing to Win: New Research on Union Strategies* (Ithaca, NY: Cornell University Press, 1998).

27. Cited in Gapasin and Yates, "Organizing the Unorganized": 53.

28. Yates, *Power on the Job*, 7–11; Toni Gilpin et al., *On Strike for Respect: The Clerical and Technical Workers' Strike at Yale* University (Chicago:

Charles H. Kerr, 1988). On the famous sanitation workers' strike, see the moving video, *At the River I Stand*, available at <http://www.news reel.org/nav/title.asp?tc=CN0007>. A good book on this is Michael K. Honey's *Going Down Jericho Road: The Memphis Strike, Martin Luther King's Last Campaign* (New York: W.W. Norton and Company, 2008).

29. A union can negotiate a "union shop" in which all members of the bargaining unit must become members of the union within a certain number of days. However, if a member of the unit challenges this, all that the union can do is force this person to become a "financial core" member, paying to the union a dues equivalent but not actually becoming a member. See Yates, *Power on the Job*, 136–37, and the legal cases cited therein.

### 3. UNION STRUCTURES AND DEMOCRACY

1. For example, a poll conducted by the United Food and Commercial Workers Union revealed among members "extreme disrespect and hostility toward the international union leadership" and "universal demoralization throughout the UFCW." This is cited in Association for Union Democracy, "How Do You Feel About the UFCW? Don't Ask!," *50+ Club News* 56 (June 1997): 8–9. On public's view of unions, see <http://www.aflcio.org/mediacenter/resources/polls.cfm>.

2. See the interview with Carey by Chris Kutalik, then editor of *Labor Notes*, available at <http://labornotes.org/node/211>.

3. Steven Brill, *The Teamsters* (New York: Simon & Schuster, 1978); Kenneth C. Crowe, *Collision: How the Rank and File Took Back the Teamsters* (New York: Charles Scribner's Sons, 1993); and Dan La Botz, *Rank-and-File Rebellion: Teamsters for a Democratic Union* (London: Verso, 1990).

4. Bureau of National Affairs, *Directory of U. S. Labor Organizations* (Washington, D.C.: Bureau of National Affairs, 2008).

5. For a list of AFL-CIO unions, including contact information, visit <http://www.aflcio.org/aboutus/unions/>. The CTW unions can be found at <http://www.changetowin.org/about-us.html>. For comprehensive data on all unions, see the Bureau of National Affairs book cited in the previous end note.

6. The rebuilding of militant central labor councils is a theme of Bill Fletcher, Jr. and Fernando Gapasin's *Solidarity Divided: the Crisis in Organized Labor and a New Path Toward Social Justice*. See too Fernando Gapasin and Howard Wial, "The Role of Central Labor Councils in Union Organizing in the 1990s," in Kate Bronfenbrenner et. al. (eds.), *Organizing to Win*.

7. For an account of the Landrum-Griffin Act's provisions, see Yates, *Power on the Job*, chap. 7; Bruce Feldacker, *Labor Guide to Labor Law*, 4th ed.

(Englewood Cliffs, N.J.: Prentice Hall, 1990), chap. 11; H. W. Benson, *Democratic Rights for Union Members* (New York: Association for Union Democracy, 1979).

8. See <http://www.monthlyreview.org/mrzine/clawson200508.html> for a discussion of trusteeship.

9. Paul F. Clark, *The Miners' Fight for Democracy: Arnold Miller and the Reform of the United Mine Workers* (Ithaca, N.Y.: ILR Press, 1981).

10. On the UE, see Ronald W. Schatz, *The Electrical Workers: A History of Labor at General Electric and Westinghouse, 1923–60* (Urbana: University of Illinois Press, 1983); and Ronald L. Filipelli and Mark D. McColloch, *Cold War in the Working Class: The Rise and Decline of the United Electrical Workers* (Albany: State University of New York Press, 1994). Much of this section is based upon the contents of various UE constitutions. I am grateful to UE District Council 6 for giving me copies of these.

11. For a good summary of the role of Communist Party activists in the labor movement, see Roger Keeran, "The Communist Influence on American Labor," in Michael E. Brown et al., eds., *New Studies in the Politics and Culture of U.S. Communism* (New York: Monthly Review Press, 1993), 163–98.

12. Michael Goldfield argues persuasively that the poor choices made by organized labor were important to the outcome of the attempt to organize the South after the Second World War. See "Race and the CIO: The Possibilities for Racial Egalitarianism during the 1930s and 1940s," *International Labor and Working-Class History* no. 44 (Fall 1993 ): 1–32; "Race and the CIO: Reply to Critics," *International Labor and Working-Class History* no. 46 (Fall 1994): 142–60; and "The Failure of Operation Dixie: A Critical Turning Point in American Political Development?," in *Race, Class, and Community in Southern Labor History*, eds. Gary M. Fink and Merl E. Reed (Tuscaloosa: University of Alabama Press, 1994), 166–88.

13. For details, see <http://www.nccouncilofchurches.org/areasofwork /committees/economic_justice/IWJC%20Questions%20And%20Answ ers.pdf>. See also the UE newspaper, *UE News*, available online at <http://www.ranknfile-ue.org/uenews.html>.

14. The quotes are taken from the UE constitutions.

15. Email sent to author on May 27, 2008. This is the source for the quotation from Lambiase in the previous paragraph.

16. See the following articles by Judith Stepan-Norris and Maurice Zeitlin: "'Red' Unions and 'Bourgeois' Contracts?," *American Journal of Sociology* 96 (1991): 1151–1200; "Union Democracy, Radical Leadership, and the Hegemony of Capital," *American Sociological Review* 60 (December 1995): 829–50; "Insurgency, Radicalism, and

Democracy in America's Industrial Unions," *Social Forces* 75 (September 1996): 1–32.

## 4. COLLECTIVE BARGAINING

1. The legal duties of the parties to bargain collectively are spelled out in Sections 8(a)(5), 8(b)(3), and 9(a) of the National Labor Relations Act.

2. On the legal aspects of collective bargaining, see Michael D. Yates, *Power on the Job: The Legal Rights of Working People*, chap. 5, and Bruce Feldacker, *Labor Guide to Labor Law*, 4th ed., chap. 5.

3. U.S. Department of Labor, *Fact Finding Report: Commission on the Future of Worker-Management Relations* (Washington, D.C.: Government Printing Office, May 1994), 81–87. More recent data is hard to come by and not reliable because more unions are avoiding the NLRB.

4. Kate Bronfenbrenner and Tom Juravich, "The Impact of Employer Opposition on Union Certification Win Rates: A Private/Public Comparison," working paper no. 113, Economic Policy Institute, February 1995; Bronfenbrenner and Juravich, "Union Tactics Matter: The Impact of Union Tactics on Certification Elections, First Contracts, and Membership Rates," working paper, Institute for the Study of Labor Organizations, no date; Bronfenbrenner, "Organizing in the NAFTA Environment: How Companies Use 'Free Trade' to Stop Unions," *New Labor Forum* no. 1 (Fall 1997): 50–60.

5. Many books and articles have been written on the IWW. A good starting point is Melvyn Dubofsky, *We Shall Be All: A History of the IWW* (New York: Quadrangle/The New York Times Book Co., 1969).

6. See <http://www.starbucksunion.org/> for details.

7. Rick Hurd, "New Deal Labor Policy and the Containment of Radical Union Activity," *The Review of Radical Political Economics* 8 (Fall 1976), 32–44.

8. Paul F. Clark, Peter Gottlieb, and Donald Kennedy, eds., *Forging a Union in Steel: Philip Murray, SWOC, and the United Steelworkers* (Ithaca, N.Y.:ILR Press, 1987).

9. Kim Moody, *An Injury to All: The Decline of American Unionism* (New York: Verso, 1988).

10. "UAW Steamrolled," *Multinational Monitor* 16 (December 1995): 5; Tom Johnson, "Caterpillar Bulldozed the United Auto Workers," *Business and Society Review*, Winter 1990: 38; Peter Elstrom, "This Cat Keeps on Purring: Caterpillar's Plan Is Paying Off," *Business Week*, 20 January 1997: 82.

11. See Sam Gindin, "Concessions in Oshawa: The End of an Era?," available at <http://mrzine.monthlyreview.org/gindin310306.html>.

12. Service Employees International Union, *Contract Campaign Manual*

(Washington, D.C.: Service Employees International Union, 1988).

13. The Bureau of National Affairs, *2008 Source Book on Collective Bargaining: Wages, Benefits, and Other Contract Issues* (Washington, D.C.: The Bureau of National Affairs, 2008). Other BNA books include *Contract Bargaining Handbook* and *Negotiating a Labor Contract.* These can be ordered at <http://storefront.bnabooks.com>.

14. Yates, *Power on the Job*, chap. 5; Feldacker, *Labor Guide to Labor Law*, chap. 5; Robert M. Schwartz and Nick Thorkelson, *The Legal Rights of Union Stewards*, 4th ed. (Cambridge, Mass.: Work Rights Press, 2006), chap. 4. Schwartz, who is a labor law attorney, has written many other useful and practical books for working people. See them at <http://www.workrightspress.com/index.html>.

15 Service Employees International Union, *Contract Campaign Manual*, parts 2 and 4.

16. For a good description of a corporate campaign, see Peter Rachleff, *Hard Pressed in the Heartland: The Hormel Strike and the Future of the Labor Movement* (Boston: South End Press, 1993). See also "Labor's Corporate Campaigns," *Labor Research Review* no. 21 (Fall/Winter 1993). See too the example of questions a union must ask and answer when preparing a corporate campaign, at <http://www.troublemaker shandbook.org/Text/Corporate%20Campaigns/Corporate%20Campai gn%20Questionaire.htm>. There is much else of interest on this web site, which is connected to the book *The Troublemaker's Handbook*, published by *Labor Notes* and available for purchase at <http://www.trou blemakershandbook.org/>.

17. Thomas A. Kochan and Harry C. Katz, *Collective Bargaining and Industrial Relations*, 2nd ed. (Homewood, Ill.: Richard D. Irwin, 1985), 102–48.

18. See Sam Gindin, *Canadian Auto Workers: The Birth and Transformation of a Union* (Toronto: James Lorimer, 1995). Sam Gindin was the chief economist of the CAW. In the last few years, he has become critical of what he sees as the growing conservatism of the CAW and the abandonment of some of its progressive politics. See an exchange between Gindin and former CAW president Robert White at <http://www.labournet.net/world/0805/caw3.html>.

19. See Philip S. Foner, *U.S. Labor and the Vietnam War* (New York: International Publishers, 1989), 1–8.

20. On this and on the repression of labor generally, see Robert Justin Goldstein, *Political Repression in Modern America* (New York: Schenkman Publishing Co., Inc., 1978). On Haywood's escape to Russia, see Dubofsky, *We Shall Be All*, 459–61.

21. American Social History Project, *Who Built America?* vol. 2 (New York: Pantheon Books, 1992), 461–63.

22. An interesting reference on this period is Ann Fagen Ginger and David Christiano, eds., *The Cold War Against Labor*, 2 vols. (Berkeley, Calif.: Meiklejohn Civil Liberties Institute, 1987). See also Steve Rosswurm, ed., *The CIO's Left-Led Unions* (New Brunswick, N.J.: Rutgers University Press, 1992).

23. For a good summary of this position, as well as the alternative view, see Victor G. Devinatz, "An Alternative Strategy: Lessons from the UAW Local 6 and the FE, 1946–52," in Cyrus Bina, Laurie Clements, and Chuck Davis, eds., *Beyond Survival: Wage Labor in the Late Twentieth Century* (Armonk, N.Y.: M. E. Sharpe, 1996), 145–60.

24. Interesting, useful, and accessible to nonspecialists are William Ury and Roger Fisher, *Getting to Yes: Negotiating Agreement Without Giving In* (Boston: Houghton Mifflin, 1981) and William Ury, *Getting Past No: Negotiating Your Way from Confrontation to Cooperation* (New York: Bantam Books, 1993).

25. Ury, *Getting Past No*, 31–51.

26. Ibid., pp. 21–26.

27. The negotiations described in the text can be seen in a remarkable video, *Final Offer*, available from California Newsreel at <http://www.newsreel.org/nav/title.asp?tc=CN0031>.

28. Ury and Fisher, *Getting to Yes*, chap. 5.

29. Ellen Dannin, "Legislative Intent and Impasse Resolution under the National Labor Relations Act: Does It Matter?," *Hofstra Labor & Employment Law Journal* 15 (Fall 1997): 11–43. Also, Dannin, *Taking Back the Workers' Law*.

30. See Ellen Dannin, "Law Reform, Collective Bargaining, and the Balance of Power," 2008, available along with many other insightful articles by Dannin, at <http://search.ssrn.com/sol3/cf_dev/AbsByAuth.cfm?per_id=111709>.

31. Michael D. Yates, "From the Coal Wars to the Pittston Strike," *Monthly Review* 42 (June 1990): 25–39. See also many articles on the subject of strikes in *Labor Notes*. These can be found online at <http://www.labor-notes.org>.

32. Max H. Bazeman, "The General Basis of Arbitrator Behavior: An Empirical Analysis of Conventional and Final-Offer Arbitration," *Econometrica* 54 (July 1986): 819–44; Orley Ashenfelter and David Bloom, "Models of Arbitration Behavior: Theory and Evidence," *American Economic Review* 74 (March 1984): 111–24.

33. Edwin F. Beal, Edward D. Wickersham, and Philip K. Kienast, *The Practice of Collective Bargaining*, 5th ed. (Homewood, Ill.: Richard D. Irwin, 1976), chaps. 9–13.

34. The NLRB and the courts have ruled that union shops cannot be enforced, as long as a bargaining unit member is willing to pay a dues

equivalent to the union. See Yates, *Power on the Job*, chap. 5.

35   Staughton Lynd, *Solidarity Unionism* (Chicago: Charles H. Kerr, 1992).

36.  See the enlightening article by Leo Panitch and Sam Gindin, "The Current Crisis: A Socialist Perspective," 2008, available at <http://www.socialistproject.ca/bullet/bullet142.html>.

37.  Bureau of National Affairs, *Basic Patterns in Union Contracts*, 14th ed. (Washington, D.C.: Bureau of National Affairs, 1995), 34. This source states that 98 percent of all agreements have arbitration clauses. Since the courts generally consider, as does management, that a no-strike clause is the quid pro quo for the arbitration clause, it is safe to say that nearly all contracts have explicit or implied no-strike agreements. There is no reason to suppose that these numbers have changed since this was written. I have studied hundreds of agreements, and I have been a labor arbitrator. I have never seen a contract without both a no-strike clause and an arbitration clause.

38.  Mike Parker and Jane Slaughter, *Working Smart: A Union Guide to Participation Programs and Reengineering* (Detroit: Labor Education and Research Project, 1994).

39.  William DiFazio, *Longshoremen: Community and Resistance on the Brooklyn Waterfront* (Hadley, Mass.: Bergin and Garvey, 1985).

40.  David W. Ewing, *Justice on the Job: Resolving Grievances in the Nonunion Workplace* (Boston: Harvard Business School Press, 1989). See too Peter Feuille and Denise R. Chachere, "Looking Fair or Being Fair: Remedial Voice Procedures in Nonunion Workplaces," *Journal of Management* 21 (1995), 27–42.

41.  Gertrude Ezorsky, *Racism and Justice: The Case for Affirmative Action* (Ithaca, N.Y.: ILR Press, 1991); Steven Briggs, "Allocating Available Work in a Union Environment: Seniority vs. Work Sharing," *Labor Law Journal* 38 (October 1987): 650–57; Michele M. Hoyman, "Alternative Models of Compliance by Unions with Civil Rights Legislation," *Law & Policy* 8 (January 1986): 77–103; Casey Ichniowski, "Have Angels Done More?: The Steel Industry Consent Decree," *Industrial and Labor Relations Review* 36 (January 1983): 182–98.

42.  Schwartz, *The Legal Rights of Shop Stewards*, chap. 4.

43.  Frank Elkouri and Edna A. Elkouri, *How Arbitration Works*, 6th ed. with 2008 Supplement (Washington, D.C.: BNA Books, 2008).

44.  Yates, *Power on the Job*, chap. 7.

45.  Devinatz, "An Alternative Strategy."

46.  Judith Stepan-Norris and Maurice Zeitlin, "'Red' Unions and 'Bourgeois' Contracts?," *American Journal of Sociology* 96 (1991): 1151–1200; "Union Democracy, Radical Leadership, and the Hegemony of Capital," *American Sociological Review* 60 (December 1995): 829–850; "Insurgency, Radicalism, and Democracy in America's Industrial

Unions," *Social Forces* 75 (September 1996): 1–32. See their book, *Left Out: Reds and America's Industrial Unions* (New York: Cambridge University Press, 2002).

## 5. UNIONS AND POLITICS

1.  Michael D. Yates, *Longer Hours, Fewer Jobs: Employment and Unemployment in the United States* (New York: Monthly Review Press, 1994), chap. 5.

2.  Don J. Lofgren, *Dangerous Premises: An Insider's View of OSHA Enforcement* (Ithaca, N.Y.: ILR Press, 1989).

3.  According to the U.S. Bureau of the Census, nearly 46,000,000 people were without health insurance in 2007. See story at <http://www.latimes. com/business/la-fi-census272008aug27,1,274 3262.story>. For more detailed data and the consequences of poor or no health insurance, see Mishel, Bernstein, and Shierholz, *The State of Working America, 2008/2009*, chap. 7.

4.  Richard B. Freemen, "Unionism Comes to the Public Sector," *Journal of Economic Literature* 24 (March 1986): 41–86.

5.  Among many others, see these books by G. William Domhoff: *Who Rules America?* (Englewood Cliffs, N.J.: Prentice Hall, 1967); *The Higher Circles: The Governing Class in America* (New York: Random House, 1970); *The Power Elite and the State: How Policy Is Made in America* (New York: A. de Gruyter, 1990).

6.  William Forbath, "The Shaping of the American Labor Movement," *Harvard Law Review* 102 (January 1987).

7.  Wolfgang Abendroth, *A Short History of the European Working Class* (New York: Monthly Review Press, 1972).

8.  Isaiah Berlin, *Karl Marx: His Life and Environment* (New York: Oxford University Press, 1996).

9.  Selig Perlman, *The Theory of the Labor Movement* (New York: Augustus M. Kelley, 1973); Mark Perlman, *Labor Union Theories in America: Background and Development* (Evanston, Ill.: Row Peterson, 1958); James Weinstein, *The Decline of Socialism in America, 1912–1925* (New York: Monthly Review Press, 1967); David Milton, *The Politics of U.S. Labor: From the Great Depression to the New Deal* (New York: Monthly Review Press, 1982); Mike Davis, *Prisoners of the American Dream: Politics and Economy in the History of the U.S. Working Class* (London: Verso, 1986).

10. David Montgomery, *Citizen Worker: The Experience of Workers in the United States with Democracy and the Free Market during the Nineteenth Century* (New York: Cambridge University Press, 1993); Christopher L. Tomlins, *Law, Labor and Ideology in the Early American Republic* (New York: Cambridge University Press, 1993).

11.  David R. Roediger, *The Wages of Whiteness: Race and the Making of the American Working Class* (London: Verso, 1991); Philip S. Foner, *Organized Labor and the Black Worker: 1619–1973* (New York: Praeger, 1974).

12.  Seymour Martin Lipset, *Continental Divide: The Values and Institutions of the United States and Canada* (New York: Routledge, 1990); Seymour Martin Lipset, *The First New Nation: The United States in Historical and Comparative Perspective* (New York: Basic Books, 1963).

13.  Robert Justin Goldstein, *Political Repression in Modern America* (New York: Schenkman Publishing Co., Inc., 1978).

14.  American Social History Project, *Who Built America?*, vol. 2 (New York: Pantheon Books, 1992), 144–52, 184–88; Philip S. Foner, *History of the Labor Movement in the United States*, vols. 3 and 4 (New York: International Publishers, 1964, 1965); Samuel Gompers, *Seventy Years of Life and Labor: An Autobiography* (Ithaca, N.Y.: ILR Press, 1984).

15.  Michael Rogin, "Volunteerism: The Political Functions of an Anti-Political Doctrine," *Industrial and Labor Relations Review* 15 (July 1962).

16.  There have been numerous Congressional hearings and commissions concerning labor racketeering. See, for example, President's Commission on Organized Crime, *The Edge: Organized Crime, Business, and Labor Unions* (Washington, D.C.: Government Printing Office, 1986). See also Philip Taft, *Corruption and Racketeering in the Labor Movement* (Ithaca, N.Y.: New York State School of Industrial and Labor Relations, 1970).

17.  Milton, *The Politics of U.S. Labor.*

18.  Ibid.; Melvyn Dubofsky and Warren Van Tine, *John L. Lewis* (New York: Quadrangle/The New York Times Book Co., 1977).

19.  Kim Moody, *An Injury to All: The Decline of American Unionism* (New York: Verso, 1988).

20.  For example, see the AFL-CIO booklet, *America Needs a Raise* (Washington, D.C.: AFL-CIO Department of Economic Research, 1996).

21.  See <http://www.aflcio.org/mediacenter/prsptm/03162007a.cfm>.

22.  *America Needs a Raise*, 21–28.

23.  Such jobs were featured in Tony Horowitz, "9 to Nowhere," *Wall Street Journal*, 1 December 1994: AI.

24.  U.S. House of Representatives Committee on Government Operations, *High Skills, Low Wages: Productivity and the False Promise of NAFTA* (Washington, D.C.: Government Printing Office, 1993); Ricardo Grinspun and Maxwell Cameron, eds., *The Political Economy of Free Trade* (New York: St. Martin's Press, 1993). The Economic Policy Institute (EPI) has published many studies detailing the harm NAFTA

has done to workers in all three nations. Go to <http://www.epinet.org> to see them.

25.  Sarah Anderson and Ken Silverstein, "All the President's Handouts," *Harper's* 288 (March 1994): 21–23.

26.  Robert B. Reich, *Locked in the Cabinet* (New York: Alfred A. Knopf, 1997).

27.  Michael D. Yates, "Does the U.S. Labor Movement Have a Future?," *Monthly Review* 48, no. 9 (February 1997); Michael D. Yates, "The Revitalization of the Labor Movement and the Creation of a Good Society: Some Notes on the Political Economy of the AFL-CIO," *The Review of Radical Political Economy*, Fall 1999; Michael D. Yates and Fernando Gapasin, "Labor Movements: Is There Hope?" *Monthly Review* 56 (June 2005).

28.  Taken from Yates, *Labor Law Handbook*, chap. 6.

29.  David Ellwood and Glenn Fine, "The Impact of Right-to-Work Laws on Union Organizing," *Journal of Political Economy* 95 (April 1987): 250–73.

30.  See Foner, *History of the Labor Movement in the United States*, vols. 2 through 5; Foner, *U.S. Labor and the Vietnam War* (New York: International Publishers, 1989); Ronald Radosh, *American Labor and United States Foreign Policy* (New York: Random House, 1969); Buhle, *Taking Care of Business*. See the excellent and up-to-date bibliography on labor's foreign policy and many other labor-related issues constructed by Kim Scipes at <http://faculty.pnc.edu/kscipes/LaborBib.htm>.

31.  AFL actually helped the government in its war against the radical unions. See Goldstein, *Political Repression in Modern America*, 124.

32.  Gabriel Kolko, *The Roots of American Foreign Policy: An Analysis of Power and Purpose* (Boston: Beacon Press, 1969); John Lewis Gaddis, *The United States and the Origins of the Cold War, 1941–1947* (New York: Columbia University Press, 1972); Marty Jezer, *The Dark Ages: Life in the United States, 1945–1960* (Boston: South End Press, 1982); Gabriel Kolko, *The United States Confronts the World* (Boulder, CO: Lynne Rienner Publishers, 2006).

33.  This section draws from the following: Edward S. Herman and Noam Chomsky, *The Political Economy of Human Rights*, 2 vols. (Boston: South End Press, 1979); Jenny Pearce, *Under the Eagle: U. S. Intervention in Central America and the Caribbean* (Boston: South End Press, 1982); Stephan Slesinger and Stephen Kinzer, *Bitter Fruit: The Untold Story of the American Coup in Guatemala* (Garden City, N.J.: Doubleday, 1982); Jenny Pearce, *Promised Land: Peasant Rebellion in Chalatenango, El Salvador* (London: Latin America Bureau, 1986); Carlos Vilas, *The Sandinista Revolution: National Liberation and Social Transformation* (New York: Monthly Review Press, 1986); Paul Buhle, *Taking Care of Business*.

34.   See Steve Early, "EFCA, the Economy, Obama, and Labor," available at
      <http://www.zmag.org/znet/viewArticlePrint/19102> and James Gray
      Pope, Peter Kellman, and Ed Bruno, "The Employee Free Choice Act
      and a Long-Term Strategy for Winning Workers' Rights," *WorkingUSA*
      11 (March 2008), 125–144.

35.   Early, "EFCA, the Economy . . .," 2.

36.   Cited in Early, 5.

37.   See the Labor Party's platform at <http://lpa.igc.org/documents/pro-
      gram.html#Restore%20Workers%20Rights>.

## 6. RACE, GENDER, ETHNICITY

1.    Peter Meiksens, "Same as It Ever Was?: The Structure of the Working
      Class," *Monthly Review* 49 (July-August 1997): 31–45; Harry
      Braverman, *Labor and Monopoly Capital: The Degradation of Labor in
      the Twentieth Century* (New York: Monthly Review Press, 1974);
      Michael D. Yates (ed.), *More Unequal: Aspects of Class in the United
      States* (New York: Monthly Review Press, 2007).

2.    Roger Horowitz, *"Negro and White, Unite and Fight": A Social History of
      Industrial Unionism in Meatpacking, 1930–1990* (Urbana and Chicago:
      University of Illinois Press, 1997).

3.    Teresa Amott and Julie Matthaei, *Race, Gender, and Work: A Multi-
      Cultural Economic History of Women in the United States* (Boston: South
      End Press, 1996).

4.    American Social History Project, *Who Built America?*, vol. 2 (New York:
      Pantheon Books, 1992), 167–84.

5.    Philip S. Foner, *Organized Labor and the Black Worker: 1619–1973* (New
      York: Praeger, 1974); Eric Foner, *Nothing But Freedom: Emancipation
      and Its Legacy* (Baton Rouge: Louisiana State University Press, 1983);
      Robin D. G. Kelley, *Race Rebels: Culture, Politics, and the Black Working
      Class* (New York: The Free Press, 1996); Yates (ed.), *More Unequal:
      Aspects of Class in the United States.*

6.    Warren Whatley, "African-American Strikebreaking from the Civil War
      to the New Deal," *Social Science History* 17 (Winter 1993): 525–58.

7.    Amott and Matthaei, *Race, Gender, and Work.* For detailed data on the
      labor force, wages, and other worker characteristics, see the January
      issues of the Department of Labor publication, *Employment and
      Earnings.* For historical data, see United States Bureau of the Census,
      *Historical Statistics of the United States, Colonial Times to 1970*
      (Washington, D.C.: Government Printing Office, 1975).

8.    Bureau of Labor Statistics, "Union Membership in 2007," available at
      <http://www.bls.gov/news.release/union2.nr0.htm>.

9.    See, for example, Lynn C. Burbridge, "The Reliance of African-
      American Women on Government and Third-Sector Employment,"

*The American Economic Review* 84 (May 1994): 103–107.

10.   See <http://www.bls.gov/news.release/History/ecopro_12032001.txt>.

11.   See Ruth Milkman, "Two Worlds of Unionism: Women and the New Labor Movement," in Dorothy Sue Cobble (ed.), *The Sex of Class: Women Transforming American Labor* (Ithaca, NY: Cornell University Press, 2007), 63–80; Kate Bronfenbrenner, "Organizing Women: The Nature and Process of Union Organizing Efforts among U.S. Women Workers since the mid-1990s," *Work and Occupations* 32 (Nov. 2005), 1–23.

12.   The data for black women is taken from Bronfenbrenner, op. cit.

13.   Michael Goldfield, "Race and Labor Organization in the United States," *Monthly Review* 49 (July-August 1997): 80–97; Robert H. Zieger, *For Jobs and Freedom: Race and Labor in America since 1865* (Lexington, KY: University of Kentucky Press, 2007).

14.   Eric Arnesen, *Waterfront Workers of New Orleans: Race, Class, and Politics, 1893–1923* (New York: Oxford University Press, 1991).

15.   Amott and Matthaei, *Race, Gender, and Work.*

16.   Roger Keeran, "The Communist Influence on American Labor," in Michael E. Brown et al., eds., *New Studies in the Politics and Culture of U.S. Communism* (New York: Monthly Review Press, 1993); Steve Rosswurm, ed., *The CIO's Left-Led Unions* (New Brunswick, N.J.: Rutgers University Press, 1992); Bert Cochran, *Labor and Communism: The Conflict that Shaped American Unions* (Princeton, N.J.: Princeton University Press, 1977).

17.   Herbert G. Gutman, "The Negro and the United Mine Workers of America: The Career and Letters of Richard L. Davis and Something of Their Meaning," in Julius Jacobson, ed., *The Negro and the American Labor Movement* (Garden City, N.J.: Anchor Books, 1968); John William Trotter, *Coal, Class, and Color: Blacks in Southern West Virginia* (Urbana: University of Illinois Press, 1990).

18.   Cited in Michael Goldfield, "Race and the CIO: Reply to Critics," *International Labor and Working-Class History* no. 46 (Fall 1994): 2.

19.   Ibid.: 20–21; Bruce Nelson, "Class and Race in the Crescent City: The ILWU from San Francisco to New Orleans," in Rosswurm, ed., *The CIO's Left-Led Unions,* 19–46.

20.   On this issue, see the fine documentary film by Tony Buba, *Struggles in Steel,* 58 min., California Newsreel, 1996, videocassette. Available at <http://www.newsreel.org/nav/title.asp?tc=CN0090>.

21.   This section relies upon Horowitz, "Negro and White, Unite and Fight."

22.   Ibid., 223.

23.   On the porters, see William H. Harris, *Keeping the Faith: A. Philip Randolph, Milton P. Webster, and the Brotherhood of Sleeping Car Porters, 1925–37* (Urbana: University of Illinois Press, 1977).

24. For an excellent introduction, see Barbara Mayer Wertheimer, *We Were There: The Story of Working Women in America* (New York: Pantheon Books, 1977).

25. It is important to note here that data similar to that in Table 4 are not available for racial and ethnic minorities. I feel comfortable in saying, however, that these groups are much more underrepresented in union leadership positions than are women. Unions, especially those in the service and government sectors, have made progress in appointing minorities to staff positions, but much more needs to be done.

26. This table is taken from Ruth Milkman, "Two Worlds of Unionism: Women and the New Labor Movement."

27. Horowitz, "Negro and White, Unite and Fight," 227–42.

28. Taken from Kate Bronfenbrenner, "Organizing Women . . ." The quote is from the electronic version, so I don't have the page number. Available at <http://digitalcommons.ilr.cornell.edu/articles/3>.

29. Susan Cowell, "Family Policy: A Union Approach," in Dorothy Sue Cobble, ed., *Women and Unions: Forging a Partnership* (Ithaca, N.Y.: ILR Press, 1993), 115–28; Carolyn York, "Bargaining for Work and Family Benefits," in ibid., 129–43. For another view, see Alice H. Cook, "Comments," in ibid., 148–56.

30. Mary Harris Jones, *The Autobiography of Mother Jones* (1925; reprint, ed. Mary Field Parton, Chicago: Illinois Labor History Society, 1972).

31. Tera Hunter, "Domination and Resistance: The Politics of Wage Household Labor in New South Atlanta," *Labor History* 34 (Spring-Summer 1993): 205–20.

32. Wertheimer, *We Were There*, 293–317.

33. Ibid., pp. 353–68; Ardis Cameron, *Radicals of the Worst Sort: Laboring Women in Lawrence, Massachusetts, 1860–1912* (Urbana: University of Illinois Press, 1993).

34. Vicki L. Ruiz, *Cannery Women, Cannery Lives: Mexican Women, Unionization, and the California Food Processing Industry, 1930-1950* (Albuquerque: University of New Mexico Press, 1987).

35. Amott and Matthaei, *Race, Gender, and Work*, 90.

36. Toni Gilpin et al., *On Strike for Respect: The Clerical and Technical Workers' Strike at Yale University* (Chicago: Charles H. Kerr, 1988).

37. These examples are drawn from Ruth Needleman, "Organizing Low-Wage Workers: Building for the Long Haul between Unions and Community-Based Organizations," *Working USA* 1 (May-June 1997): 45–59. Also, see Ellen Mayock Starbird, "Organizing in Home Health Care Work: Sexism, Poverty, and Racism," paper presented at the 92nd meeting of the American Sociological Association, Toronto, Canada, 9–13 August 1997.

38. Needleman, "Organizing Low-Wage Workers": 56.

39.   Ibid.: 52-56.

40.   Ibid.: 56.

41.   On organizing home health care workers, see Linda Delp and Katie Quan, "Homecare Worker Organizing in California: An Analysis of a Successful Strategy," *Journal of Labor Studies* 27 (Spring 2002), 1-23. For a debate about SEIU strategies, see "SEIU: Debating Labor's Strategies," available at <http://www.monthlyreview.org/mrzine/seiu140708.html>.

42.   See <http://prideatwork.org/page?id=463&output=p> for a time line of important dates in LGBT labor history.

43.   Patti R. Roberts, "Comments," in Cobble, ed., *Women and Unions*, 349–56.

44.   Cowell, "Family Policy," 117.

45.   Michael Goldberg, "Affirmative Action in Union Government: The Landrum-Griffin Act Implications," *Ohio State Law Journal* 44 (1983): 649-89; Elizabeth M. Iglesias, "Structures of Subordination: Women of Color at the Intersection of Title VII and the NLRA. Not!," *Harvard Civil Rights Civil Liberties Law Review* 28 (1993): 395–503.

46.   Fernando Gapasin, "Race, Gender and Other 'Problems' of Unity for the American Working Class," *Race, Gender & Class* 4, no. 1 (1996): 41–62.

47.   Cowell, "Family Policy."

48.   Ruth Milkman, "Organizing Immigrant Women in New York's Chinatown: An Interview with Katie Quan," in Cobble, ed., *Women and Unions*, 281–98.

49.   Camille Colatosi and Elaine Karg, *Stopping Sexual Harassment* (Detroit: The Labor Education and Research Project, 1992).

50.   *Collective Agreement between the Ontario Public Service Employees Union and the Crown in Right of Ontario* (1992–1993), 30–32.

51.   Herbert Hill, "Black Workers, Organized Labor, and Title VII of the 1964 Civil Rights Act: Legislative History and Litigation Record," in Herbert Hill and James E. Jones, eds., *Race in America: The Struggle for Equality* (Madison: University of Wisconsin Press, 1993), 263–344.

## 7. IMMIGRANT WORKERS

1.   Kim Moody, *Labor in Trouble and Transition*, chap. 4.

2.   The labor force includes all persons sixteen and older who are either employed or unemployed. See <http://www.bls.gov/news.release/pdf/forbrn.pdf> for data on foreign-born workers; see the Pew Hispanic Trust for these and other data on undocumented workers, e.g. <http://pewhispanic.org/files/reports/6.pdf>. Also, <http://pewhispanic.org/files/execsum/61.pdf>.

3.   See Mishel, Bernstein, and Shierholz, *The State of Working America, 2008/2009*, Table 3.30; Kim Moody, *Labor in Trouble and Transition*, 71.

4.   Derrick Z. Jackson, "Undocumented Workers Contribute Plenty,"

*Boston Globe*, 12 April 2006, available at <http://www.boston.com/news/globe/editorial_opinion/oped/articles/2006/04/12/undocumented_workers_contribute_plenty/>.

5.   Kim Moody, op. cit., chap. 4.

6.   On the farmworkers, see Sam Kushner, *The Long Road to Delano* (New York: International Publishers, 1975). Many books have been written about César Chávez. For a list of them, see <http://www.amazon.com/s/ref=nb_ss_gw?url=search-alias%3Dstripbooks&field-keywords=cesar+chavez&x=14&y=20>.

7.   See Michael D. Yates, "A Union Is Not a Movement," published originally in the November 19, 1977, issue of *The Nation* and available at <http://mrzine.monthlyreview.org/yates160106.html>. Here you can link to a series of articles about the UFW published in the *Los Angeles Times* in January 2006. On the failure of the Watsonville strawberry strike, see <http://www.allacademic.com/meta/p107388_index.html.>.

8.   Ibid., 214–215. See also Immanuel Ness, *Immigrants, Unions, and the New U. S. Labor Market* (Philadelphia: Temple University Press, 2005).

9.   See <http://www.migrationpolicy.org/pubs/7_Immigrant_Union_Membership.pdf> for details.

10.  David Bacon, "Did a Mississippi Raid Protect Right-wing Politicians?," available at <http://www.truthout.org/article/did-a-mississippi-raid-protect-rightwing-politicians>. Also Simone Landon, "Immigration Raid Breaks Up Organizing Drive at Iowa Meatpacking Plant," available at <http://www.alternet.org/story/97842>.

11.  Michael D. Yates, *Cheap Motels and a Hot Plate: an Economist's Travelogue* (New York; Monthly Review Press, 2007), p. 159.

12.  My remarks on the CIW rely very heavily upon the research of labor organizer and activist Elly Leary. See Elly Leary, "Immokalee Workers Take Down Taco Bell," *Monthly Review* (Vol. 57, October 2005) and Elly Leary, "Florida Farmworkers Chop Up Burger King," available at <www.monthlyreview.org/mrzine/leary300508.html >.

13.  This is from the CIW website: <http://www.ciw-online.org>.

14.  Janice Fine, *Worker Centers: Organizing Communities at the Edge of the Dream*, 1–2.

## 8. THE TASKS AHEAD

1.   For union membership, see Bureau of Labor Statistics, "Union Membership in 2007." On union mergers, see Elizabeth A. Ashack, "Major Union Mergers, Alliances, and Disaffiliations, 1995–2007," available at <http://www.bls.gov/opub/cwc/cb20080919ar01p1.htm>.

2.   Jelle Visser, "Union Membership Statistics in 24 Countries," *Monthly Labor Review* (Jan. 2006), available at <http://www.bls.gov/opub/mlr/2006/01/art3full.pdf>. The data in this article have been

adjusted to be comparable with the way union density is calculated in the United States.

3.  The data in the final chapter of *The State of Working America, 2008/2009* (the chapter is titled "International Comparisons") make for sobering reading. We hear so much that the United States is "Number One." This chapter shows that we are Number One is some dubious categories.

4.  This section relies heavily upon the following sources: Michael D. Yates, "Does the U.S. Labor Movement Have a Future?," *Monthly Review* 48, no. 9 (February 1997); Fernando Gapasin and Michael Yates, "Organizing the Unorganized: Will Promises Become Practices?," *Monthly Review* 49 (July/August 1997): 46–62; Kim Moody, *An Injury to All: The Decline of American Unionism* (New York: Verso, 1988); Bina, Clements, and Davis, eds., *Beyond Survival;* Doug Henwood, "Talking About Work," *Monthly Review* 49 (July-August 1997): 18–30; Jim Crotty and Gerald Epstein, "In Defense of Capital Controls," in *Are There Alternatives? Socialist Register 1996*, ed. Leo Panitch (London: Merlin Press, 1996), 118–49; Howard Botwinnick, *Persistent Inequalities* (Princeton, N.J.: Princeton University Press, 1994); Richard Freeman and Joel Rogers, "Worker Representation and Participation Survey: First Report of Findings," *Proceedings of the 47th Annual Industrial Relations Research Association Meeting, 1994* (Madison, Wis.: Industrial Relations Research Association, 1995),336–45; Center for Popular Economics, *Common Sense Economics* (Washington, D.C.: AFL-CIO, 1997); Michael Goldfield, *The Decline of Organized Labor in the United States* (Chicago: University of Chicago Press, 1987). Two additional, recently written, sources are Kim Moody, *U.S. Labor in Trouble and Transition* and Bill Fletcher, Jr., and Fernando Gapasin, *Solidarity Divided*.

5.  Moody, op. cit., chap. 3.

6.  Ibid.

7.  David Bacon, "West Coast Janitors Get Ready to Fight," *Z Magazine* 10 (April 1997): 16–18; Paul Johnson, *Success While Others Fail* (Ithaca, N.Y.: Cornell University Press, 1994); Marc Cooper, "Labor Deals a New Hand," *The Nation* 264 (24 March 1997): 11–16.

8.  D. M. Kotz, T. McDonough, and M. Reich, *Social Structures of Accumulation: The Political Economy of Growth and Crisis* (New York: Cambridge University Press, 1994).

9.  AFL-CIO Department of Economic Research, *America Needs a Raise*, 1.

10. Harry Braverman, *Labor and Monopoly Capital: The Degradation of Labor in the Twentieth Century* (New York: Monthly Review Press, 1974).

11. Paul F. Clark, *The Miners' Fight for Democracy: Arnold Miller and the Reform of the United Mine Workers* (Ithaca, N.Y.: ILR Press, 1981).

12. Kim Moody, "American Labor: A Movement Again?," *Monthly Review* 49 (July-August 1997): 63-79.

13.   Robert Fitch, "America Needs a Raise," *The Nation* 263 (25 November 1996): 25–28; Moody, *Labor in Trouble and Transition,* 170.

14.   Joseph C. Goulden, *Meany* (New York: Atheneum, 1972), 466-67.

15.   Ben Hamper, *Rivethead* (New York: Warner Books, 1991).

16.   Michael Goldfield, "Race and the CIO: The Possibilities for Racial Egalitarianism during the 1930s and 1940s," *International Labor and Working Class History* no. 44 (Fall 1993): 1–32; "Race and the cia: Reply to Critics," *International Labor and Working-Class History* no. 46 (Fall 1994): 142–160; "The Failure of Operation Dixie: A Critical Turning Point in American Political Development?" in *Race, Class, and Community in Southern Labor History,* eds. Gary M. Fink and Merl E. Reed (Tuscaloosa: University of Alabama Press, 1994), 166–88.

17.   Cooper, "Labor Deals a New Hand": 12-14.

18.   Ibid., 14.

19.   Gapasin and Yates, "Organizing the Unorganized": 54–57. The regeneration of central labor councils is a basic theme of Bill Fletcher and Fernando Gapasin's *Solidarity Divided.*

20.   David Bacon, "Evening the Odds: Cross-Border Organizing Gives Labor a Chance," *The Progressive* 61 (July 1997): 29–33; Sumner M. Rosen, "Renewing Labor's Power and Vision," in *A World that Works: Building Blocks for a Just and Sustainable Society,* ed. Trent Schroyer (New York: The Bootstrap Press, 1997), 136–37; Andrew Herod, "The Practice of International Labor Solidarity and the Geography of the Global Economy," *Economic Geography* 71 (October 1995): 341.

21.   See Kim Moody, *Labor in a Lean World: Unions in the International Economy* (New York: Verso, 1997).

22.   Fletcher, Jr., and Gapasin, *Solidarity Divided,* 196.

23.   Andrew Stern, *A Country that Works: Getting America Back on Track* (New York: Free Press, 2006).

24.   Ben Hamper, *Rivethead: Tales from the Assembly Line* (New York: Grand Central Publishing, 1992). Also, Dan La Botz, "What's to Be Done about the Auto Industry?", available at http://mrzine.monthlyreview.org/labotz181108.html.

# INDEX